Indian Higher Education

Perspective from the Margin

Indian Higher Education

Perspective from the Margin

Raosaheb K. Kale

AAKAR

INDIAN HIGHER EDUCATION: Perspective from the Margin
Raosaheb K. Kale

First Published 2018

ISBN 978-93-5002-550-5

Published by
AAKAR BOOKS
28 E Pocket IV, Mayur Vihar Phase I
Delhi 110 091 India
aakarbooks@gmail.com

Laser Typeset at
Arpit Printographers, Delhi 110 032

Printed at
Sapra Brothers, Delhi 110 092

To
Rekha & Parents

Contents

Preface

I had spent most of the time in learning, teaching and carrying out research in science. At the same time, my long stay, as a student and then faculty member, at the Jawaharlal Nehru University, interaction with students and teachers on the campus, listening to scholarly talks and presentations further enhanced and kept my interest alive in social issues. Apart from this, I had been a member of the standing committee of the University Grants Commission (UGC) to oversee the implementation of reservation policies in the Indian universities, which gave me an opportunity to interact with officers of many universities and understand the way various schemes of the UGC and Government of India for SCs and STs were implemented. In addition, I have conducted inquiries against some colleges and universities in matters related to violation of reservation policies in admissions and appointments, which also gave me a clear picture about the mindset of highly educated people on the campuses and their attitude towards the SC and ST communities. With some exceptions, most of them are either against reservation or see it as an anti-poverty drive, or redistribution of resources and wealth. Very few understand or accept that the reservation was a conscious decision taken by the founding fathers of the nation, to undo the historic wrongs and bring social equality. Indian education, unfortunately, failed to a great extent to inculcate the idea and importance of social responsibility and sensitivity among some of the educated and learned people on the campuses as well as to liberate their minds entrapped by socio-religious beliefs, traditions and customs. During the visits to colleges and universities in the country, I could talk to individuals, groups and organizations who had been fighting for rights and against discriminations on campuses, which helped to understand the nature and extent of detrimental implementation of reservations and welfare policies making the beneficiaries as victims. An experience as a member of committees of the Planning Commission, Ministry of Human Resource Development, UGC and other organizations provided some glimpses of the bureaucratic approach towards welfare schemes for SCs and STs. They are, to an extent, still British in thought, taste and action. However, it did not occur to me that I would write on the subject other than science.

One day I received a telephonic call from Dr. Rama Devi Pani, an Editor of the *University News*, a biweekly Journal of Higher Education published by the Association of Indian Universities, with a request to contribute an article to one of its special issues. At the outset I politely declined, and then reluctantly agreed. On her suggestion, I wrote on welfare schemes of the UGC for the underprivileged section of society. Subsequently, I wrote a few more articles on reservation to SCs and STs, and related topics. The feedback of some of these articles was quite encouraging and satisfying. A few friends advised me to compile these articles in the book form. However, I ignored their request.

One day in Gandhinagar, during a discussion on education problems with Prof. Ajay Dandekar, I mentioned these articles, including an unpublished one on the exclusive nature of education in the British period. He went through the articles and suggested that I should bring them out in book form. Because of my ignorance about the grammar of book writing in social science or social issues, and other related aspects, I was reluctant to do so. His persuasion as well as assurance to look into and take care of all such matters including finding a publisher, made me agree. Not to have broken the sequence in the story, the new chapter on the status of higher education in independent India was written and added. As the landscape of higher education has been changing very fast, to keep space with time and change, the developments of the recent past were included in the last chapter. I must mention that owing to the keen interest and efforts of Prof. Dandekar, these articles finally emerged in book form. I do not have words to express my thanks to Prof. Dandekar.

I will be failing in my duty if I do not express my appreciation to Dr. Dhananjay Rai, who was kind enough to introduce me to Mr. K.K. Saxena of Aakar Books. Without this introduction the manuscript would not have seen the light of day.

Discussion, from time to time, with Prof. Sukhdeo Thorat, Prof. Nandu Ram, Prof. Tulsi Ram and Dr. Raja Sekhar Vundru helped to enrich the content of the present volume. I would like to express my grateful thanks to them. Many friends like Prof. Rajen Harshe, Prof. Promod Kumar Yadava, Prof. Rana Pratap Singh, Prof. P.G. Jogdand, Prof. Gautam Gawali, Prof. Vivek Kumar, Prof. D.K. Lobiyal, Prof. Y.S. Alone, Dr. Chinna Rao Yagati, Dr. Ramchandra, Dr. Sheetal Sharma, Dr. Rajan Kumar, Dr. Milind Awad and others gave several suggestions and also kept insisting on compiling the writings and publish. I would like to record my sincere thanks to all of them. I would also like to express my thanks to Prof. E.V. Ramakrishanan, Prof. N. Rajaram, Prof. Man Singh, Prof. M.H. Fulekar, Prof. Alok Gupta and Prof. Chandra Mohan, for their constructive suggestions, as well as Dr. Ramesh C. Gaur and Shri Somesh Vishwakarma for checking the similarity index.

While searching for literature on education, I came across the writings of many scholars such as S.K. Thorat, J.P. Naik, R.V. Parulekar, Eleanor Zelliot, Sekhar Bandyopadhyay, Bhagwan Das, G. Aloysius, K.S. Chalam, B.M. Sankhdher, A. Satyanarayana, A.K. Biswas, C.L. Bakshi, Ravi Srivastva, S. Sinha, A. Dubey, S. Raju, K.B. Powar, Deepak Kumar, Pawan Agarwal, Vivek Kumar, Chinna Rao Yagati and many more. I hereby acknowledge that their scholarly contributions gave me more clarity on educational and social issues related to the unprivileged section of society. Their work was very useful to place educational issues in the historical and social perspective.

How can I forget Mukesh Parmar and Mohammad Nauman. Both, very warm and affectionate, I thank them for their secretarial assistance and other related work. Their help enabled me to complete the present volume on time.

My family Dr. Rekha, Prachee, Pratyush and Prakruti always stood by me in all weathers. Because of their continued support, it became possible to complete this manuscript.

As education converts a person into a national asset, the countries which provided education to its people, have developed and progressed. However, this did not happen in the case of India, and instead education, particularly higher education, remained confined to a small section of society, mainly because of its hierarchical caste-ridden social structure. Although the successive governments, after independence, took some measures, as part of nation building, education was not easily accessible to the majority of people. To realize the dream to be a developed nation, education has to be democratized by spreading evenly among the masses. SCs and STs are major constituents of the large uneducated masses and are around twenty-five per cent of the total population. In the interest of the nation, SCs and STs, have to be educated to make them a national asset, without which it would be difficult for India to be a developed country. The reservations for SCs and STs in educational institutions should be seen in this context. Therefore, the future of India, to a great extent, is intimately linked with the educational status of SCs and STs. Most importantly, being a great equalizer, the education of SCs and STs would contribute in achieving social equality and in turn strengthen the base of our democracy making it sustainable and strong.These and such other aspects were kept in mind while preparing this volume.

Raosaheb K. Kale

1

Introduction

People belonging to Scheduled Caste (SC) communities, earlier called untouchables, were exploited by the upper caste people as social slaves. They had no rights but duties. Further, traditions and customs did not allow them to accumulate or generate wealth. As a result, they always remained entirely dependent on the support of upper castes. The caste system imposed several economic and social sanctions against untouchable communities which continued for centuries. Even today, they have been carrying with them a historic burden and the stigma of their caste. The present socio-economic prosperity of the upper caste people, to a great extent, is a result of exploitation of untouchables in the past. To undo these historic wrongs and bring social equality, the founding fathers of the nation, immediately after independence, had taken several constitutional measures; and introduced and implemented welfare schemes, including reservation in the academic institutions, scholarships, fellowships and other facilities. However, some of the members of upper caste communities have been opposing such welfare measures.

An opposition by upper caste people to the educational schemes for SC and Scheduled Tribes (ST) is rooted in the caste system itself. In the past, untouchables were not allowed to take education as part of the traditions of the caste system. Refusal to teach Eklavya in the *Mahabharata* and not allowing Shambhuk to obtain knowledge in the *Ramayana* were perhaps examples of such tradition. The same tradition continues today in the changed form. The ST community was geographically and culturally isolated and remained educationally backward and neglected. The opposition to their education is not different in the form and magnitude from that of the SCs.

Indian society is a heterogeneous cluster of castes, hierarchically arranged in four groups called *Varna.* Brahmins placed themselves at the top of the pyramid, followed by the Kshatriyas and the Vaishyas. The *Shudras* were at the bottom of the pyramid as the fourth *varna*. There was also the fifth group of castes called *Panchamas* or *Ati-shudra,* although not initially part of the *Varna* system, was placed below the *Shudras*. The terms such as depressed classes, downtrodden and untouchables were also used to identify them in the British period; and as Dalit in the present time. All these terms appear in the present volume.

According to the Hindu religion, the *Varna* has a divine origin. Being part of religious faith and belief, this theory of divine origin of the *Varna* system had been beyond scientific sruitiny, logical questioning and critical evaluation. Therefore, the hierarchical order of Hindu society remained unchallenged and continued to maintain its rigidity in terms of form and function, even today. Unlike the Brahminical scholars, the minds of Westerns were not conditioned and approached the *Varna* and caste system more rationally, away from the religious domain. On arrival, out of curiosity, necessity or both, the British made an effort to understand and interpret the present and past of Indian society. These and other Western writers relied on the Sanskrit texts for their search and studies; and subsequently suggested that the *Aryans* invaded India. As, the theory of *Aryan* invasion proves the supremacy, the Brahmin scholarship accepted it gladly. Further, these Brahmin scholars also believed in the invasion theory because of the intimate link between English and Sankrit shown by the Western scholars, which helped them to identify with the Aryans and also to shape their thinking accordingly. Alignment with the Western mindset was evident, for example, from their view that the Shudras had been the descendants of the Indus valley people, who were vanquished by the *Aryans* and term them *Anaryas* or Dassas. It was also assumed that some *Aryans* who intermarried with Dassas became part of *Shudras* (Ghosh, 2001). Importantly, the Western and Brahminical scholarship, while interpreting the past, tried to show the Aryans as a superior and civilized race and glorified their past. However,

Dr. Ambedkar (1946) rejected both the theories. He extensively wrote and critically analysed the differentiation of Indian society into Varnas and castes.

Dr. Ambedkar (1946) provided a detailed account of the origin of *Shudras*. According to him, there was a time when Indo-Aryan society recognized three *Varnas,* namely *Brahmins, Kshatriyas* and *Vaishyas*. Importantly, he considered the *Shudras* to be the part of *Kshatriyas*. The continued feud between *Shudra* Kings and *Brahmins* generated hatred towards the *Shudras,* and consequently, Brahmins refused to perform the *Upanayana* of the *Shudras*. Denial of *Upanayana* resulted in the social degradation of *Shudras* and fell below the rank of the *Vaishyas,* and in turn came to form the fourth *Varna*. On the other hand, the untouchables are considered to be original descendants of people who continued to follow Buddhism and did not convert under pressure or threat or both, to Hinduism, after the downfall of Asoka the great. In this context, Charles Allen (2012) in his book *Asoka,* p. 400, has stated, 'the downside for Buddhism was that in India its holy places were absorbed, its history excised and those who clung to its heresies declared untouchables'. Allen's observation supports the views of Dr. Ambedkar expressed more than sixty-five years ago that the untouchables had been Buddhist. According to him the sheer historical circumstances pulled them back, and relegated them to the status of downtrodden (Ambedkar, 1946, 1948). Also, Ayodhee Thass Pandithar (1845-1914), an intellectual who anticipated Dr. Ambedkar by two generations; was of the view that Dalits were original Buddhists and had been stigmatized as 'untouchables' by Brahmins for resisting the caste system (Venkatachalapathy, 2014).

Very little is known about education in the ancient period. Even existing books on Ancient India including several volumes published by organizations like Bharatiya Vidya Bhawan and Ramakrishna Mission, almost ignored education (Gosh 2001). Radha Kumud Mookerjee (1918-20), A.S. Altekar (1934) and recently Suresh Chandra Ghosh (2001) tried to throw some light on the history of education in Ancient India. Their writings were based mainly on religious texts. Sometimes, the findings based on such sources cannot be related to time and space, and therefore, difficult to consider as historical facts. In the past the tradition of history writing in India vastly differed from that of the West, and hence was distinctly different. The colonial experience homogenized and slotted our past. Interestingly, the Officers of the East India Company took great interest in understanding Indian history, particularly of the period prior to the arrival of Muslims to India (Allen, 2012). Anyway, the writing on the history of education in ancient India, for example Altekar (1934), was confined to education of Brahmins in Vedic schools and associated rituals. Although Sankhdher (1999) covers education in the British period, he provides glimpses of the ancient period. Importantly, education was forbidden for *Shudras*. This situation must have developed post-Mahabharata, as we have references to the *Shudra* kings and their regions. In the social context, *Shudras* were supposed to serve other *varnas*. Placed below the *Shudras* and also being social slaves, the conditions of people belonging to untouchable castes were worse which forced them to live as sub-humans, completely at the mercy of upper castes. As education, by design, was for the upper castes, particularly for Brahmins, closed the doors of education to untouchables. The exclusion in education, started in an ancient time and thereafter, continued for centuries.

On arrival of the British, education became available, in the real sense, to the untouchable castes. However, they could not access the same due to caste barriers and steep resistance from the upper castes. The British when felt a need to create a servile class started the so-called modern education system in India. The 'British came as traders and gradually mastered the resources of the country and finally emerged as the rulers. Their sole purpose was to earn profits, to promote the development of agriculture, industry, trade and commerce in order to bring prosperity to England, the home country in Europe' (Bandyopadhyay, 2007). The need of effective governance and administration forced the British to introduce the present education system and, in turn, created, by default, almost tailor-made opportunities for Brahmins and other higher caste communities to further consolidate their hold over knowledge. Interestingly, when the British introduced modern English education, *Brahmins* resisted and protested against the same, as they perceived it as a threat to their social status.

In course of time, Brahmins in large numbers joined the British administration and military service at various levels and, protected and promoted the interest, mainly, of their own community. Indeed, 'the British Raj sometimes used to be dubbed as Brahmin-Company Raj' (Pratap Bhanu Mehta, 2012). They not only monopolized education but closed the doors of education to depressed classes. The indigenous ruling class opposed every move made by the British to extend education to untouchables under the pretext of religious traditions and laws. They had used all possible means such as snatching slates and books from school-going children of depressed classes, threatened masses, burnt houses, imposed social boycott and even killed depressed classes, aspiring for education. It is important to note that the British were criticized 'for not providing education to Indians, not eradicating mass illiteracy and not producing even a single graduate in one hundred years after the Battle of Plassey. The petitions were submitted and prayers were made to British rulers for the education of the Indian masses'. It is a matter of sheer travesty that the Indian elite class which demanded education from the British denied the same to the depressed classes, to secure the hold over knowledge production.

It should be remembered that the British were not here, in India, for social reformation thus expectedly spent almost nothing on education for the first 50 years. However, in the year 1813, the East India Company sanctioned Rs one lakh for education, and further raised to Rs ten lakh in 1833. Interestingly, British Parliament was supposed to enhance this grant ten times after 20 years to Rs one crore, but failed to do so. The actions of the empire were guided by the interests of the colonial masters. It was necessary for the British to seek the help of people who had status and control over the society, to run the country of vast diversity. Therefore, they established the Madrasa at Calcutta (now Kolkata), and Sanskrit College at Banaras and Pune, and subsequently at other places for erstwhile rulers, elites and Brahmins, but ignored the interests of the downtrodden, making education as an exclusive entity, in their time. The downtrodden simultaneously experienced the British as well as Brahminical discrimination and deprivation. Indeed, as early as 1830, the untouchable communities could not even dream of education. We have dealt with this aspect in Chapter 2. It gives a glimpse of the British policy in terms of educational issues, such

against th[illegible]
higher castes towards th[illegible]
struggle of downtrodden communiti[illegible]
access to education.

National leaders were aware of the importance of higher education as it was evident from the appointment of the Education Commission under the Chairmanship of Dr. Radhakrishnan immediately after independence. Prior to that, there were a number of resolutions of the All India Congress Committee (AICC) pertaining to education and its context that were passed during various sessions of the AICC. However, thereafter, without formulating long-term perspectives education policy and developing the road-map for its implementations, successive governments continued to appoint commissions and committees without giving any serious thoughts to the issue on the table. Further, instead of giving autonomy and academic freedom, the government started regulating education, a tendency that only increased over a period. As a result, the growth of higher education was relatively slow and Gross Enrolment Ratio (GER) did not cross beyond 10% till the year 2000. As a part of the expansion of education, between the 1950s and 60s, the country established five IITs with the help of overseas countries. The main purpose here was to develop technology indigenously in order to make the country self-sufficient in basic technologies. This type of expansion was based on the rationale that progress and self-sufficiency depended on such an approach. Although the nation invested heavily to establish and run these IITs, their social returns were not satisfactory. The IIT-trained graduates, instead of serving their own country, migrated to Western countries where they contributed in developing technologies which India has had to buy. This migration of skilled human resources from IITs adversely affected the development of indigenous technology. It would be pertinent to mention that the US, in its developmental stage, did send many students to Germany, who came back after their studies and helped the US to establish universities and develop technologies, and in turn contributed to make the US a developed administration and military service at various levels and, protected and promoted the interest, mainly, of their own community. Indeed, 'the British Raj sometimes used to be dubbed as Brahmin-Company Raj' (Pratap Bhanu Mehta, 2012). They not only monopolized education but closed the doors of education to depressed classes. The indigenous ruling class opposed every move made by the British to extend education to untouchables under the pretext of religious traditions and laws. They had used all possible means such as snatching slates and books from school-going children of depressed classes, threatened masses, burnt houses, imposed social boycott and even killed depressed classes, aspiring for education. It is important to note that the British were criticized 'for not providing education to Indians, not eradicating mass illiteracy and not producing even a single graduate in one hundred years after the Battle of Plassey. The petitions were submitted and prayers were made to British rulers for the education of the Indian masses'. It is a matter of sheer travesty that the Indian elite class which demanded education from the British denied the same to the depressed classes, to secure the hold over knowledge production.

It should be remembered that the British were not here, in India, for social reformation thus expectedly spent almost nothing on education for the first 50 years. However, in the year 1813, the East India Company sanctioned Rs one lakh for education, and further raised to Rs ten lakh in 1833. Interestingly, British Parliament was supposed to enhance this grant ten times after 20 years to Rs one crore, but failed to do so. The actions of the empire were guided by the interests of the colonial masters. It was necessary for the British to seek the help of people who had status and control over the society, to run the country of vast diversity. Therefore, they established the Madrasa at Calcutta (now Kolkata), and Sanskrit College at Banaras and Pune, and subsequently at other places for erstwhile rulers, elites and Brahmins, but ignored the interests of the downtrodden, making education as an exclusive entity, in their time. The downtrodden simultaneously experienced the British as well as Brahminical discrimination and deprivation. Indeed, as early as 1830, the untouchable communities could not even dream of education. We have dealt with this aspect in Chapter 2. It gives a glimpse of the British policy in terms of educational issues, such as reluctance of the British to provide education to the downtrodden, to avoid the protest and hostility of higher castes against the East India Company and British empire, mindset of higher castes towards the education of the downtrodden and struggle of downtrodden communities and their leaders to get access to education.

National leaders were aware of the importance of higher education as it was evident from the appointment of the Education Commission under the Chairmanship of Dr. Radhakrishnan immediately after independence. Prior to that, there were a number of resolutions of the All India Congress Committee (AICC) pertaining to education and its context that were passed during various sessions of the AICC. However, thereafter, without formulating long-term perspectives education policy and developing the road-map for its implementations, successive governments continued to appoint commissions and committees without giving any serious thoughts to the issue on the table. Further, instead of giving autonomy and academic freedom, the government started regulating education, a tendency that only increased over a period. As a result, the growth of higher education was relatively slow and Gross Enrolment Ratio (GER) did not cross beyond 10% till the year 2000. As a part of the expansion of education, between the 1950s and 60s, the country established five IITs with the help of overseas countries. The main purpose here was to develop technology indigenously in order to make the country self-sufficient in basic technologies. This type of expansion was based on the rationale that progress and self-sufficiency depended on such an approach. Although the nation invested heavily to establish and run these IITs, their social returns were not satisfactory. The IIT-trained graduates, instead of serving their own country, migrated to Western countries where they contributed in developing technologies which India has had to buy. This migration of skilled human resources from IITs adversely affected the development of indigenous technology. It would be pertinent to mention that the US, in its developmental stage, did send many students to Germany, who came back after their studies and helped the US to establish universities and develop technologies, and in turn contributed to make the US a developed institutions and governance (*The Finance Express*, 2012). The generation of human capital to build and run institutions and, govern and administer the country we need, at least, a critical mass of educated and skilled people, which at present India does not have. In such a situation, as suggested by Rodrik, the economic growth will remain slow. In other words, considering the small and confined educational base as well as social diversity and dynamics, it would be difficult for India to become a developed nation before or after 2020, unless education is democratized. Keeping these aspects in mind, Chapter 7 may be read. It may be mentioned that JNU adopted the Government of India Policy (2006) which provides twenty-seven per cent reservation for the OBC students in admission without much delay, which helped further to achieve greater diversity. However, a section of students and teachers opposed the same. Subsequently, JNU became the nerve centre of the anti-reservation movement. The anti-reservation group emerged on the campus during the first agitation against OBC reservation in services; and continued to be visible, vocal and active since then.

Way back in the late 1960s, in my Marathi medium school, an English teacher, while explaining the word 'develop' (to make us understand), stated, 'India is a developing country and going to be a developed one very soon.' From that day, I have, like many others, been dreaming to see India as a developed nation. With curiosity, therefore, I read a book entitled, *India 2020: A Vision for the New Millennium*, written by Dr. A.P.J. Abdul Kalam. He has been promoting the idea of India as a developed nation by 2020 for some time now. As Chairman of the Technology Information, Forecasting and Assessment Council (TIFAC), with the help of many, he prepared the 2020 India vision, thus gave a road map for transforming India into a developed nation. On becoming the President of India, he used every opportunity to put forth the India 2020 vision in front of the nation and Parliament. He spoke nine times on the India 2020 Vision in Parliament, addressed twelve State Assemblies (Abdul Kalam, 2012) and many times at various other forums.

Dr. Kalam also mentioned in his book entitled, *Turning Point* (2012) that he took a conscious decision not to contest for a second term for the post of President of India, and decided to go back to his career in academic and research and confine to work with passion for transforming developed India by 2020. Even before he died Dr. Kalam promoted the idea of a developed nation although 2020 is just a few years away. The writings and speeches of Dr. Kalam have influenced and are influencing the programmes and policies of the government. Therefore, an attempt has been made in Chapter 8, to understand transforming India by 2020, keeping the role of higher education in mind.

The education is a tool for development, progress and prosperity. Therefore, to make the country developed, then to run and maintain it, the education system should create at least a critical mass of educated and skilled human resource. However, the education system failed on this account as it remained highly un-democratized resulting in disparities—geographical, gender and social. Low GER and low-quality education created acute shortage of educated and skilled human resources, which are essentially required for a developed nation.

These problems, faced by the country due to social disparities, need to be addressed on priority to transform India into a developed nation. The large population consisting of 16.2 per cent SC, 8.2 per cent ST, 13-15 per cent minorities, around 40 per cent OBC and many rural and urban poor have no easy access to quality education. Indeed, their educational and socio-economic progress is a prerequisite for the transformation of the country. The social disparity causes educational disparity and in turn economic disparity. It may be noticed that unlike other public personalities Dr. Abdul Kalam never protested empathetically about the social disparities, caste-based discrimination, and suffering and pain of the downtrodden. Instead, he linked the transformation of India to spirituality (Abdul Kalam, 2002). The spirituality has an importance and significance in the life of people; however, in the context of development of the nation, social realities cannot be ignored. However, Dr. Abdul Kalam conveniently preferred to remain silent on social issues and caste practices. He was also silent to great extent on the suffering of STs who have been victims of cultural isolation.

As Indian society mostly consists of castes, arranged in

institutes to the diversity index. With this background, the UGC was asked to develop the mechanism to measure the diversity index. Accordingly, the UGC constituted the Committee for this purpose under the Chairmanship of Prof. G.K. Chaddha, of which I was also a member. At the very first meeting, a few issues related to the diversity were discussed in some detail and also shared experiences and ideas. At the end, the Chairman suggested to prepare a brief note individually to be discussed in the next meeting. I prepared a three to four page note highlighting the efforts made by JNU to get students from different parts of the country with different socio-economic backgrounds.

The work of the Committee was progressing quite well, and expected to complete the same at the earliest. In between, the Ministry dealing with welfare and issues of the minority communities probably claimed that the preparation of the diversity index was its job and not that of the UGC. Most probably because of this, the Committee had to stop work abruptly. Although, the Committee stopped functioning, the note prepared on JNU continued to remind me about the idea of diversity on campuses. The diversity has great significance for SCs and STs. On achieving the same, the SCs and STs are likely to get their fair representation in the sphere of academic life on the campus.

In this context, the experience of JNU and its diversity was interesting. Available data and information showed that JNU was a microcosm of mini-India, with fifteen per cent SC, eight per cent ST, more than twenty-three per cent, non-creamy layer, OBC and more than thirteen per cent minority students from every part of the country. It also revealed that a large number of students were from rural, non-public schooling and low-income backgrounds. Similarly, women in a significant number were also enrolled in JNU. The JNU experience suggested that reservations for SC, ST and OBC and affirmative action for others did not lower the academic standard but on the contrary contributed to enhancement of academic excellence. It was found that the social diversity on campuses and academic excellence were not mutually exclusive.

Accordingly to Dani Rodrik, Professor of International Political Economy at Harvard University, economic growth relies to a much greater extent on sustained improvements in human capital, own statistical section for compilation of all information. It is difficult to understand the blackout.

The UGC has a section which deals with central universities. It procures various information on a regular basis from these universities including on enrolment of SC and ST students. In addition, the UGC has a section called SCT Cell to deal with implementation of reservation policies and other affirmative actions in the form of various schemes. These sections provide reliable information related to enrolment of SC and ST students in central universities, which could be useful to understand the implementation of the reservation policy of the Government of India in admissions in central universities. This source surprisingly, with few exceptions, showed that the enrolment of SC and ST students in the central universities was quite low. It is known that relatively the quality of education is better in these universities. However, the same was not easily accessible to SC and ST students. As a result our aim to provide access to quality education with equity could not be completely realized. Importantly, the problems faced by the SC and ST students are not confined only to getting admission. Their arrival and presence on the campuses are not welcomed by some section of the students and teachers mainly belonging to so-called upper castes. They experience discrimination and humiliation during the period of their studies. It became more visible when 27 per cent reservations for non-creamy layer of OBC was extended to the centrally funded educational institutions. There was almost a revolt against the reservations for OBC. During the revolt and thereafter SC and ST students become soft targets of the anti-reservation agitators. Some of these aspects are discussed in Chapter 6.

Meanwhile, in the year 2005, the Sachar Committee was appointed to find out the latest social, economic and educational status of the Muslim community, which submitted its report on November 30, 2006. The Report revealed the educational backwardness of the Muslim community and suggested several measures to bridge the gap between them and other sections of the society. Importantly, the Committee also suggested to achieve diversity on campuses including the institutes run and maintained by the minorities, and to link the financial aid to the educational on a meagre salary; in some cases, it was even less than minimum wages of skilled labourers in the cities. The shortage of eligible candidates also adversely affected the education system. Most importantly, the NET has made PG degrees and PhD degrees redundant as NET is an essential qualification for the appointment of teachers at the level of Assistant Professor. The State Level Elegibility Test (SLET) and the UGC guidelines 2009 on a PhD as an essential qualification for the appointments could not be considered as the right substitute for the NET.

The NET examination, if passed, makes a candidate eligible for the post of Assistant Professor. The suitability is finally decided by the selection committee. Therefore for SC and ST candidates, NET may be advantageous. Since, NET certifies the potential to be a teacher, the probability to be selected is enhanced to a great extent. In case of SC and ST candidates with NET, it becomes quite difficult for the selection committee to reject them outright. Sometimes NET certification compels the committee to select. Thus NET may immunize SC and ST candidates against the caste biasness in the selection process. However, on the other hand, it is also seen that many SC and ST students armed with NET certificates are wandering about in search of jobs. Often the mindset of members of the selection committee decides the fate of SC and ST candidates and not their certificates.

Chapters from 4 to 9 were published in the *University News*, a weekly Journal of Higher Education, published by the Association of Indian Universities, New Delhi, during 2006. Thereafter, higher education of India experienced some expansion in terms of number of universities, colleges, teachers and students without any significant impact on its quality. Most importantly, these increased numbers did not change the exclusive nature of education. It remained un-democratized as before and was not easily accessible to underprivileged sections of society particularly, SC and ST communities. Therefore, basic aspects, assessments, meaning, message and conclusion of these publications remained unchanged. Because of this, the original data embodied in these publications is retained. However, minor changes have been made to update the content wherever necessary.

The last chapter deals briefly with new initiatives taken by the

Government of India in the Eleventh and Twelfth Five Year Plans. When the British transferred power in 1947, they left behind a small education system, with nineteen universities, 695 colleges and more than 270,000 students. At present there are more than 564 universities, 33,000 colleges, 8 lakh teachers and 1.69 crore students. This increase looks quite large. However, the expansion of higher education was slow and took more than 55 years to achieve 10.84 per cent GER, significantly lower than many other countries. Unfortunately, education was mainly confined to a select and small section of society, particularly, urban rich and elite as well as upper castes, which resulted in disparities like social, gender and spatial. The SC, ST and other socially backward castes being located mainly in the rural part of the country, the education was not easily accessible to them. Considering this aspect, it should not be surprising that the GER for more than 370 districts of India was less than the national average of 10.84 per cent during the year 2006-07. Further, out of these, nearly twenty-seven per cent districts had GER just three to nine per cent.

Indeed, to provide education to all is a responsibility of the government. However, the government started withdrawing from higher education, particularly from 1970 to the early 2000s. Budgetary allocation was around one per cent of GDP in 1970 which came down to 0.4 per cent of GDP around 2000. It amounted to twenty per cent reduction every 10 years. The situation became worse for the state universities. The under-funding has thrown higher education into a crisis and pushed India back in time. In the same period, the government encouraged establishing private colleges and universities, which mainly offered professional courses. As a fall out, the students in large numbers moved to these privately established academic institutes and did not significantly increase the overall GER.

The slow or limited expansion created a shortage of educated and skilled human resource which the country needed for the growing economy in the time of globalization. To meet such a demand the government established several institutes of higher learning. For the reformation and preparation of the road map for its Higher Education, the government appointed the National Knowledge Commission (2006-09), and a Committee to Advise on

Renovation and Rejuvenation of Higher Education (2008-09). Another committee popularly known as the Sachar Committee (2005) was also constituted to find out the latest social, economic and educational condition of the Muslim community of India. In addition, the government also followed the legal route to reform the higher education and introduced several bills in Parliament. Recently (2013) the government has constituted the Committee chaired by Prof. A.M. Pathan to draft the bill with the aim to bring all central universities under the single Act. It appeared that the government recognized the significance of higher education and became proactive around 2004-05. It increased funding which was nine to ten times higher than the earlier years. Although the country is passing through financial difficulties, the higher education was expected to get liberal financial support of at least 1.5 per cent of GDP during the Twelfth Five Year Plan. However, allocation is not enhanced and kept at the level of the Eleventh Plan.

After independence, in the last sixty-five years, more than five major and several committees were appointed one after another by the successive governments, with the aim to reform and expand higher education. It seemed that these commissions and committees considered Indian society as homogeneous. Further, their approach to Indian education appeared to be influenced by the education systems of European and North American countries, mainly the UK and US. India is a country of diversity and disparity; it is unique and not to be compared with any other country. Problems of Indian education needed Indian solutions. While making recommendations and then their implementation, Indian social complexities were ignored. As a result, the section of society which has been accessing education from the British time, differentially benefited and the large population, mainly unprivileged, remained outside the purview of higher education. Had the higher education planned and targeted benefits to the rural masses, the situation would have been completely different, in terms of GER, social disparities and availability of educated and skilled working population to reap the demographic advantage. Very pertinently, Pulpare Balakrishnan (2015) in his recent article in *The Hindu* referred to the writings of Dr. Amartya Sen which suggested that 'higher education in India was being expanded largely only in response to middle class pressure'. However, socially, as we know, the major and dominant constituents of the Indian middle class are Brahmins and a few upper caste people whose share in the total population is between ten and fifteen per cent.

In the Constitution of India, as mentioned elsewhere, the provision has been made to protect the educational interest of SCs and STs, and for its translation into benefits, the reservations have been provided in admission in the government and government-aided academic institutes. The reservation in admissions have also been extended recently to non-creamy layer OBCs which was perceived by the upper castes as a threat to their social status and dominance in education, administration and governance. They resisted under the pretext of dilution of merit, lowering the quality of education and shrinkage of employment opportunities.

The merit is a relative rank and not necessarily the measure of talent and wisdom. It could, perhaps, be defined as an ability to score more. The merit as an outcome in interview, interaction, viva-voce examination or written test, is dependent on various factors. Further merit cannot predict or assure better performance in jobs, service or assigned work. It is known that the meritocracy greatly (or exclusively) contributed to the collapse of the famous Enron Company of the US. The so-called best brains that studied and trained in the best institutes of technology and business of the US could not save Enron. In the similar line, despite appointment of teachers and admission of students, purely on merit, the IITs failed in terms of social return. Till the recent past, securing more than fifty per cent marks in the examination was considered to be an academic achievement. In the present days, the candidates with ninety to ninety-five per cent marks are found to be unemployable. These numbers as a form of merit do not reflect the potential of the person. It would not, perhaps, be completely out of context to refer to Sachin Tendulkar who has been described as the God of Cricket. This world would never get another Sachin Tendulkar in future, as it would not be possible for other players to achieve what he has achieved, particularly as a century of centuries. However, there is another record of a century against his name. He was out more than 100 times, for the score below ten, which was always ignored conveniently. This unique century, scoring below ten runs shows his high degree of tendency to fail. As far as the century of centuries is concerned, Tendulkar took thirty-three innings and 368 days, to move from his 99 to 100 centuries. Further, he was nineteen times and seventeen times out for the score between 90 and 99 runs, and 80 and 89 runs respectively, which is indicative of his fear of failure. If assessed in term of Locus of Control (Chugh et al., 2012) and compared, Rahul Dravid is likely to be more internally controlled than Sachin Tendulker and in turn a better batsman. This possibility is supported by the observation of Glenn McGrath, former Australian aggressive fast bowler with more Test wickets (563) than any other fast bowler in the world. He placed Rahul Dravid above Sachin Tendulker and Brian Lara. At a function held in Delhi on June 3, 2015, he said, "If I had to choose among Lara, Sachin or Dravid to bat for my life, I would choose Rahul Dravid every time" (*Hindustan Times, HT City*, 2015). It is important that Vinod Kambli, who played with Sachin Tendulkar in the early days, was equally talented. However equal talents did not prosper and flourish equally. The answer to this difference is beyond the number of runs and centuries scored. One must understand the difference between perception and reality. The nature and nurture shape the person and personality. Lack of right patronization and grooming in cricket, adversely affected the performance of Vinod Kambli, otherwise a very rare talented cricketer. Naturally, we are all the same with the genetic makeup and brains. However, we are different in terms of nurture. The socio-economic conditions imposed by customs and traditions kept SCs, STs and other underprivileged people did not allow them to grow and flourish.

It would be pertinent to mention the story carried by the *Sunday Times* (Ahmedabad), on June 9, 2013, on the witty and radical speech delivered by Ben Bernanke at his alma matter, Princeton University, on the occasion of Graduation Day. He reportedly said, "A meritocracy is a system in which the people who are luckiest in their health and genetic endowment; luckiest in terms of family support, encouragement and probably income; luckiest in their educational and career opportunities; and luckiest in so many other ways difficult to enumerate—those are the folks who reap the largest rewards." This description also perfectly fits the Indian meritocrâcy.

It is always assumed by the upper castes that reservations lower the quality of education. Let us take the examples of some universities. Delhi University was known to be the centre of excellence in the 1950s and 60s which subsequently deteriorated when there was no reservation. Even today, DU is perhaps the only central university which has resisted and not implemented the reservation policy completely. The UGC had withheld its grant at least twice in the past for non-compliance of the reservation policy. Banaras Hindu University (BHU) slipped from its academic glory around the same time. The reservations were not implemented in BHU during this phase. BHU always resisted the implementation of reservations. In the recent past, UGC conducted an enquiry against BHU on reservation issues. The University of Allahabad and University of Rajasthan were two other centres of academic excellence which also experienced the downfall. The University of Calcutta, University of Mumbai (now Mumbai University) and University of Madras, were established in 1857 and lost their academic glory in course of time. All these three universities were almost completely free from the reservation at the time of their downfall. Indeed, during the academic downfall, these universities were governed, administered and run by the people belonging to higher castes and descendants of beneficiaries of the British Raj. On the other hand, JNU implemented reservations and also introduced additional affirmative action of its own in admissions; and appointment to teaching and non-teaching posts, almost from its inception. It was able to attract students in large numbers and some teachers from the underprivileged section of society, particularly SC and ST communities. Most importantly, even with the large population of underprivileged on campus, JNU achieved academic excellence. Today, perhaps it is the best University in the country. Thus, it is quite clear that the reservations do not adversely affect academic standards. On the other hand, the JNU experience indicated that the reservation contributes to achieving academic excellence. However, surprisingly, very recently, the reservations were also opposed in JNU unsuccessfully by certain sections of teachers and students. It confirms the mindset of some people belonging to dominant castes who want to continue their control over education and society even in the changed time.

The JNU experience confirmed that the secular and progressive peoples could also be casteist. There is no other word to define them. Some of the teachers who claimed to be secular and progresive were at the forefront to oppose the reservations at the level of associate professor and professor for SCs and STs, and at the level of assistant professor for OBCs. Their unsuccessful fight against reservations divided the JNU community particularly teachers vertically on caste lines. The cracks that have thus occurred need to be cemented. However, only the time as a mason would be able to do so.

While protesting against reservations, the students particularly from the institutes offering professional courses took brooms and started sweeping the roads or took brushes and started polishing the shoes to show what could happen to them, if reservations are implemented. Indeed, in present days there is no dearth of opportunities and availability of vacancies. The educated and skilled human resource is required in large numbers in different sectors from the lowest to highest rung. It may be mentioned that education is not easily accessible to the SCs and STs. As a result their presence in the employment market is not adequate. Therefore, SCs and STs seeking jobs do not really pose a threat to others. Even if, eligible and available, they are not selected rather declared as not found suitable, whether a post is reserved or unreserved. Those who oppose the reservations mainly belong to dominant higher castes whose share in population may not exceed fifteen per cent but occupy eighty to eighty-five per cent space of every sphere of life, leaving almost nothing for the remaining and still create the illusion of scarcity of jobs due to reservations.

The central government extended twenty-seven per cent reservation in admissions in centrally funded institutes of higher education in 2006 for OBCs. There was a revolt all over the country against the same. The policy was criticized on the ground that it would adversely affect the interest of the general category students because of twenty-seven per cent reduction in the general seats. Considering this aspect, the government also increased the intake capacity by twenty-seven per cent for the general category students to protect their educational interest. After this gesture of the government, there was no need, reason and scope to continue the agitation. However, the students and teachers belonging to higher castes continued their protest. They further intensified their agitation and opened different fronts including a legal one to stop the implementation of OBC reservations. SC and ST students were also targeted and suffered collateral damage. The approach and nature of protest clearly indicated that the upper castes wanted to keep education exclusively for them and oppose it for others with the aim to maintain the status and continue to control the society and country as was done in the past.

An approach and tendency of exclusiveness in education is detrimental to the country as it would create educational disparities and in turn a further imbalance in the society leading to an unimaginable crisis. The time has changed. The victims of disparities would not allow themselves to suffer passively as in the past and would certainly revolt. To avoid the same and its consequences, the conditions should be created in which all the sections of society should progress, prosper and flourish together. For the progress of society and in turn development of the nation, education is needed to be democratized. India being a country of disparities, to achieve equality in an unequal society is a challenge. In this context, it would be quite relevant to refer to Dr. B.R. Ambedkar while pleading for education for depressed classes, he argued, 'I must here emphasize that this country is composed of different communities. All these communities are unequal in status and progress. If they too are brought to the level of equality, then, the only remedy is to adopt the principle of inequality and give favoured treatment to those who are below the level.' Further he went on, 'for I honestly believe that equality of treatment to people who are unequal is simply another name for indifferentism and neglect'. In the light of Dr. Ambedkar's observations, it is quite clear that the government has applied the same principle to provide educational opportunities to those sections of society which were kept away, historically from education.

We need to understand that the reservations and the affirmative actions in education are aimed to bring equality in society which is crucial for the future of the country, as it would convert the majority of the population into a national asset. Therefore, educational, social and economic progress of SC, ST, OBC and other underprivileged sections is intimately linked to development of the nation and its future. The day this is realized by the upper castes and the people who have been opposing the reservations and affirmative actions, India as a country would be completely different. The reservations are in the interest of the nation and its future and not only that of beneficiaries. This book may be read in this context. While doing so, it may be also remembered that the educated people belonging to upper castes and the elite class themselves are products of an unfair system in an unequal society.

REFERENCES

Abdul Kalam, A.P.J. with Rajan, Y.S. (1998). *India 2020: A Vision for New Millennium*, Penguin Books, New Delhi.

Abdul Kalam, A.P.J. (2002). *Ignited Mind*, Viking, New Delhi, pp. 96-97.

Abdul Kalam, A.P.J. (2012). *Turning Point*, Harper Collins, India, New Delhi.

Allen, Charles (2012). *Ashoka*, Hachette Digital, London.

Altekar, A.S. (1934). *Education in Ancient India*, Isha Books (Reprinted in 2010), Delhi.

Ambedkar, B.R. (1940). Who Were the Shudras? How They Became the Fourth Varna in the Indo-Aryan Society. Reprinted in: *Dr. Babasaheb Ambedkar: Writings and Speeches*, Vasant Moon (ed.), The Education Department, Government of Maharashtra, Mumbai, 1990, Vol. 7, pp. 1-227.

Ambedkar, B.R. (1948). The Untouchables: Who Were They and Why They Became Untouchables. Reprinted in: *Dr. Babasaheb Ambedkar: Writings and Speeches*, Vasant Moon (ed.), The Education Department, Government of Maharashtra, Mumbai, 1990, Vol. 7, pp. 231-382.

Bandyopadhyay, Sekhar (2007). *From Plassey to Partition: A History of Modern India*, Orient Blackswan, New Delhi.

Chug, Ganesh Dutt, Kale, R.K. and Jha, Prakash (2013). Locus of Control of Cricket Players. *The Scientific Journal of Sport-Science and Practice*, Vol. 2, No. 5, 2012, str-29-38.

Ghosh, Suresh Chandra (2001). *The History of Education in Ancient India*, Munshiram Manoharlal Publishers Pvt. Ltd., New Delhi.

Ghosh, Suresh Chandra (2009). *History of Education in Modern India, 1757-2007*, Orient Blackswan, New Delhi.

Hindustan Times, Report: I'd to choose Dravid to bat for my life, HT City, New Delhi, Thursday, June 4, 2015, p. 1.

Mehta, Pratap Bhanu (2012). *The Indian Express*, June 29.

Mookerjee, Radha Kumud (1918-20). Cited by Ghosh, Suresh Chandra (2001).

Pulapre, Balakrishnan (2015). We Do Not Want No Education, *The Hindu*, Saturday, June 27, p. 8.

Rodrik, Dani (2012). *The Financial Express*, Ahmedabad, Tuesday, August 14.

Sankhdher, B.M. (1999). *Education System from 1857 to William Hunter's Commission 1882*, Deep & Deep Publications, New Delhi.

The Hindu, Tuesday, June 6, 2013, p. 5.

Venkatachalapathy, A.R. (2014). From Footnote to the Forefront, *The Hindu*, Wednesday, December 24, p. 9.

2

Exclusion in Education in British India

The East India Company came into existence by a royal charter on December 31, 1600, 'to trade in the eastern part of the world including India'. The Company reached the Indian shore at Surat, a coastal town of Gujarat State, in 1612, where it established its factory, a term then used for an office. On obtaining trading rights *(farman)* from the Mughal Emperor Jahangir who ruled from Delhi, the company started trading in India from 1613. Within four years, the Company established its relations with the Mughal Emperor and sent Sir Thomas Roe in 1617 as the Resident English envoy in to imperial court at Delhi. Thomas Roe subsequently succeeded in securing more liberal trading rights for the Company. With this modest beginning, 'the Company gradually expanded' its trade and could make Bombay, Madras and Calcutta as main centres of its trading activities (Bandyopadhyay, 2007).

The expansion of territorial empire in India was neither planned nor directed from Britain (Marshall, 1998). Indeed, to begin with, the company had no intent or mandate to conquer or colonize India. Bandyopadhyay (2007), while referring to the work of Sen (1971), has rightly inferred that 'the decline of the Mughals, dynastic feuds, and lust for power among the members of the royal families or their relatives to dethrone the occupant and capture the power, created conditions to intervene in the royal disputes' and in turn 'provided opportunities for intervening in disputes of the Indian rulers and acquiring political control over vast territory. 'The Company perfected the art of creating opportunities to intervene and conquer.' With this backdrop, the Battle of Plassey (1757) provided an opportunity to the Company to establish its political supremacy. The British who came as traders, and the Battle of Plassey (1857) made them rulers. Thereafter, they went on expanding their wings all over the country and ruled for one hundred and ninety years.

Being engaged in trade, the East India Company, expectedly was not interested in the education of the native Indians. Therefore, there was little or no reason to introduce education in India. The education system in India, in the form of indigenous schools, as well as seats of Sanskrit and Arabic learning were already in place. However, the earliest efforts to introduce education other than the indigenous system began with the Christian missionaries, private societies and individuals including the Company officials (Sharp, 1920).

Through private initiative, the Calcutta Free School Society was founded (1789) solely for the education of Europeans. Others such as the Calcutta Benevolent Institution were the outcome of missionary enterprises. Later on, the Calcutta School Book Society (1817), Calcutta School Society (1819), the Society for promoting the education of the poor within the Government of Bombay, Bombay Native School Book, and School Society (1815) and a few others came into existence.

Although not being part of their duties, the Company officials founded educational institutions. Captain John Deveton, General Claude Martin, David Hare, and others were some of the individuals who strove to introduce education different from the indigenous system. The growing interest in 'Indians themselves' was exemplified by Raja Rammohun Roy (1823) and others (*Selections from Educational Records, Part-I, 1781-1839*). Swartz established schools in Tanjore. He is remembered as a pioneer of education in Madras Presidency. Kiernander and others also established schools at Cuddalore (Dispatch of the Court of Directors, dated February 16, 1787). The Asiatic Society at Calcutta was founded in 1784 by British scholars. Sir William Jones was one of the founders and first President of the Society.

The Company had been established to undertake trade in the eastern part of the world and no other activities. However, its officials started institutes using funds of the Company and emphasized oriental learning. Importantly, these officials provided educational opportunities only to the upper castes, elite, dominant and aristocratic section of population, to get their support and involvement direct or indirect, to administer and govern smoothly and effectively, and in turn to bring the vast and diverse country under the complete control of the British. For continuance of hold over the country and its society, it was necessary for the British to earn the good will particularly of Brahmins as well as the upper section of the Muslim community. Expectedly, Warren Hastings established the *Madrasa* at Culcutta, in 1781, to study Arabic and Persian languages as well Muslim law. His aim was to prepare experts in these areas from the Muslim community and appoint and give them responsible and lucrative positions in offices like the courts of justice, to settle social, religious and other disputes. After him, in 1792, Jonathan Duncan established the Banaras Sanskrit College, Chaplin, the Commissioner of Deccan, started a Sanskrit College for Hindu Learning (1821) at Poona (now Pune), and College at Agra (1824). The aim of these two Sanskrit colleges was 'to preserve and cultivate the laws, literature, and religion of Hindus'; and use the scholars who emerged from these colleges to run the adminsration smoothly. In Delhi F. Franser started schools (1823) 'for the instruction of children of zamindars or peasantry in reading and writing the Persian language' (Sharp, 1920).

The Company officials also made an attempt to learn Indian culture by studying the scriptures in Sanskrit, Arabic and Persian languages, and to use that knowledge to govern and administer the country smoothly and effectively (Bandyopadhyay, 2007). The Company tried to rule the Indian people and keep them under the clutches of their own laws, and also to legitimize British Raj in India (Majeed, 1992), which was evident from the establishment of the Fort William College at Calcutta in 1800 AD, to train civil servants in the Indian languages and traditions.

English education was first introduced in India in the 18th century AD. The schools were established in Calcutta, Madras, and Bombay, exclusively for the education of European and Anglo-Indian children. On other hand, till 1813 the Company ignored the similar needs of English education of the native Indians. The Company made two streams in education quite early. Earlier Charles Grant, a servant of the Company in India, who later became one of the Directors of the Company and a Member of Parliament, showed interest in the education of Indians. In 1792, he wrote a treatise entitled, 'Observations on the State of Society among the Asiatic Subjects of Great Britain, particularly with Respect of Morals and on the Means of Improving it'. He pleaded therein for English education for Indians. However, his request was rejected, when the Charter Act was renewed in 1793. William Wilberforce, a Member of Parliament had unsuccessfully advocated on behalf of Grant, to start English education for Indians. The Charter of the Company came up again, after 20 years, for its renewal. Wilberforce in his second attempt could 'succeed in getting his resolution on English education for Indians passed'. As a result, a clause (number 43) was incorporated in the East India Company Act of 1813. It was the first legislation on the right of education in India and also made the company responsible for the education of Indians. The budgetary allocation of Rs. one lakh per year was made for its implementation. This legislation made the East India Company responsible for education and its spread to the Indian masses. Because of this, 1813 is considered as a year of the beginning of Westernized education in India (Trautman, 2004).

Indeed, the treaties written by Charles Grant (1792) could be considered as an educational policy, in which he made a strong case for aggressive Anglicization and Christianization of India and its culture. Grant completely opposed the then prevailing Orientalist policy introduced by Warren Hastings and others, and planned to replace the same at the earliest. There is no scope to deal with the controversy between the Anglicists and the Orientalists and its influence on education. It is important to note that, clause 43 of the Charter Act 1813 dealing with 'Indian education was vague' and 'was open to interpretation'. As a result, the nature of Indian education was not immediately decided. The Orientalists, who dominated the General Committee of Public Instruction at that time, used this delay as an 'opportunity to push forward their agenda of orientalist education', which was evident from establishment of a Sanskrit college in Calcutta, and Oriental college at Agra and Delhi, and also 'patronage for the *tols* (*pathshalas*) and *madrasas* as institutions of indigenous teaching' (Trautman 2004).

It was significant that two events, perhaps, determined the fate of Indian education. First, the strong protest of Raja Rammohun Roy (1823) against the establishment of the Sanskrit College at Calcutta, in the form of a memorandum submitted to the Governor General, he pleaded therein for modernization of India through English education, and dissemination of knowledge of Western science. The memorandum, indicative of growing interest and aspiration of Indians in Western education, considerably helped to tilt the balance between the Orientalist and Anglicist approach in favour of the latter. Second, Lord William Bentinck took over as the Governor General in 1828, and the subsequent appointment of Thomas Babington Macaulay as a Law Member in his Council, who later on became the President of the General Committee of Public Instruction. On February 2, 1835, Macaulay wrote the minutes on Indian education, which Bentinck immediately approved and issued an executive order on March 7, 1835 despite strong protest from the Orientalists (Bandyopadhyay, 2007). Thus Macaulay laid the foundation for Anglicist education, with the aim to form an elite class that was, 'Indian in blood and colour, but English in taste, in opinion, in morals, and in intellect'. The education policy given by Macaulay had no plan to spread education among the masses. Instead, he targeted the educational interest of the elite section of society. It was assumed that this elite section, also termed as Middle Anglicized class, would take the responsibility to educate the masses. According to the British, education was expected to be spread among the masses through the process of filtration. Amazingly, this was nothing but the British shifting their responsibility to Indian elites, to educate the Indian masses, which were traditionally against the education of lower classes and castes. Bentinck's order issued on March 7, 1835 eventually determined the aim, content, and medium of Indian education. The legacy of exclusive education introduced by the British, to a great extent, is still continued even after their departure long back, in 1947.

At the early stage, Brahmins particularly from Pune-Mumbai region, opposed and protested against English education, which was perceived by them as an attack on their social status. However, when English was made the language of the administration in 1837, and employment opportunities made available at the level of subordinate positions to Indians through a Government Resolution of 1844, the same people in large numbers started learning English. As a result, English education rapidly expanded and took firm roots in the Indian soil. However, the education remained confined to wealthy urbanized and upper castes. Despite this limitation the period between 1839 and 1859 witnessed many educational activities including gradual evolution of provincial systems of education as well as two important dispatches. The first dispatch from the court of directors, in 1854, is considered to be the Magna Carta as it made provision for English education to Indian masses, replacing the earlier education policy which was beneficially targeted to provide education to a small section of the population belonging mainly to the upper castes. Another was from Lord Stanley, Secretary of State in 1859, which outlined a general education policy for India and establishment of the provincial departments of education to implement the same. The immediate outcome of the dispatch of 1839 was enacting the three University Acts of 1857. Accordingly, the three Universities were established, in Calcutta (now Kolkata), Bombay (now Mumbai), and Madras (now Chennai). The form, governance, and function of these three universities were based on London University. Consequently, the period from 1857 to 1947 witnessed a slow but significant expansion of higher education. The number increased from three universities, 27 colleges with 5,399 students in 1857 to 19 universities, 496 colleges and 2,41,369 students by 1947. Thus there was an addition of sixteen new universities, 469 colleges and 2,35,970 students during the period of 90 years.

Social Exclusion in Education

A long period of 190 years, between the Battle of Plassey (1757) and the independence of India (1947), witnessed a slow growth of education. During this period, the social character of education was not very different from the indigenous system. The indigenous educational institutions in all the Provinces of British India were essentially religious in nature. The people belonging to the untouchable castes had no education system of their own, and the available education was non-accessible to them as they were not admitted to the schools because of their social status (Hunter, 1882).

By design, the British started the educational institutes almost exclusively for the elite groups and the upper caste people. It also appeared from several reports that these institutions were kept socially exclusive, perhaps to please the dominant sections of the society who mattered more for the British in the smooth running of the administration. It is evident from some of the representative examples from the following official reports:

Ardeshir Dhanjishah Bahadoor, the Kotwal of Surat City and Member of the Examination Committee, in his report dated November 29, 1836 submitted to James Sutherland, Session Judge of Surat, on functioning of 167 schools and educational institutes with a total enrolment of 4,620 students, had clearly mentioned that, in general the students comprised children of *Banias* and Brahmins 'by far the most numerous and regular'. Further he reported that '16 schools were exclusively run for Brahmins'.

W. Elliot, Sub-Collector of Dharwad, wrote on October 12, 1833 and reported to Nesbet, Principal Collector and Agent in the Carnatic (Dharwad) that the school of Dharwad (established in 1826), 'provided instruction only to Brahmins while the great mass of the people derived no benefit from it'. Thus for the people other than the Brahmin community had no access to education.

Thomas Candy, the Superintendent of Native Schools (Government schools) in the Deccan, in his second inspection report dated May 1, 1839, had narrated the incident which occurred during his visit to the school No. 20 (Akola). Although, the population of *Koonbee* community was high but their children were not enrolled in the school. When he pleaded with the people belonging to the *Koonbee* community to send their children to the schools, the entire Brahmin community almost revolted against his suggestion (Parulekar and Bakshi, 1955). Brahmins did not want even *Koonbee* children in the school. *Koonbee* is a peasant community mainly involved in cultivation of land, and considered to be upper caste in the social order. If this was the attitude of Brahmins towards the communities like *Koonbee,* then one can well imagine what could have been their attitude towards the people belonging to untouchable castes.

Surprisingly, the Brahmin community was also agitated against the establishment of Poona Sanskrit College (1921) and the appointment of Captain Candy as its Superintendent. Indeed, the Brahmins would have been happy and welcomed, had the British started the college exclusively for them using the *Dakshina* Fund, the charitable grant that the Peshwa used to distribute among the Brahmins as rewards. This charitable grant was originally endowed by Dabharay Senapatee of the Maratha Empire from the Revenue of the State (Richey, 1921). Making the provision for the salary of Captain Candy from this fund seemed to have resulted in great anger and unrest among the Brahmins, who were known for not sharing their benefits and privileges with others. Captain Candy was evidently non-Brahmin, and that too a Christian and foreigner. Paying his salary from the *Dakshina* Fund was probably seen by Brahmins as an attack on their rights. The circumstances, historical and social, strongly supported this possibility and not any other. Until Mr. Elphinstone had continued to spend this grant for some time as per past practice, after the conquest of the Peshwa Empire (1818), everything was normal and smooth for the Brahmins. The day, a deviation was made by the British and they had used the *Dakshina* Fund for establishment of the college and particularly the payment of salary of its British Superintendent, instead of giving awards and rewards as well as community meals to Brahmins, it led to a controversy and agitation. It was expected as Brahmins lost their direct and targeted beneficial schemes.

Apart from these, one more case needs to be mentioned. In 1856, a boy who belonged to the Mahar caste was denied admission in the Dharwar Government School. He was willing to pay the prescribed fees and other charges. Following the denail, he approached the Government of Bombay with a petition, which in turn refused to intervene and ruled that: 'It would not be right, for the sake of a single individual, the only Mahar who had ever come forward to beg for admission into a school attended only by the pupils of higher castes and to force him into association with them, at the probable risk of making the institution practically useless for the great mass of natives' (Report of the Director of Public Instruction for Bombay Presidency for the year 1856-57). From the proceedings of the Government of Bombay, the case was to be referred to the Government of India which instead of finding a solution remarked: 'The Governor General in Council thinks it very probable that the Bombay Government has acted wisely in the matter; but it desires me (i.e. Secretary to the Government of India) to say that the boy would not have been refused admission to any Government school in the Presidency of Bengal' (Government of India, Letter No. 111, dated January 23, 1857). However, in reality the practice prevalent in Bengal was contrary to the 'supposition' of the Government of India. The Bengal authorities 'had left it to the District Committees of Institutions to grant or refuse admittance to candidates of inferior castes, with reference to the state of local native feeling in each case'. As a result, the depressed classes were left in the cold, even in Bengal (Moon, 1982; 1993).

According to Dr. B.R. Ambedkar, the policy of the British Government was deliberately designed to provide education to the higher castes, mainly the Brahmins (Moon, 1993). This fact could be ascertained from the Report of the Hunter Commission (1882), which Dr. Ambedkar had always used to criticize the Britsh and their education policy, detrimental to the downtrodden. It is mentioned therein that 'Even twenty-eight years after the introduction of Mass Education Policy (1854), the masses, particularly the untouchable castes, and the tribes remained outside the pale of education'. This fact is quite clear from Table 1 which shows the social composition of education at different levels in Bombay Presidency for the year 1881-82. It is amply clear that the main beneficiaries of British Education in India were Brahmins. The students belonging to the Brahmin community were 20.17 per cent at Primary School level, 30.70 per cent at Middle School level, 40.29 per cent at High School level, and 50.2 per cent at College level. Thus the enrolment of Brahmin children was very high compared to their share in population.

One of the important features of education was that the number of Brahmin children progressively increased right from the primary level up to the college level. The rate of increase of their enrolment from one level to the next remained constantly at ten per cent, which was the highest compared to other social groups. In case of children belonging to other Hindu castes, their presence in terms of percentage was 64.69 at primary level schooling. However, their enrolment declined gradually to 22.5 per cent, as they reached the college level. The dropout rates of students belonging to other

Table 1: Students Belonging to Different Social Groups in Education at Various Levels in Bombay Presidency (1881-82)

Social Groups	*Number of Students*			
	Primary School	*Middle School*	*High School*	*College*
Brahmins	63071 (20.17%)	3639 (30.70%)	1978 (40.29%)	241 (50.21%)
Other Hindus	202345 (64.69%)	4447 (37.51%)	1713 (34.89%)	108 (22.50%)
Lower Caste Hindus	2862 (0.87%)	17 (0.14%)	Nil (0%)	Nil (0%)
Aboriginal and Hill Tribes	2713 (0.87%)	6 (0.05%)	Nil (0%)	Nil (0%)
Christians	1521 (0.49%)	1429 (12.06%)	111 (2.26%)	14 (2.92%)
Muslims	39231 (12.54%)	687 (5.80%)	100 (2.04%)	7 (1.50%)
Parsis	3517 (1.12%)	1526 (12.87%)	965 (19.66%)	108 (22.50%)
Jews and Others	373 (0.12%)	103 (0.875)	92 (0.86%)	2 (0.42%)
Total	314248 (100%)	11854 (100%)	4959 (100%)	480 (100%)

Source: Compiled from three tables given in *Dr. Babasaheb Ambedkar: Writing and Speeches*. Vol. 12, pp. 102-103, 1993; Government of Maharashtra.

Hindu castes, which mainly comprised the rich and elite, were very high compared to Brahmins. The presence of untouchable castes, aboriginal and Hill Tribes students remained very low in education, so much so that there was no student from those communities either in the high schools or in the colleges of Bombay Presidency. Even at the primary level, their presence was negligible, i.e. less than one per cent. In case of the middle school, out of a total of 11,854 enrolments, there were just seventeen and six students belonging to the untouchable castes and Hill Tribes, respectively, which comes to 0.14 and 0.05 per cent, respectively, for them.

As suggested in the Dispatch of 1854, education was thrown open to masses. However, it remained inaccessible to untouchable castes. After the Hunter Commission Report (1882-1883) the government started separate schools for depressed classes in order to provide them access to education, particularly in Madras Presidency. The government also asked missionary bodies to provide education to these depressed class people. To encourage the missionaries, the government relaxed some of the grant-in-aid rules related to their educational institutes. However, there was no improvement in the educational status of depressed classes for more than 40 years between the Hunter Commission (1882) and the year 1923. It needs to be mentioned that primary education was transferred from the control of the Provincial Government of Bombay to the control of local bodies, in 1923. These local bodies were completely under the control of upper castes. It was known that upper caste people were against the education of Depressed Classes. This move adversely affected the educational interest of Depressed Classes of Bombay Province. For this very reason, Dr. Ambedkar protested against the transfer of primary education from government control to the control of local bodies.

The Report of Director of Public Instruction, Bombay Presidency, for the year 1923-24, revealed the disparity that existed in the educational advancement of the social groups. There was not even one student belonging to the depressed classes, enrolled in a college. Only 14 students belonging to depressed classes per one lakh of the population were reported to be enrolled for the secondary school education. At the primary level, there were eighteen depressed class students per one thousand of the population. On the other hand, the Brahmin students were 119 per one thousand of the population at primary level, three thousand per one lakh of the population at secondary level, and one thousand per two lakh of the population at the level of higher education. It could be noted that, Brahmins were smallest in number in terms of population but were ahead of others in education at all levels, whereas the depressed classes, second highest in terms of population, their presence was lowest in education. These facts indicated that the status of education of depressed classes, at least in Bombay Presidency, was deplorable, and remained the same for several years.

The educational conditions of untouchable castes in other Presidencies were also not very different. For example, Chinna Rao (2002) has shown that, in Madras Presidency education was under the control of Brahmins and was largely based on the Hindu religion in content, with the share less than five per cent in population the enrolment of Brahmins in education was 60 to 70 per cent outnumbering other non-Brahmin communities. Further, Yagati stated that the books used in the educational institutions contained lessons that were directly derived from the Vedas and various Shastras, Puranas, and other epic literature, which as a tradition the untouchables were not supposed to read. Most importantly, the teachers were all Brahmins. Another striking feature was the virtual exclusion of untouchable castes from the sphere of education. Apart from the above, according to him, on the basis of the Dispatch of 1854, which threw open education to all classes, the Government of Madras, in 1893, passed the legalization for 'Rate Schools,' called the Madras Education Act of 1863, and took a series of measures which were widely hailed as the Magna Carta of Panchama Education, did not yield desirable results. Indeed, these measures should have enhanced the educational status of the untouchable castes, but could not! In another study, Satyanarayana (2002) has shown that the growth of education between 1893 and 1947 in Andhra almost reflected the prevailing caste hierarchy, which means higher the caste, easy to access education, and on the other hand, lower the caste difficult to access education. Thus the accessibility to education was inversely proportional to the caste hierarchy.

Table 2 shows the literacy among the *Namasudras* of Bengal between the years 1901 and 1931 (Census of India, 1901; 1921; and 1931). In 1901, literacy among *Namasudras* was 3.3 per cent, while in 1911 it was 4.9 per cent. Expectedly, the literacy level was quite low and made slow progress. It took ten years to increase by 1.6 per cent. The schools were located mostly in the localities of caste Hindus, who resisted the entry of low caste children to these schools. It practically resulted in the denial of admission to untouchables even in government schools. Admissions were also denied to untouchables in the colleges in Calcutta. In the schools, the children of untouchables were not allowed to sit with their shoes on. They were supposed to remove them before entering the school. These children were provided with separate benches or had to sit in isolation on the floor. It may be mentioned that unlike other presidencies, no special or separate schools were established for the depressed classes in West Bengal Presidency. In the hostels, started and run with grants from the government, students belonging to depressed classes were not admitted; and when admitted, separate arrangements were made for their accommodation and food. In Bengal, also, education was not easily accessible to the depressed classes, i.e. the people who needed them the most.

Table 2: Literacy Among the Namasudras of Bengal

Year	*Population*			*Literate*		
	Total	*Male*	*Female*	*Total*	*Male*	*Female*
1901	1,796,220	905,292	890,928	59,344 (3.3%)	58,153 (6.42%)	1,191 (0.13%)
1911	1,860,705	941,851	918,854	91,625 (4.92%)	89,613 (9.51%)	2,012 (0.21%)
1921	2,004,911	1,018,013	986,808	150,548 (7.50%)	144,832 (4.22%)	5,716 (0.57%)
1931	2,094,936	1,067,386	1,027,550	139,016 (6.63%)	126,001 (11.80%)	37,551 (3.65%)

Source: Census of India, 1901, 1911, 1921 and 1931.

Table 2 also indicates the sharp rise in the literacy rates of the *Namasudras* from 4.92 to 7.50 per cent in the year 1921. *Namasudras* were perhaps the most awakened community at that time among the untouchable castes of Bengal and fought for their rights. They had started their own schools to educate their own community, which might have contributed to rise in their literacy.

It should be noted that the literacy had been defined as the capacity of a person to sign and identify the alphabets. Therefore, the actual number of people who were educated might be very low. Indeed, in the 1870s W.W. Hunter found in Faridpur district that, '...out of a total population of more than 156,000 of this curious race in Faridpur, less than 200 boys are to be found at school'. It comes to around just 0.13 per cent. This fact supports the exclusive and discriminatory nature of education in Bengal in the British period. The first census had classified around 26 castes in Bengal as being untouchable. Among these, except the *Namashudra* community, the spread of education was expected to be very low.

It must be mentioned that Chaudhury (2002) had carried out a detailed statistical analysis of the Census data (1901-1921) of different Presidencies and Princely States, and found that the literary rates of castes were strongly and positively correlated with the hierarchical positions of castes. These findings are similar to that of Satyanarayana (2002) for Andhra Pradesh. In other words, the high castes had high rates of literacy and the low castes had low rates of literacy. As a result, the small but dominant sections of the society managed to monopolize English education and other related opportunities (Aloysius, 2007).

Mindset of So-Called Upper Castes

Indian society is heterogeneous in nature, layered in graded inequality, and separated with non-permeable barriers in terms of social interactions. The people at the bottom had been forced to be social slaves with absolutely no basic human rights which lead to their suppression and exploitation by the upper caste Hindus in the name of religion, customs, and divine sanctions. The caste Hindus worshipped animals, plants, and also non-living objects, and believed in the concept of God's existence in every atom and molecule. The living or non-living, existence of god is believed in everything. With this belief, then god should be in the untouchable. However, those belonging to untouchable castes were treated differently by these same people. Even their presence could make them polluted. Hindus dehumanized and pushed untouchables to a status even lower than animals. Dogs, cats, and cattle could move and mix with high caste people, but just the touch or mere sight of the Dalits would make them polluted. Caste Hindus seemed to have forgotten that all human beings share a common biological origin and evolution.

The hierarchical structure of society was made extremely rigid in form and function; with no possibility for the downtrodden to move upward. The social inequalities were assumed to have religious sanctions and any effort made to bring social equality was considered to be an act of sin and losing salvation. Therefore whenever attempts were made to provide education to the downtrodden that met with a stiff or violent resistance.

'Traditionally, in the past, the caste Hindus believed that knowledge was sacred and could not be imparted to the untouchables. The high caste people objected to imparting education to lower castes on the ground that it would lead to their advancement in life and induce them to seek emancipation from their social slavery'. Such a mindset of caste Hindus is discussed below with some relevant examples. These and other aspects of graded social inequality have been addressed elsewhere in detail by Thorat and Kumar (2008).

The British Government was not very keen to provide education to the depressed classes. However, whenever the British tried to implement its educational policy of providing educational access to untouchables, it encountered strong opposition in all the provinces. According to Satyanarayana (2002), in Andhra when the government insisted on strict implementation, and opened schools for untouchable castes, the upper caste resistance found expression in the form of withdrawal of their children from schools [G.O. Law (Education) 15; January 25, 1929]. In case admitted to common schools, untouchable students were forced to sit outside the building, on separate benches or at a separate place with or without communities mat on the floor, despite the warnings being issued to teachers against such a practice. The study of Chinna Rao (2002) on the educational status of depressed classes during the 1930s also supports these facts.

As per the report, for the year 1896-97, by the Director of Public Instruction, Bombay, when the local officer of Kaira District gave admission to lower caste children, the caste Hindus closed down the schools for years. Further, the huts and crops of the low caste people were burnt and heavy penalties were imposed on the depressed classes for two years (Moon,1982,1993). While referring to the Census of 1901, Misra (1961) has reported the regular and common use of various terror tactics against the depressed castes, to prevent their access to education. Indeed, Brahmin opposition to the education of the lower castes was the prominent feature of Indian society of those days (Keer, 1964).

Higher castes in Kerala, particularly Nambudaris and Nayars, prevented the lower caste children from joining the schools. They disruptively opposed all efforts of the untouchables to secure education. These intolerant caste Hindus did not stop here. They even burnt down their schools (Aloysius, 2005). The untouchable castes had to face the horror and terror of the upper castes. For example when, the people belonging to the Izhava community attempted to enter a temple at Vaikkom in 1800, they were butchered and their bodies were buried in a tank near the temple (Rao, 1979). This horror act indicated the mindset of upper caste Hindus. It was also quite clear from the observations of Sir W.W. Hunter, Chairman of the Education Commission in 1882 that almost a similar situation also prevailed in Bengal. Hunter found that the Bengali high caste Hindus very strongly opposed any attempt made by the government to provide education to the untouchables. It was not surprising that the untouchables of Bengal, particularly *Namasudras*, held the *Bhadralok* responsible for their social degradation and educational backwardness. Even in the most hostile conditions, *Namasudras* fought back decisively for their rights and dignity. The *Namasudras* called a strike in 1873 against the *Bhadralok* who subjected them to their humiliation and persecution (Bandyopadhyay, 2005). This strike is considered to be the first general strike in India. As a mark of protest against the higher castes, the *Namasudras* preferred British rule to home rule, remained aloof from *Swadeshi* boycott, Non-cooperation and even the independent movement, and also did not join the agitation launched in 1905 following the Partition of Bengal by Curzon (Biswas, 2000). These facts showed the anger harboured by *Namasudras* against the Bhadralok.

In view of the Non-cooperation movement, protest, and resentment of caste Hindus, the British had established separate schools for the untouchables in some provinces. Even this act of the British was seen as an attack on Hindu religion and customs. For example, on establishing, the school of Cherumans, an untouchable caste at Calicut, 'the angry Nayars and Tiyas used to waylay the boys as they went to school and snatch the books from their hands' (Aloysius, 2007). The higher caste teachers refused to teach them in such separate schools established exclusively for the untouchables. 'On appointment or transfer, Brahmin teachers declined to join or even resigned from the service to avoid teaching untouchable children in the schools called Adi-Andhra schools exclusively for untouchable castes' (Satyanarayana, 2002). Because of caste prejudices, according to Chinna Rao (2002), the inspecting officials were reluctant to enter untouchable localities, to inspect the schools established exclusively for them. These officials use to call the students out well beyond the village from their localities, examine their answers from a distance more than ten feet. Such behaviour of caste Hindu teachers was not unexpected as they were enslaved by the teaching of their religion. The orthodox Hindus believed that learning was forbidden for untouchables. Its violation was believed to be a sin and a person who commits such a sin was assumed to be denied salvation. Therefore, any caste Hindu would make every possible effort to keep the religious customs intact and also not lose salvation.

Importantly, the representatives of depressed classes in local bodies, particularly in the Andhra region of Madras Presidency, had insisted upon the implementation of the principle of equality in education. Upon refusal by the upper castes, depressed classes made an attempt to establish educational institutions for themselves through their own efforts. When caught between the orthodoxy of Hindus and apathy of the British, self-emancipation was the best way that the untouchables could find. The *Namasudras* of Bengal did it quite effectively. Amazingly, the rich and higher caste people also opposed the establishment of schools by untouchables for themselves (Moon, 1982; 1993). It was evident that caste Hindus were determined to crush every hope and educational move of the untouchables. For example, in 1920, an appeal in the form of application of Swami Sahajanandan, an Adi-Dravidian saint, for a piece of government waste land to establish such a school was rejected by the high caste revenue official on false grounds. Sahajanandan decisively fought this case by taking it to higher authorities. On making enquiries, the British District Collector found all reports in the file misleading (D Dis No. 2395-20-A-4, Proceedings of the Collector of South Arcot, dated September 3, 1920).

Another example was more shocking. In 1923, M.C. Rajah, a renowned Dalit leader from the South and contemporary of Dr. Ambedkar moved a resolution in the local Legislative Council, Madras Presidency, 'asking for an increase in the number of scholarships for the children of the depressed classes'. The caste

Hindu Minister of Education vehemently opposed the resolution on the ground that 'poverty was not the monopoly of depressed classes' (Rajah, 1925). The caste Hindu minister failed to understand that poverty does not make a person socially backward. Indeed, it is the other way round. Poverty is just one of the symptoms of *Dalitness*. The sociology of poverty of *Dalits* is different from Brahmins and upper castes. In the British period, Brahmins in Madras Presidency, around three per cent of the total population, occupied more than eighty per cent of the posts (Bhagwan Das, 2007). This fact seemed to be conveniently ignored by the Minister. According to the Indian Public Service Commission (1887), that of 1866 Hindu members who joined judicial and executive services, as many as 904 (nearly 50 per cent) were Brahmins and 454 (nearly 25 per cent) were Kayasths (Misra, 1961). Can one compare the depressed classes with the Brahmins and upper castes.

Even the minds of some of the social reformers, politicians, and progressive people belonging to upper castes were trapped and enslaved by their Hindu traditions and beliefs. In 1916, when Sir Maneckji Dadabhoy, a Parsi member who represented the Hindu constituency, moved a resolution in the Central Legislature 'seeking amelioration in the moral, material, and educational conditions of the depressed classes and requested them to formulate schemes for the same, the Hindu members were upset and very angry with him'. Even Pandit Madan Mohan Malaviya, great freedom fighter, social worker, and educationist who founded the Banaras Hindu University, considered it as an attack on the Hindu community. It is surprising and unbelievable that he objected and opposed the resolution. A social reformer like Sir Surendranath Banerjee also took a similar line. In 1928, another resolution was moved by M.R. Jayakar asking the government to provide special facilities for the education of untouchables; it met the same fate as the earlier resolution mentioned above (Moon, 1993).

The social reformer should propagate messages that could help in social homogenization, by annihilating the castes, leading to social equality. Similarly, the educationist should spread the education in such a way that every section of society is equally benefited. Being a renowned social reformer and also an educationist, the same was expected from Pandit Ishwar Chandra

Vidyasagar. However, in his letter to Sir John Peter Grant, Lieutenant Governor of Bengal, written on September 29, 1859, he 'humbly' opined therein that 'education should be confined to the "higher classes on a comprehensive scale' (Biswas, 2000). Since, in India, traditionally, education was always confined to higher castes only, Vidyasagar perhaps wanted to continue the same, even in the modern period. The other possibility was that he was supportive of the trickle-down theory in education introduced by Macaulay. Both his ideas of confinement of education to the higher caste people and his support to spread education through the permeability were against the educational interests of the depressed classes.

In contrast, Lord Mayo, Governor General of India (1869-72), was of the view that the higher education would never reach the lower strata of the society (Basu, 1933), through the process of percolation. Similarly, Lord Rippon, in the Convocation address to Calcutta University, had clearly mentioned 'the non-desirability, in any country, to have a small highly educated class and a large uneducated class'. He stressed the equal distribution of education in society (Palit, 1882). Surprisingly, the British officials could see the importance and social relevance of education, but not some of the Indian social reformers and educationist. It is difficult to believe that a person like Vidyasagar could have such a negative and narrow view as mentioned earlier on the scope and spread of Indian education. In this context, it is also pertinent to note that the memorandum submitted by the Bengal Depressed Class Association to the Simon Commission in 1929, in which mention has been made about one of the observations of the Village Commission, on their condition of education. The Village Commission observed that: 'speaking generally, it is still the case that the casteman not only does nothing for the enlightenment of the outcaste, but puts positive obstacles in his way knowing that if he is enlightened, he can no longer be exploited'. The observation had presented the ground reality which needed no elaboration.

There were many people who could not or did not notice the educational backwardness of depressed classes. At one of the meetings of the British India Association, Calcutta, Baboo Kissory Chand Mitter in his speech mentioned that, 'Educate the upper and middle classes and the lower class will be instructed and elevated'. According to Mitter, once the upper and middle classes are educated they would educate the lower classes. He was sure that the education would percolate from top to bottom. The context in which Mitter made a statement was very clear. One could read upper and middle classes as upper caste, and lower classes as lower castes. However, it should be remembered that the theory of the down filtration of education had never been verified in the context of history, but still it was vigorously propagated in India. 'Indeed in no country in the world had knowledge filtered naturally from the highest to the lowest class. In India the higher castes were an educated class, a thousand years before the Christian era, and yet not a drop of knowledge descended to educationally thirsty people' (Dey, 1868). Therefore, indirectly, the trickle-down theory had been used very conveniently by some of the caste Hindus to oppose education to the downtrodden people.

The Arya Samaj was established for the purpose of social reformation. People working in this organization were supposed to be above caste prejudices. However, some of the caste Hindus associated with the Arya Samaj retained their deep-rooted prejudices. Chinna Rao (2002), narrated the incident that occurred in 1914 at the Arya Samaj anniversary function at the Begampet Vaidik Ashram. A competition was organized for the children from the various schools to recite Vedic Mantras and explain their meanings. When an untouchable student, from one of the schools called Adi-Hindu Primary School, performed very wel, stood first and received appreciation from the audience, the Secretary of the Vaidik Ashram was shocked as a Brahmin student had not won. He objected to the results with rude and vulgar remarks against the untouchable student. He was of the opinion that the *Chandal,* derogatery term used for untouchable, was not supposed to deserve such an honour. Subsequently, the prize was not given to the untouchable student. The moral of the story is that even if one adds sugar or applies butter to bitter gourd, it still remains bitter. Similarly, the teachings of socio-religious reformers did not change the mindset of some people and retained their caste prejudices. The secretary of the Ashram had forgotten the social background of Valmiki and Vyas who wrote the *Ramayana* and *Mahabharata.*

There was no doubt that the caste Hindus had been rigid in their observance of the religious rites and social customs. Any violation of these religious rites and social customs particularly by the untouchables was never tolerated by them. Even for the smallest fault or mistake, the untouchables were severely punished. Therefore, it was not at all surprising that the caste Hindus continued to resist the education for the untouchables, most of the times violently. Although, the higher castes did not allow untouchables to either change or claim benefits including education, they themselves had however changed and adjusted quickly with changing times to grab the newly emerging opportunities without showing respect to their own religious and social customs. For example, when the Grant Medical College was opened in Bombay in 1845, 'initially the upper castes, particularly Brahmins, did not come forward for medical education for the fear of polluting dissections, etc'. (Deepak Kumar, 2006). They agitated over this matter and made a hue and cry. It could be one of the reasons behind closing down the Medical School founded in 1826 in Bombay, by Elphinstone, the Governor of the Presidency. However, the upper castes themselves had opted to enrol once they found that, it would bring better fortune, jobs and more money. For the same reason, the influential section of the natives welcomed the establishment of the Calcutta Medical College (1835), where Madhusudan Gupta had become the first Indian to dissect a human body. He was given a 21-gun salute in Fort William for this act by the British (Deepak Kumar, 2006). Gupta went against traditions, customs and religion. For better opportunities upper castes, particularly Brahmins always went against their own religion. It must be noted that crossing the sea for a Hindu meant loss of his religion. But in course of time, this religious restriction faded away (Talukdar, 1998). Now everyone knows that Brahmins and trading castes were the first ones to cross the sea to reach Europe and USA for education, jobs and money. Although, there could be a long list of violations of religious and social codes by the upper caste Hindus for their own benefit, the same was not permitted in the case of the untouchables, so as to continue their exploitation. The upper castes resisted the provision and spread of education to the untouchables in the name of Hindu religion and the hierarchical social order.

Asking for educational rights for the untouchable castes was considered as an attack on the Hindu religion, even by few highly respected politicians, freedom fighters, and social reformers of that period.

Attitude of the British Towards the Education of Untouchables

The adage that it is not possible to fool all the people all the time, however, was proved wrong by the British Government. 'It had created an illusion in the minds of untouchables and made them believe that the British Government was greatly concerned about their condition and that all possible efforts would be made for their upliftment including providing education. However, at the same time, the British Government focused on the rich and elite of the classes and upper castes, mainly Brahmins from the Hindu community'. This attitude of the British Government was described by Zelliot (2004), as self-protective, and maintained the same as a policy by the British for a long time. Therefore, the educational efforts made by the British Government for the untouchables had always been weak and insincere. Indeed, from the beginning, the educational needs of untouchables were almost completely ignored by the British.

When the Grant Medical College was established in Bombay in 1845, the Principal wanted to open its doors to the downtroddens, as high castes were reluctant to opt for medical education as it perceived polluting and causing religious sin. He approached the Director of Public Instructions (DPI) for such permission, who replied in panic that 'we have come here to rule and not to cause social upheavals' (Deepak Kumar, 2006). The response of the DPI was a confirmative test of the governmental plan to keep the untouchables away from education.

Lord Warren Hastings took a similar line way back in the year 1781. He established a *Madrassa* to gain the sympathy, support, and cooperation of the elite Muslims. The same policy was followed by Jonathan Duccan who established a Sanskrit College at Banaras in 1891. Thus, the former appeased the Muslim elites, whereas the latter appeased the Brahmins. This possibility was strongly supported by the warning given by Randle Jackson, a British Member of Parliament. He said that 'we have lost our colonies in

America by imparting our education there, we need not do so in India too' (Sankhdher, 1999). The British seemed to have learned from their past mistakes and were very selective in spreading education among the various sections of Indian society.

Keeping their own interest in mind, the British focused on the small but dominant upper castes particularly Brahmins who had traditionally complete control over the hierarchical society. It was the dispatch of the Court of Directors, dated June 3, 1814, to the Governor General in Council, prescribing therein the plan for effective implementation of the Section 43 of the Statute 1813, and asking to encourage and promote Sanskrit learning among the Hindus so as to 'fulfil the purpose which the Parliament had in mind' (Moon, 1982, 1993). It obviously implied that the purpose in the mind of Parliament was just to keep the Brahmins happy and ignore the interest of the other sections of the society particularly the untouchables. The British, soon, understood the reality that for centuries, Indian society remained under the control of Brahmins. Therefore, keeping them happy, promoting and protecting their interest and taking care of their needs was essential to get the support and cooperation of Brahmins, to rule the country. This approach reflected in every action the British had taken. With this background, it was significant to refer to the communication from the Court to Madras in 1830, upholding the expediency of educating the upper castes. The Court ruled that 'the improvements in education are those which concern the education of high classes, which have natural influence over the minds of their countrymen. By raising the standard of instruction among these classes, it would eventually produce much greater and more beneficial change in the ideas and feelings of the community than one can hope to produce by acting directly on the more numerous classes'. It was an anxious desire of the Court to have 'at their disposal a body of natives qualified by their habits and acquirement to take a larger share and occupy high positions in the civil administration'. The Court firmly believed that to keep the country under the British control, it was necessary to create a space for the upper castes, particularly Brahmins in administration. Therefore, this could be reason for introducing Sanskrit as one of the eligibility criteria for addmission in the Medical College, in the Madras Province, making this education exclusively for the Brahmins and upper castes, and shutting the doors for the socially backword castes which had prohibited by the practice of Hindu religion, to learn Sanskrit (Veermani, 2015). Due to this very reason Dr. Ambedkar could not take Sanskrit and instead had to opt for Persian during his early education. On the other hand, the fear of the Court was that 'education would change the untouchables into 'men of superior intelligence and nothing would prevent them to join the higher offices open to native talent, which might anger many benevolent men and also could be perceived by them as the height of rigidity and weakness in the British Government to succumb to the social prejudice' (Moon, 1982, 1993).

A similar mindset is emitted from the communication of Lord Monstuart Elphinstone (1823), Governor of Bombay Presidency, to the Commissioner of Indian Affairs. Therein, he wrote, 'I consider it is more important to impart a high degree of education to the upper classes than to diffuse a lower sort of it among the common people' (Sankhdher, 1999). Surprisingly, Lord Elphinstone was considered to be a most liberal and noble-minded administrator, even when he held views such as these. The college established in Bombay to provide English education to Brahmins and upper castes, was named after him to recognize the service he had rendered to the people of Bombay Presidency. On the education of the untouchables, he observed in 1824 that 'the lower castes are not only the most despised, but among the least numerous of the great division of society, and it could be feared that if our system of education first took roots among them, it would never spread further' (Zelliot, 2004). Apart from taking keen interest in the education of upper castes particularly the Brahmins, he restricted the teaching profession exclusively to the Brahmins. He went to extent to select the first batch of Brahmins and appoint as the government teachers (Elphinstone, 1823; Rao, 2016).

Although, the British by design oriented their education policy towards Brahmins who at the beginning did not show much interest in English education. It was evident from low enrolment of Brahmin students in Elphistone College of Bombay. Out of the total number of students one hundred and sixty-one, between the years 1827 to 1842 Brahmins were just twelve. Even Parsis were more than double (twenty-eight) than them. The college was dominated by Pathare Prabhu with their enrolment of seventy-one. Brahmins perceived English education as detrimental to Indian tradition as well as their own interest and social status.

On the other hand, the British were, perhaps, more worried about the unexpected low strength of Brahmin students which remained almost at the same level for more than twenty years after establishment of the college. To push and implement their educational agenda successfully, the British had taken several measures around 1851 to attract Brahmin students to the college. At the same time, educational interest of untouchable castes like Mahars, Mangs and Chamars was ignored. Although, the British did not believe in the caste system, they followed customs, traditions and religious sanctions of not permitting untouchable castes to seek education. It took the British almost nine years from 1851 to 1860 to get Brahmin students enrolled in significant number. Brahmins became the single largest caste in terms of numbers in college and remained more than fifty from 1867 onwards. Around 1885, the strength of Brahmin students reached 43 per cent of the total enrolments. In 1890, out of a total of 218 students, Brahmins were 65, and Prabhus were just 12. Finally the dominance of Brahmins in the college could be successfully established which the British always wanted (Chavan, 2013, and references therein)

Similarly, Brahmins of Poona, very conservative and orthodox in nature, perceived English education as a great threat to their culture and social status. Mastery of Sanskrit had enabled them to keep the society under their clutches for centuries. Deviation from Sanskrit meant losing their grip over the society and lowering their own status. Therefore, when the British established the English school in Poona in 1823, they boycotted and did not enrol the their children. Aggressive protests exihibited their disapproval and anger against English education. The pressure built by Brahmins had forced the British to close down the English school. Interestingly, just after two years the same Brahmins changed their position on realizing the importance of English education.The introduction of Enlish, in 1825, in the Sanskrit College, was welcomed with open arms. Whenever found beneficial, Brahmins were the first to avail of the opportunities. The English education was not the exception. It could be noted that 'a new class emerged around 1850 could foresee the material gains the English could offer, started submitting appeals and petitions for English education' (Chavan, 2013, and references therein). In changed circumstances Sanskrit lost its relevance. Soon, Brahmins mastered English and continued to hold their grip over society.

British English education, opened the doors of employment opportunities for Indians. Because of their own selfish interest and British agenda, the Brahmins and other upper castes could access English education and harvested its benefits. On the contrary, the barriers of religious sanctions, traditions and customs, the differentially favourable attitude of the British, kept the untouchable caste educationally backward. As a result, 'the Brahmins in the Madras Presidency and Bhadralok in the Bengal Presidency took advantage of the new educational policy and occupied most of the posts available in the administration' (Bhagwan Das, 2007). A similar situation prevailed in the other presidencies.

Thus, the British Government skilfully navigated the system of Indian education. It differentially favoured upper castes, particularly Brahmins and at the same time kept the untouchables at a safe distance from the purview of education. No schools were opened for the untouchables until 1855 in the Bombay Presidency (Moon, 1982, 1993).

Bhagwan Das (2007) described lucidly the educational opportunities availed by the downtrodden despite adverse conditions created by social traditions, religious sanctions and the negative approach of Brahmins as well as lack of interest shown by the British. He mentioned in some detail that 'the untouchables had joined the Presidency armies and fought battles along with others under the command of British officers. Military service provided the first opportunity to the soldiers belonging to the untouchable castes to learn, read, and write'. Being camp followers and domestic servants for British families in their cantonments (Bhagwan Das, 2007) untouchables could listen and learn and subsequently read and write English. The keen interest shown by missionaries in educating downtroddens, enabled them to overcome the official neglect and apathy.

Bhagwan Das (2007) has also observed that 'their interaction with missionaries, as soldiers in the army, as camp-followers, and as domestic servants of British families made lower caste communities to understand the value and significance of education which encouraged them to demand educational opportunities'. In the course of time, the untouchables organized and launched movements in various parts of the country, to realize their dream of education. However, the British continued their predetermined educational policy of neglect towards the untouchables. For more information, refer to the work of Richter, 1908; Ambedkar, 1928; Ramaswamy, 1974 and Chinna Rao, 2007.

Individual efforts of officials of the East India Company (1780s-90s), treaties of Grant (1813), minutes of Macaulay (1835), and Dispatch of 1854 were some milestones of the education policy of the British. All these four policies differentially favoured the elite and upper castes. On the other hand, these policies particularly the latter two had a long-lasting adverse effect on the untouchables. Macaulay's minutes were targeted to groom the elite class to make them eligible and involve them, which could help the British to administer the country. For others, particularly the under-privileged, Macaulay planned education through the 'down filtration'. The policy of 1854 opened avenues for the under-privileged to access education. However, its implementation was detrimental to the interest of untouchables. The implementation and implications of policies of 1835 and 1854 have been briefly discussed.

For the massification, a mandate given by the Dispatch of 1854, the British government had prepared a plan to educate the Indian masses indirectly through the elite class identified by Macaulay which was also termed as middle anglicized class (Smith, 1857); by the process called 'filtration' or 'interpretation'. Thus, Western education was expected to be imparted to the Indian masses by their own Anglicized class (John, 1973). Amazingly, the British had undertaken the massification by the 'trickle-down' process, through the 'elite few' which had been traditionally against the education for others particularly, downtroddens. Indian society consists of hierarchically arranged four *Varnas*. In which *Brahmins* at the top could learn and teach. Next in order, *Kshatriyas* and *Vaishyas*, respectively, who could only learn. However, the *Shudras* and *ati-Shudras*, at the bottom could neither learn nor teach. Because of the religious sanctions, the people at the lowest rung had been completely excluded from education. Any deviation from this tradition was considered to be contempt and the violator could be socially boycotted and at the same time exterminated from his caste. As every social group had well-defined duties, making changes in its form and function was also considered to be a sin of a serious nature. The *varna* is not a homogeneous group of people. It is made of a cluster of castes. Because of these strict religious rules, and social traditions Brahmins did not teach people who were at the bottom and neither did the upper caste people allow the untouchables to learn. This rigid practice continued for thousands of years, preventing the untouchables from receiving education. With this background, the British government adopted a policy of non-interference in the social and religious affairs of Indian society, and shifted its responsibility to the Indian elite to educate the downtrodden. The British rescued themselves and introduced and propagated the theory called 'down filtration'. The knowledge never trickled-down from the *Brahmins* to untouchables in the past in Indian society, and neither did it percolate down from the higher to lower classes in any country in the world earlier. It was, perhaps, a false hope given by the clever British government to the untouchables. Indeed, the British as mentioned earlier were against the education of untouchables which could also be seen from Para 21, in the Communication from the Court to Madras in 1830. It is included in the Report of the Board of Education of Bombay Presidency for the year 1850-51. It stated therein: 'If the children of the poor are admitted freely to government institutions, what is there to prevent all the despised castes—the Dheds, Mahars, etc., from flocking in number to their walls' (Moon, 1982, 1993).

The mandate of dispatch of the Court of Directors of the year 1854 aimed at providing access to education to the masses, had violated while implementing the same as untouchables were deliberately excluded and, therefore, never really benefited. Many British officials were upset and unhappy, and agitated against the massification of education, which assured its failure. In their opinion the new education policy would, 'give a high degree of mental cultivation to the lower classes, while leaving the more wealthy in ignorance'. Expectedly, the British officials were more concerned about educational need and status of upper castes, the elite and the rich. Educating the untouchables was perceived to be detrimental to the interest of the British as it could lead to discontent and possible revolt by the general public which might make conditions difficult for them to run the administration. Such anticipated or imaginary dire consequences to British rule probably resulted in the general antipathy of its officials towards the education of the untouchable castes.

An attitude and insistence of British officials to establish colleges and schools for higher castes and classes forced the Secretary of State for India in his dispatch of 1859 to write and reiterate again the responsibility of the government towards the education of masses. British officials had no option but to obey the orders which came from Britain. Accordingly, the schools were opened for the masses in the various districts. However, the stiff resistance of caste Hindus to the admissions of the children of untouchables in these schools, and antipathy of British officials again contributed to the failure of the education policy of massification, making the Dispatch of 1859 a wasteful exercise. When reviewed the education policy of 1854, the Hunter Commission (1882) observed that 'the untouchables were found to be outside the pale of education as they were before the year 1854'. No significant improvement was seen in the educational status and condition of untouchables, at least, in Bombay Presidency till 1923.

Thus the British, by design, restricted education to higher castes, mainly to Brahmins, and in turn empowered the already powerful, and deprived those who were already depressed.

Indigenous Initiatives and Efforts

Mahatma Jotiba Phule (1827-1890), Savitribai Phule (1831-97), Sayajirao Gaikwad (1875-1939) of Baroda, Chhatrapati Shahu Maharaj (1874-1922) of Kolhapur, Maharshi Vithal Ramji Shinde (1873-1944), B.R. Ambedkar (1891-1956), Karmaveer Bhaurao Patil (1887-1959) and many others made all possible efforts to spread education among the depressed classes. Phule in his entire life worked and fought for the cause of depressed classes. He started a school for the untouchables in 1852, the first of its kind at least in Bombay Presidency, even before the efforts made by the Christians or the British (Zelliot, 2002). Even before this, he opened a school for girls, in 1848, and subsequently two more for girls in 1851. He attributed the social and economic backwardness of depressed classes to the lack of their education. He observed, 'the lower castes were sunk deep in ignorance and misery, which could arise only by getting education' (O'Hanlon, 1985). Phule continued to plead with the British Government for the education of the downtrodden, which was evident from the memorandum, dated October 19, 1882 he had submitted to the Education Commission, (1882) popularly known as the Hunter Commission, to draw attention towards the neglect of primary and higher education among the poor and backward masses and also urged to open separate schools, for Mahar, Mang, and such other communities, to make primary education compulsory, to provide scholarships and other incentives, not to withdraw government aid to higher education, not to entrust higher education to private agencies and keep primary and higher education under control of government and many other related matters. It can be mentioned that Phule's letter, unlike that of Raja Rammohun Roy (1823), was ignored mostly by the scholars in the field of Indian education. It did not get a place in the educational records compiled by the British like Sharp (1920) and Richey (1921). Phule was the first social reformer in the country to start a movement for the education of masses (Chalam, 2007). Phule used every opportunity to draw the attention of the Queen and other British authorities towards the education needs of the masses, particularly the downtrodden. During the visit of the Prince of Wales to Poona (now Pune) in 1889, Phule adopted a novel approach to welcome him and in turn to convey to the Queen the need for education of the socially backward communities. He made the first generation school children of Mahar and Mali castes receive him with the message, 'Tell Grandma, we are a happy nation, but 19 crores are without education' (Keer, 1964).

The contribution of Sayajirao Gaikwad of Baroda towards the welfare of depressed classes and their education is well known. As early as 1883, he opened 18 special schools for the depressed classes (Nurullah and Naik, 1951). He made education free. Slates, pencils, textbooks, etc., were provided free. He also introduced compulsory primary education around the year 1892-93. Probably, the Gaikwad of Baroda was the first one in the country to take such measures. He provided financial assistance in the form of a scholarship to Dr. B.R. Ambedkar for pursuing his education in the US.

Measures taken by Chhatrapati Shahuji Maharaj for the upliftment of the depressed classes were also exemplary. He was against the caste system and defied its rules. Shahuji Maharaj himself was a victim of the caste system. Brahmins opposed his recitation of *Vedic mantras*. According to them, being a Shudra, Shahuji Maharaj had no right to chant the *Vedic mantras*. This incident was not the first one in the history of the Maratha kingdom. Earlier even the coronation of Shivaji Maharaj was opposed by the Brahmins on the same ground. Shahuji Maharaj mingled with depressed classes and accepted tea from them. If seen in retrospect such an act of Shahuji Maharaj was revolutionary. More significantly, he had not just encouraged, but also participated in social reformation movements such as the eradication of untouchability. In the month of February, 1908, he founded an education society with the objective to spread education among the untouchable classes of the Kolhapur state (RAKS 1907-08). He also opened hostels and schools for the depressed classes. As a result, the number of students of untouchable castes in the primary schools increased from 234 in 1894 to 27,830 by 1921-22. Further, importantly, in 1911, out of 507 students, 26 belonged to the Mahar community were enrolled in Rajaram High School (Latthe, 1924). Considering the time, this number (26) was quite high in terms of percentage (5.13 per cent). It could be mentioned that these 26 students were from just one caste and that too in one school. Therefore, the actual number of students was expected to be high as the depressed classes were a cluster of many castes and there were many schools in the state of Kolhapur at that time. He believed in social equality and equal opportunity. Perhaps, because of this he closed all the separate schools meant for the lower castes, and then opened all the Public Schools for the untouchables. He issued an order on September 30, 1919 for this purpose. It might not be out of context to mention here that while the scholarship provided by the Gaikwad of Baroda made possible for Dr. Ambedkar to pursue MA and PhD level education in the United States, that one provided by Shahuji Maharaj of Kolhapur enabled Dr. Ambedkar to complete DSc and Bar-at-Law degrees in London.

Both Vitthal Ramji Shinde and Bhaurao Patil also worked in their lifetime to spread education among untouchables. Considering their times it was not easy to establish and run the schools for the poor and underprivileged. Raising the funds in a ruler setting itself was a challenge. Most importantly, it was essential to mobilize people, convince them about the significance of education and importance of making children educated. The children, at school going age, were one of the sources of earning for their parents. Sending children to school could put an additional burden to their miseries. Further, for schooling, the children had to go to distant places and stay there which needed financial support for maintenance. Poverty did not allow parents to support such education. Educating the child was an unbearable double financial burden for the parents. To succeed in spreading education it become essential to start the hostels with free lodging and boarding facilities for the children of the underprivileged. Additionally, Shinde and Patil had to face the anger of higher castes, who resisted the education of children of the poor and underprivileged. Shinde established a night school in 1905, he subsequently opened more schools for the underprivileged. He also established an organization called the Depressed Classes Mission, and according to its report for the year 1912, 1,100 students were enrolled in 23 schools run by the mission. Thus, many from the untouchable communities could access the education and reaped its benefits. He also established an Ahilya Ashram at Pune (then Poona) which remained an important centre of activities related to the education of Dalits.

Patil, affectionately called Karamveer, made efforts to spread education in Maharashtra, particularly in the western region. He established the education society called Rayat Shikshan Sanstha in 1919, and opened the schools. As he recognized the need of taking care of lodging and boarding of students started hostels so that the children of the poor and underprivileged could come and stay to pursue their education. As a result, a large number of students came from the different villages and availed of hostel facilities which enabled them to complete their education. With such efforts, Patil could spread education among the poor and unprivileged. He tried to improve the conditions of the life of the rural masses. Rayat Shikshan Sanstha continues to function even today. The untouchables, large in number, benefited because of Patil's education society. The efforts of Shinde and Patil changed the educational landscape of Maharashtra.

As pointed out by Zelliot (2002), the educational reformers, who made early efforts and established institutions to provide opportunities for education to lower caste people, were all non-Brahmins. Although the Brahmins, it is stated further, did not establish any educational institutions, the social reformers and progressives among them supported the upliftment of untouchables in general, and their education in particular.

Dr. Ambedkar, who considered the education as a panacea for all ills of depressed classes, took forward and continued the social reformation movement started by Chhatrapati Shahuji Maharaj and Mahatma Phule. Dr. Ambedkar was a great social reformer who used politics as an instrument and fought on several fronts for the rights of untouchables, breaking the shackles of social slavery, annihilating caste differences and bringing equality in society where the members of untouchable communities could live in honour and dignity. Even with such a hectic, busy and eventful life, Dr. Ambedkar accorded equal importance to the education and educational issues of untouchables. As he was always thirsty and hungry for knowledge, Dr. Ambedkar read and wrote extensively on various topics and subjects including education in the newspapers from *Mook Nayak*, to *Prabudha Bharat* which he started and published from time to time and in the form of scholarly books. In his last days, though not keeping well and needed rest, he wrote books like *Revolution and Counter Revolution* and *Budhha and His Dhamma*. In a fragile health condition he planned to launch a national political party which he named the Republican Party of India, to bring all like-minded progressive national leaders under its wings. He himself drafted its constitution. Dr. Ambedkar, perhaps the only leader of his time, who was highly educated, with extraordinary talent, wisdom and vision. He wrote or spoke on every issue. While mobilizing people to fight for social justice, Dr. Ambedkar asked his followers to educate their children for emancipation and socio-economic progress. Indeed, his message, 'educate, organize and agitate' spread in all directions and reached every part of the country and galvanized the entire Dalit community.

As evidence before the University Reformed Committee (1924), appeal in the Bombay Assembly (1927) and in other numerous memorandums as well as interventions, presentations, evidences, debates and discussions in the Governor General's Assembly, Constitution Assembly and Parliament, Dr. Ambedkar pleaded and protected the educational interest of Dalits. He severely criticized the British for their educational policy which completely and continuously neglected the untouchables. He used the British sources like the Hunter Commission Report (1882) and Report of Board of Education of Bombay Presidency (1850-51) for his arguments. He opposed the Compulsory Primary Education Act (1923) (Bombay Act No. IV of 1923) and called it a 'fraud'. Some people misunderstood Dr. Ambedkar and falsely propagated that he had been against compulsory primary education. Being detriment to the interest of the downtrodden, he rightly opposed certain clauses. He was against the provision in the Act of 1923 to shift primary education from the Province Government to the Local School Boards under the members belonging to higher castes who were too uneducated to understand the necessity of education, and were traditionally against the education of depressed classes. The keen interest of Dr. Ambedkar in the compulsory primary education to the masses and significance he attached to it was evident from his memorandum submitted to the Indian Statutory Commission which visited India in 1928. He therein pleaded for compulsory primary education for the general masses and depressed classes. Dr. Ambedkar who pleaded with the British for compulsory primary education under the control of the Provincial Government, after independence, while drafting the constitution he himself got an opportunity to deal with this important issue. It is important to mention that Article 45 incorporated under the directive principles of the Constitution of India was his sole contribution. It reads as, 'The State shall endeavour to provide within a period of ten years from the commencement of the Constitution, for free and compulsory education for all children who complete the age of 14 years'. When seen in the context of the recently promulgated the Right to Education Act, 2009, it shows the vision of Dr. Ambedkar and importance he has given to primary education. Dr. Ambedkar always accorded priority to primary education which could also be seen from his promise of free and compulsory primary education given in the manifesto of his Independent Labour Party. Perhaps, he was the first who emphasized education in its election manifesto, especially in the early days (Chalam, 2007). He emphasized the significance and importance of education for the downtrodden, and argued that, 'when communities are unequal in their status and progress, and are to be brought to the level of equality, then the only remedy is to adopt the principle of inequality and give favoured treatment to those who are below the level' (Moon, 1986). Education being the great equalizer, Dr. Ambedkar assured access to it by the underprivileged through making a provision in the Constitution. According to Article 46, the state is required 'to promote with a special care of the educational and economic interest of weaker sections of the people, and in particular of the Schedule Castes and Schedule Tribes and to protect them from social injustice and all forms of exploitation.' Apart from education, the provision of reservation in legislation and services were also made in the Constitution for SCs and STs. Had Dr. Ambedkar not been there in the Constitution Assembly, the possibility was quite high of not making provision for such welfare measures in the Constitution, and SCs and STs could have been completely at the mercy of higher castes.

On becoming the member of the Governor General's Council, Dr. Ambedkar submitted memorandum 'on education and other grievances of Schedule Castes' in 1942. Therein, he pointed out almost non-accessibility of sciences, engineering and technology education and non-availability of opportunities to advanced education in foreign universities. In support of this observation he gave an example of the School of Mines at Dhanbad stating that out of ninety-seven registered students none were from SC, and demanded reserved seats for them. He emphasized science and technology education to enhance the employment opportunities for the underprivileged. Further, therein he pleaded for, among other things, an annual grant of Rs. 200,000 for scholarships for SC students and another annual grant of Rs. 100,000 for scholarships for SC students to go abroad to get science and technology education in the US and other European countries, including England. It may be mentioned that Dr. Ambedkar himself was a beneficiary of scholarships given by Sayajirao Gaikwad of Baroda and Shahuji Maharaj of Kohlapur, which enabled him to complete his education in the US and England respectively. Who can understand the importance and necessity of scholarships other than him and therefore pleaded with emphasis for the same. The representation of Dr. Ambedkar demanding scholarships and stipends for studies in India and abroad as well as reservations in the public services yielded the desired effect. On the recommendation of the Viceroy, the Secretary of State accepted these demands in 1942, and 'the first time in history the Scheduled Castes were provided 8.5 per cent reservation in central services and other facilities' (Bhagwan Das, 2007).

Dr. Ambedkar did not solely depend on the British for the education of the downtrodden. He founded the People's Education Society, on 8th July 1945 with its headquarters in Bombay, to provide access and spread education, particularly higher education among the Dalits. He started Sidhartha College (1946) in the prime Fort locality of Bombay. Subsequently, he acquired a huge piece of land (more than three hundred acres which is enough, even today, to establish the multi-faculty traditional university) at Aurangabad in Marathwada region then Marathi-speaking parts of Nizam State which remained backward till recently in all respects, being remote and neglected. He started Milind College there in 1950 with hostel facilities. It was the first college of this region. Soon, Dalit students, in large numbers, joined these colleges where not just imparted education but also trained for social responsibility. During and after completion of their studies, these motivated and inspired students went back to society and carried forward the work of Dr. Ambedkar in their own way, and awakened and mobilized the masses for their rights. After Dr. Ambedkar, this Society expanded its work by opening more colleges. Even today, this society is very active and making several efforts to realize the dream of Dr. Ambedkar. The students of these institutions, particularly after the death of Dr. Ambedkar, have been carrying his message, 'educate, unite and agitate' across the nation and around the world. 'The life and mission of Ambedkar in itself is a case that reflects the history of how education can shape a leader and destiny of the people whom he represented' (Chalam, 2007), as well as the destiny of the nation. The perspective of Dr. Ambedkar on various issues including the history, question of Hindu women, education, and his response to social exclusion can be referred to in the work of Thorat and Aryama, 2007. His social movement for emancipation of depressed classes and efforts he made for their education for more than forty years changed the life of millions of people who suffered for centuries as social slaves of the upper castes.

Similarly, many social reformers from the Madras Presidency took initiatives and made efforts to spread education among the untouchable communities. Expectedly, as mentioned earlier, the British focused on upper castes and ignored the aspirations of the underprivileged. According to Chinna Rao (2002), who undertook a survey for the period 1823-25, in the Madras Presidency, there were 12,498 schools and 1, 88,000 students in a population of 12,850,941. Almost all these students belonged to the upper castes. The British made education, by design or default non-accessible to untouchables. Although, the educational interest of untouchables was ignored by the British, in colonial Andhra of Madras Presidency, social reformers like Kandukuri Viresalingam (1848-1919) and Raghupati Venkatratnam Naidu (1862-1939) made efforts to educate them. Satyanarayana (1952), Appa Rao (1972) and Ramakrishna (1983) could be referred for more details. Later on, Unnava Laxminarayana and Tripuraneni Ramaswamy Choudhary carried forward the agenda of educating the untouchables. The Maharaja of Pithapuram also took an interest and supported the education of the untouchables.

The first generation of educated Dalits such as Bhagya Reddi Verma (1888-1939), Vendru Tatayya (1850-1930), Eeli Vadapalli (1911-1972), Golla Chandrayya (1888-1972), and Pandu Laxmanswamy (1892-1960) soon understood the low degree of impact of philanthropic efforts and British initiative, and took the responsibility themselves to spread education among their own community. Apart from them, organizations like Andhra Provincial Harijan Sevak Sangh which was established in 1932 worked for the education of the Adi-Andhra community. Between 1932 and 1934, this Sevak Sangh started 41 night schools, 11 day schools, 19 hostels, and 20 libraries and continued its educational service for years (Satyanarayana, 2002). Christian missionaries took more interest than other organizations in the education of the downdrodden. In this context it could be mentioned that organizations such as Prarthana Samaj, Brahmo Samaj, and Arya Samaj rejected the evils of the caste system and pleaded for the eradication of untouchability (Gautam, 1991), but failed to a great extent to support and provide education to the downtrodden who belonged to their own religion. Their activities could perhaps be considered as a reaction to counter the success of Christian missionaries in proselytizing untouchables. The Hindu reformers, the 'enlightened' caste Hindus and organizations also failed to abolish the caste system and kept a safe distance from the social movements actively involved in spreading education among Dalits. They treated symptoms and not the cause. Importantly, the first generation of educated untouchable leaders saw education as the only effective instrument to break the shackles of social slavery. These leaders formed the Adi-Andhra Mahasabha and spread education among the people of their own community. The Mahasabha held conferences for awakening the masses, passed resolutions urging the government to introduce free education for untouchable children (Satyanarayana, 2002). Similar activities were also undertaken in other parts of Madras Presidency which was evident from the petitions submitted to the East India Company in 1779 and to the British Administration at Fort St. George in 1810. Further, the Adi-Dravida Mahajan Sabha (1857), Dravida Mahajan Sabha (1891), and Dravida Educational Association (1937) had protested against untouchability, exploitation, and injustice. Apart from such protests, these organizations launched the struggle for their education.

Pandithar Ayodhee Thass (1845-1914), Rao Bahadur Rettamalai Srinivas 1860-45 and others individually or through organizations persistently demanded separate schools for the children of untouchable communities. The leaders also demanded fee concessions and scholarships to students. Because of their efforts several schools for children of untouchables were opened (GO No. 1010 Revenue dated September 30, 1892 and GO No. 1010A Revenue dated February 1, 1893). Kamalanathan (1984), (the son of renowned A.P. Periyasamy Pulavar, an associate of Pandithar Iyodhee Thass), has provided a detailed account of the movement launched by Adi Dravidas for their own emancipation. According to him a library, 12 day-schools, 2 night schools, and 2 boys' hostels were established by Adi Dravida between 1886 and 1932. Further Adi Dravida had published eleven magazines between 1869 and 1916. He also provided a detailed account of forty major political conferences and meetings organized since 1891 as well as 18 Buddhist conferences organized between 1909 and 1932 by Adi Dravidas in Madras Presidency. It is notable that Pandithar Iyodhee Thass (1845-1914) who was at the forefront for the cause of untouchables, revived Buddhism; founded the Adavaitnanda Sabha at Nilgiris in 1876 and the Dravida Mahajana Sabha in 1891, edited and published the weekly news magazine called *Oru Paisa Tamilan* through which he awakened the people (Ravikumar, 2007). He 'forged a radical identity for Dalits, and reinterpreted Indian and Tamil history through Buddhism' (Venkatachalapathy, 2014).

Chellappa Maistry, N.Y. Murugesan, R.A. Das, Swami Sahajanandan, P.V. Subramaniam, L.C. Gurusamy, B.S. Moorthi, M. Palanisamy, Rathinam, and Veeraswamy and others throughout their lives fought for social justice. They started schools, hostels and educational institutions for the depressed classes (Padmanabhan, 1996). M.C. Rajah (1883-1943) a great Dalit leader from the South, almost a contemporary of Dr. Ambedkar, occupied numerous high political positions, made continued efforts for the education of untouchables of Madras Presidency, in and outside the Madras Legislative Council as its member.

Rajah, like Dr. B.R. Ambedkar, considered education as the panacea for all the woes of the depressed classes. Apart from quality education, Rajah pursued the Madras Government to provide mid-day meals for poor Adi Dravida children in the government Elementary Schools, scholarships and liberal fee remission for the students studying in recognized schools and colleges as well as free hostels throughout the Presidency. It must be noted that, he was in favour of making elementary education compulsory for all (Rajah, 1925). Rajah's demand was the same as that of Dr. Ambedkar for free and compulsory primary education in the Bombay Province, around the same time. These similarities of demands could not be a coincidence. It is an example which showed that the Dalit leaders while fighting for the rights of their own people kept the interest of the nation and the entire people or communities in mind. The democratization of education is known to contribute, to a great extent, in progress and development of the nation. It happened in Japan and other countries.

Functionally, the hierarchical society of Kerala was at its worst. In addition to untouchability, the society of Kerala used to practise the unapproachability. The people belonging to some lower castes were not permitted to approach those of higher castes. It was like a safe distance kept between two vehicles. The Izhavas were supposed to keep 20 to 30 feet distance between them and Nambudaris. Similarly, the Cherumas, and Pulayas had to keep 64 feet, and Nayadis had to keep 72 feet distance from Nambudaris. Surprisingly, the mere sight of some tribes polluted the Nambudaris (Rao, 1979). Every problem inherently has a solution. In case of society of Kerala, the solution for its evils emerged in the form of revolution right 'from the bottom rungs of the social order at the instance and inspiration of Swamy Sri Narayan Guru', and authority on the *Vedas* as well as great social and religious reformer. Dr. Palpu, Kumaran Asan (1873-1924), Sahodharan, Aiyappan and several others who belonged to untouchable communities contributed greatly to the social movement and social change (Aloysius, 2005).

Sri Narayan Guru (1856-1928), set up a number of Vedic schools for untouchable castes. Such an act could have been termed, as a sacrilege or blasphemy as the Hindu religion did not permit untouchables to read and recite *Vedas.* He believed in the universalization of education and worked for the same. He gave equal importance to modern education and advocated its expansion. His message 'educate so that you may be free and organize so that you may be strong', had a long lasting effect as it created waves among the untouchables for their own emancipation. Expectedly, the inspired untouchables recognized the importance of education and as a result organized themselves and launched the movement for promotion of education among their own people. Their collective struggle and fight generated pressure for admission of untouchable castes in government schools (Aloysius, 2005).

Dr. Palpu, a medical doctor belonging to the Izhava community with a high degree of talent and wisdom, launched the movement for admissions in the state-run schools in the 1880s, for the children of his community. When the right to public school education was won, due to the tireless efforts of Dr. Palpu and his associates; the literacy rate among the Izhavas increased from 3.15 per cent to 12.60 per cent between 1875 and 1891. This increase was almost ten per cent. As mentioned above, Dr. Palpu was a medical doctor by profession, but did not get employment in Travancore only because he was an untouchable. He had to go to Mysore State for the same. He suffered a lot due to his social background. It was evident that the high caste people had no respect for the educated person with talent and wisdom belonging to the untouchable community.

Palayas, much lower than Ezhavas in the hierarchical social order expectedly faced worse kind of suppression, oppression and humiliation for aspiring for education. Hostility of upper castes and irresponsible and insensitive attitude of the rulers pushed Palayas and other untouchable communities towards the missionaries for their education. When children of Palayas and other untouchable castes began going to schools opened by missionaries, the upper castes and landlords particularly Syrian Christians not just opposed their education, but burned the schools, forcefully tried to take possession of acquired land for schools and made it almost impossible to get a piece of land to start new ones. Every move of the Palayas and missionaries for education of untouchables was ruthlessly crushed. Not to hurt the religious feeling of upper castes, even the government of Travancore in 1870 could not open schools for lower castes. Further, the same government in 1894 under pressure withdrew the grant-aid to missionary schools (Kawashima 1998 and Oommen 2007).

The non-supportive attitude of the government and also

suppression and oppression from upper castes, made the Palayas more determined. Therefore, they launched a movement to fight simultaneously with the upper castes and government for their rights. Consequently, the government was forced in 1904 to ensure education for socially backward castes including Palayas. However, surprisingly, the government could not enforce its own policy as upper castes withdrew their children from schools (Gladstone, 1984). It was evident from the proceedings of Mulam Popular Assembly of the year 1974, 1909 and 1911 that the right to education remained the major objective of the Palayas. Importantly, during the period from 1910 to 1930, the movement of Palayas focused and caused awakening among them. Meanwhile, the Christian Palayas also joined the general movement. The self-awakening had an enlightened impact on the Palayas. Despite numerous difficulties, the Palayas continued to take an interest in the education of their children. It was significant that educated Palayas inspired others for education and also to fight for their rights. As a result, young men and women emerged as leaders from their movement. For example, Villikara Mathan was one such leaders. He went on to become the member of Mulam Popular Assembly in 1914 (Gladstone, 1984). Ayyannkali (1846-1941) was another Palaya leader who played an important and vital role in the educational movement among Cherumas, Prayas and Palayas. He mobilized and awakened the downtroddens. He led several agitations which includes agriculture strikes to protest against refusal of the higher castes to admit Palaya children to local schools. As the long strike adversely affected the agricultural activities, the Travancore government was forced to mediate a settlement. This strike was the first of its kind in the history of Kerala, compelled higher castes to agree to allow Palaya children in the public schools (Chentharassery, 1985). Further, in 1911 and 1914, the Travancore government had to promulgate an educational code declaring the right of lower castes to get admission in government run schools. There is also a similar struggle and suffering of other untouchable castes like the Palayas in Kerala. Thus, lower castes suffered and struggled immensely to secure access to education. Although, Kerala is presently one of the progressive states, its past seemed to be bleak.

Nissim Mannuthukkaran in his article recently published in *The Hindu* (April 15, 2014), entitled 'The Echoing Silence of Caste that Slavery was Prevalent in Kerala Until the Late 19th Century', wherein he mentioned that slavery had existed in its worst form. Dalits could be sold and bought, and could be flogged like cattle to work in fields, which indicated that slavery robbed the human dignity, honour and self-respect of Dalits. Once it was abolished, the practice of slavery continued for many more decades. Furher, the account provided by Mannuthukkaran has great significance as he himself was a descendant of the family which had such slaves. According to him these slaves were bought by the friend of forefathers and subsequently relocated in the family of his forefathers. It indicated that the slaves could be offered as a gift to other families. The practice of sale, purchase and gift wuold have broken the family bonds of slaves and scattered them in all directions and lost the contacts in course of time, not to meet again.

The Namasudra of Bengal and their movement could be considered as an excellent example to understand the initiatives and efforts made in the British period to get and provide an access to education to the depressed classes themselves. The Namasudra community (known as *Chandal* before 1911) suffered immensely due to the caste system, its traditions and customs. For their own emancipation the Namasudras launched a movement (1872-73), which later gradually turned into widespread agitation. Bandyopadhyay (2005) has described, with some details, the struggle of Namasudras. According to him, a number of meetings were held by Namasudras, between 1881 and 1930 in different villages to address the social issues and achieve greater solidarity among the community. Subsequently, *Namasudra Hitaishini Samiti* was constituted to coordinate the entire movement. Its meetings were popularly known as 'uplift meetings'. The first meeting was held in 1881, and was addressed by Guruchand, one of the leading personalities who mobilized and awakened Namasudras for their rights, and more than sixteen other local leaders from different districts. A series of such meetings were held thereafter to mobilize people. As a result, thousands of people participated in subsequent meetings. The significance and need for education of both boys and girls was emphasized every time in the meeting. Even occasions like funerals or rituals were used to hold 'uplift meetings'. One such meeting, for example, was 'held in 1910 in the village of Ramshorn Plodder of Khulna, after the funeral ceremony of his mother'. 'The meeting began at 15 hours in the afternoon and continued well beyond 21 hours at night'. Perhaps, for the first time in the history of the social movement, the mourning occasions like funerals had been converted into the meetings where people were asked to unite and be prepared to fight for their rights. Thus, through informal and formal meetings, Namasudras continued their struggle for social justice. At the same time their focus remained on education. At the Jessor Conference in 1908, it was resolved to make the 'Namasudra Conference' permanent, and to organize its meetings every year to discuss the social problems, plan for the strategies for emancipation and spread of education (Bandyopadhyay, 2005).

The *Matua* sect founded by Harichand Thakur became an active centre for social mobilization and realization of the dream to educate Namasudras. Through the sect both Harichand Thakur and his son Guruchand, propagated the message of education. They established a Matuakhali Ashram in the district town of Khulna, and encouraged the Namasudra students from poor families to come, stay and complete their studies, and in turn made many Namasudra students educated. Importantly, Harichand had believed, like Mahatma Phule, that 'illiteracy and ignorance were the root cause of all degradation of the Namasudra masses'. Therefore, he asked his son Guruchand to work and protect the educational interest of the Namasudras, after him. Accordingly, Guruchand remained active for the cause of their education. He spread the message: 'educate yourself, earn money and be respectable'. He also donated land to establish the school at Orakandi (Bandyopadhyay, 1985).

Social responsibility shown by the rich towards the poor of their own community was the uniqueness of the Namasudra movement. The rich Namasudras came forward, provided moral, financial and leadership support to their social movement. Such involment like rich Namasudras is rarely seen in the social struggles. Generally, the rich section remains passive and become onlookers. The togetherness was the strength and success of the Namasudras movement.

The Education Commission of 1882 had recommended that, no admission be refused on the ground of caste in the government schools and colleges, and the authorities concerned could liberally encourage the establishment of special schools for the children of lower castes. These recommendations were not put into practice in Bengal Province. However, the Namasudras continued to remain active to organize themselves and support the educational needs of the children of their own community. In the light of these facts, it was quite significant to note that in 1921-22, out of a total of 96,552 depressed class students, 49,273 students belonged to the Namasudra community alone. During the same year, 197 students of the depressed castes were in the University College, and of that 144 were Namasudras. At the primary level also, the presence of Namasudras was relatively high (Biswas, 2000).

It was important that the depressed castes of Bengal were avid for education, as it was seen as a remedy for their degraded social, and economic conditions, which was evident from the memorandum submitted separately by the All Bengal *Namasudra* Association and the Bengal Depressed Classes Association to the Simon Commission in 1929 as well as their supplementary statement, and deputation to the said Commission, on January 29, 1929 at Calcutta.

It is noteworthy that a very high degree of orthodoxy was practised then in Bengal. Upper caste Hindus strongly opposed even change in caste names from *Chandal* to *Namasudra*. After more than 30 years of their struggle, the Bengal Government changed the name to *Namasudra* by notification in 1911 (Annual Administration Report, 1880-81; Indian Law Reporter, 1883; Census of India, 1911; S. Biswas, 1996 and A.K. Biswas, 2000). Considering such hostile social conditions, success of *Namasudras* to get an access to education and spread the same among themselves was exemplary and inspiring for other unprivileged.

It was significant that the untouchable communities realized the importance of education quite early and launched the struggle for the same. Despite the steep resistance from the upper castes and neglect by the British government, these depressed communities gained some degree of access to education, mainly due to their own efforts and of the social reformers from all the Presidencies and a few princely states.

Conclusion

It can be concluded that the form and functions of the caste system of Indian society did not permit the lower castes, particularly untouchables to take education. Because of traditions, customs and religious sanctions, the untouchables were kept out of education for thousands of years. As the British who neither practised nor believed in the caste system, the untouchables saw an opportunity to access education when the education system was introduced by them. However, the British focused their attention on the elites, rich, royal, and upper castes that too mainly the Brahmins, ignoring the educational interests of untouchables. In this context, the refusal of admission to untouchable students in the government school at Dharwad could be considered as an excellent example. Everyone, right from the lowest authority at the local level to the highest in England, seemed to have worked in tandem or in a coordinated manner to overlook the educational needs of the untouchables. Both the Orientalists and the Anglicists adopted the same approach and neglected the education of untouchables. The famous Dispatch of 1854 opened education for the masses. However, while its implementation untouchable castes were excluded from education, and restricted educational benefits to higher castes.

Because of their own awakening and owing to the efforts of the social reformers, the untouchables launched several agitations in various parts of the country to get access to education. Indeed, they made education as an important issue in their social struggle and movement. In response to their agitations, whenever the British Government tried to provide access and educational opportunities to the untouchables, the upper castes strongly resisted. Thus, the educational aspirations of the untouchables were severely crushed between the orthodoxy of higher castes and apathy of the British during the long period of 190 years from 1757 (Year of Battle of Plassey) to 1947 (Year of Independence). The spread of education, among the untouchables was mainly due to their own struggle, efforts of the various social reformers and the leaders who emerged from their own community. Had the educational opportunities been provided to the untouchables on par with those available to the upper castes, their socio-economic status would not have been the same, and India as a country would also have been very different.

REFERENCES

Aloysius, G. (2005). *Interpreting Kerala's Social Development*, Critical Quest, New Delhi.

Aloysius, G. (2007). *Nationalism Without a Nation in India*, Oxford University Press, New Delhi.

Ambedkar, B.R. (1928). *Statement Concerning the State of Education of the Depressed Classes in Bombay Presidency*, Submitted to Indian Statutory Commission on May 29, 1928.

Annual Administration Report, Presidency Division, 1880-81.

Appa Rao, M.R. (1971). *Brahmashri Raghupati Venkataratnam Naidu*, Kakinada.

Bandyopadhyay, Sekhar (1985). Social Mobility in Bengal in the Late Nineteenth and Early Twentieth Centuries, Ph.D. Thesis of University of Calcutta, Cited by G. Aloysius (2007).

Bandyopadhyay, Sekhar (2005). *The Namasudra Movement*, Critical Quest, New Delhi.

Bandyopadhyay, Sekhar (2007). *From Plassey to Partition: A History of Modern India*, Orient Blackswan, New Delhi.

Basu, B.D. (1933). *India Under the British Crown*, R. Chatterjee, Calcutta, p. 128.

Biswas, A.K. (2000). *The Namasudras of Bengal: Profile of Persecuted People*, Blumoon Books, New Delhi.

Biswas, S. (1996). *Anweshan*, Adal Badal, Calcutta, 1996, p. 275.

Census of India, 1901, Vol. VI(a), Part II, Imperial Tables, pp. 102-103; *1911*, Vol. I, Tables, p. 82; *1921*, Vol. V, Bengal, Part II, Tables, p. 96; *1931*, Vol. V, Bengal, Part II, Tables, p. 183; Cited by A.K. Biswas (2000).

Census of India, 1911, Vol. V, Report part I, Cited by A.K. Biswas (2000).

Chaudhury, Pradipta (2002). Literacy, Caste, Class and Gender in India, In: *Education and the Disprivileged*, Sabyasachi Bhattacharya (ed.), Orient Longman, New Delhi, pp. 270-289.

Chavan, Dilip (2013). Politics of Patronage and Institutionalization of Language Hierarchy in Colonial Western India, In: *Education in Colonial India: Historical Insights*, Deepak Kumar, Joseph Bara, Nandita Khadria, Ch. Radha Gayathri (eds.), Manohar Publications, New Delhi, pp. 187-226.

Chalam, K.S. (2007). Dalit Emancipation Through Education, In: *Ambedkar in Retrospect: Essays on Economics, Politics and Society*, Sukhadeo Thorat and Aryama (eds.), Indian Institute of Dalit Studies and Rawat Publications, New Delhi, pp. 339-354.

Chentharassery, T.H.P. (1985). *Ayyankali*, Prabhat, Trivandrum.

Chinna Rao, Yagati (2002). Education and Identity Formation Among Dalits in Colonial Andhra, In: *Education and the Disprivileged: Nineteenth and Twentieth Century India*, Sabyasachi Bhattacharya (ed.), Orient Longman, New Delhi, pp. 83-122.

Das, Bhagwan (2007). Moment in the History and Reservation, In: *In Search of Inclusive Policy: Addressing Graded Inequality*, Sukhadeo Thorat and Narender Kumar (eds.), Rawat Publications and Indian Institute of Dalit Studies, New Delhi, pp. 275-285.

Dey, Lalbihari (1868). Member Bethune Society, Talk given at Bethune Society, Calcutta in December 10, 1868, on Primary Education, Printed in: *Education System from 1857 to William Hunter's Commission 1882*, B.M. Sankhdher (ed.), Deep & Deep Publications, New Delhi, 1999, pp. 49-72.

Elphinstone, Mountstuart (1823). *Minutes dated 13 December, 1823*, Education Department, 1825, Vol. 1.

Elphinstone, Mountstuart (1884). Selections from the Minutes and Other Official Writings of the Hon. Mountstuart Elphinstone, George W. Forrest (ed.), Richard Bentely and Sons, London, 1884. Cited by Eleanor Zelliot, *Dr. Babasaheb Ambedkar and the Untouchable Movement*, Blumoon Books, New Delhi, p. 35.

Gautam, M.B. (1991). *Bhagyadayam: Madari Bhagyareddy Verma: Life-Sketch and Mission*, Adi-Hindu Social Service League Trust, Hyderabad, p. 2.

Gladstone, J.W. (1984). *Protestant Christianity and People's Movement of South Travancore, 1884-1914*. Centre for Asian Studies, Amsterdam. Cited by George Oomen (2007).

Gladstone, J.W. (1984). *Protestant Christianity and People's Movement in Kerala; A study of Christian Mass Movement in Kerala 1850-1936*, Seminary Publications, Trivandrum.

Howell, Arthur (1872). *Education in British India*, Office of the Superintendent of Government Printing, Calcutta.

Hunter Education Commission Report (1882).

Indian Law Reporter, 11, Calcutta, 1883, p. 176.

John, Clive (1973). *Macaulay: The Shaping of Historian*, Alfred A. Knopf, New York.

K.A.K.S. 1907-08, p. 59460, cited in *Chhatrapati Shahu's Crusade Against Untouchability*, B.D. Khane (2006), Critical Quest, New Delhi.

Kamalanathan, T.P. (1984). *Mr. K. Veeramani, M.A., B.L. is Refuted and the Historical Facts about the Scheduled Castes Struggle for Emancipation in South India*, Ambedkar Self-Respect Movement, Tirupathur.

Kawashima, Koji (1998). *Missionaries and Hindu State: Travencore 1858-1936*, Oxford University Press, Delhi.

Keer, D. (1964). *Mahatma Jotiba Phule*, Popular Prakashan, Bombay, p. 111.
Kumar, Deepak (2006). *Science and the Raj*, Oxford University Press, New Delhi.
Latthe, A.B. (1924). *Memoirs of His Highness Shri Shahu Chhatrapati Maharaja of Kolhapur*, 2 Vols., Times of India Press, Bombay.
Majeed, Javed (1992). *Ungoverned Imagining: James Mill's History of British India and Orientalism*, Clarendon Press, Oxford.
Marshall, P.J. (1998). The British in Asia: Trade to Dominion, 1700-1765, In: *The Oxford History of the English Empire, The Eighteenth Century*, P.J. Marshall (ed.), Vol. 2, Oxford University Press, London and New York, pp. 487-507.
Merno by Painter, March 31, 1908, G218/01908/26, CMSA.
Misra, B.B. (1961). *The Indian Middle Classes: Their Growth in Modern Times*, Oxford University Press, London.
Moon, Vasant (1982). *Dr. Babasaheb Ambedkar: Writings and Speeches*, Vol. 2, Department of Education, Government of Maharashtra, pp. 402-427.
Ibid.
Moon, Vasant (1993). *Dr. Babasaheb Ambedkar Writings and Speeches*, Vol. 12, Department of Education, Government of Maharashtra, pp. 93-114.
Nassim, Mannathukkaren (2014). The Echoing Silence of Caste, *The Hindu*, 15 April, p. 8.
Nurullah, Syed and Naik, J.P. (1951). *A History of Education in India During the British Period*, Macmillan, Bombay.
O'Hanlon, Rosalind (1985). *Caste, Conflict and Ideology: Mahatma Jotirao Phule and Low Caste Protest in Nineteenth Century Western India*, Cambridge University Press, Cambridge.
Oommen, George (2007). Education, Self-Perception and Identity: The Experience of the Palaya Christians of Kerala 1860-1930. In: *Education and Social Change in South Asia*, Krishna Kumar and Joachim Oesterheld (eds.), Orient Longman, New Delhi, pp. 101-126.
Padmanabhan, A. (1996). *Dalit at the Crossroads: Their Struggle—Past and Present*, Poompugar Pathippagam, Madras.
Palit, Ram Chandra (1882). *Speeches and Resolutions of Lord Rippon*. Baptist Mission Press, Calcutta, p. 268.
Parulekar, R.V. and Bakshi, C.L. (1985). *Selection from Educational Records (Bombay), Part III, 1826-1840*, pp. 42-43.
Raja Rammohun Roy (1823). Memorandum Written to His Excellency the Right Hon'ble William Pitt, Lord Amherst, on the December 11, 1823; In: *Selection from Educational Records, Part I, 1781-1839*, H. Sharp (ed.), Office of the Superintendent of Government Printing, India, 1920,

Calcutta; Reprinted by National Archives of India, Government of India, 1965, p. 99.

Rajah, M.C. (1925). *The Oppressed Hindus*, The Huxley Press, Madras; Republished in 2005 by Critical Quest, New Delhi.

Ramakrishna, V. (1983). *Social Return in Andhra*, Vikas, New Delhi.

Ramaswamy, Uma (1974). Self-Identity Among Scheduled Castes: A Study of Andhra, *Economic and Political Weekly*, Vol. IX, No. 48, pp. 1958-1964.

Rao, M.S.A. (1979). *Social Movement and Social Transformation*, Manohar Publications, New Delhi.

Rao, Parimala V. (2016). Personal discussion.

Ravikumar (2007). A Grasp of the Past, *Tehelka*, December 15, p. 57.

Richey, J.A. (1921). Selection from Educational Records, Chapter IV, *Provincial Developments*, Bombay, Government Printing, Calcutta; National Archives of India, Reprinted by National Achieves, Government of India, 1965, pp. 143-176.

Richter Julius, A. (1908). A *History of Missions in India*, Anderion and Ferier, London.

Sankhdher, B.M. (1999). *Education System from 1857 to William Hunter's Commission 1882*, Deep and Deep Publications, New Delhi.

Satyanarayana, A. (2002). Growth of Education Among Dalit-Bahujan Communities in Modern Andhra, 1893-1947. In: *Education and the Dispriviliged: Nineteenth and Twentieth Century India*. Sabyasachi Bhattacharya (ed.), Orient Longman, New Delhi, pp. 50-83.

Sen, S.P. (1971). *The French in India 1763-1816*, Munshiram Manoharlal Publishers, New Delhi.

Sharp, H. (1920). *Selection from Educational Records, Part I, 1781-1839*. Government Printing, Calcutta; Reprinted by National Archives of India, Government of India, 1985.

Smith, George (1857). Indian and Comparative Philosophy, *Calcutta Review*, 29, pp. 229-279.

Suryanarayana, K.R. (1952). *Sir R. Venkataratnam*, Rajahmundry.

Talukder, S.R. (1998). *Indian Civil Service Examination and the Savarna Merit*, Blumoon Books, New Delhi.

Thomas, F.W. (1891). *The History and Prospects of British India*, Deighton Bell, Cambridge.

Thorat, Sukhadeo and Aryama (2007). *Ambedkar in Retrospect: Essays on Economics, Politics and Society*, Indian Institute of Dalit Studies and Rawat Publications, New Delhi.

Thorat, Sukhadeo and Kumar, Narender (2008). In: *In Search of Inclusive Policy: Addressing Graded Inequality*, Indian Institute of Dalit Studies and Rawat Publications, New Delhi.

Trautmann, Thomas, R. (2004). *Aryans and British India*, Yoda Press, New Delhi.

Vankatachalapathy, A.R. (2014). From a Footnote to a Forefront. *The Hindu*, Wednesday, December 24, p. 9.

Veermani, K. (2015). Torch-Bearer of Reform, *The Hindu*, Thursday, November 19, p. 11.

Zelliot, Eleanor (2002). Experiments in Dalit Education: Maharashtra 1850-1947, In: *Education and the Disprivileged: Nineteenth and Twentieth Century India*, Sabyasachi Bhattacharya (ed.), Orient Longman, New Delhi, pp. 35-47.

Zelliot, Eleanor (2004). *Dr. Babasaheb Ambedkar and the Untouchable Movement*, Blumoon Books, New Delhi, p. 35.

3

Exclusiveness of Higher Education in Independent India

The Education Despatch of 1854 is considered to be the Magna Carta of the Indian education system (Richter 1908). As a part of its implementation, the British established three Universities in 1857, one each at Calcutta (now Kolkata), Bombay (now Mumbai) and Madras (now Chennai). Bankim Chandra Chatterjee and Indu Nath Bose were the first two graduates of the Indian University. When the British left in 1947, there were just 19 universities, 496 colleges and 2,41,369 students for 0.44 billion Indian population at that time. The British kept the Indian education system small. As a part of design, the British provided education to a selective and elite section of society, particularly to get help from them to rule this vast country. The dire consequences, of such exclusiveness of education was, recognized by the founding fathers of independent India, which was evident also from the inaugural address of Jawaharlal Nehru at the All India Education Conference, that was convened by the Union Education Minister in January 1948. In that address Nehru emphatically stated that the country needed to revolutionize the education system. Subsequently, steps were taken to restructure the university education to meet the demands of human resources needed for the socio-economic development of the country. Most importantly, the constitutional provisions were made to protect the educational interest of the weaker sections of society. According to Article 46, the State was required to "promote with special care the educational and economic interest of the weaker sections of people, and in particular of Scheduled Castes and Scheduled Tribes and (to) protect them from social injustice and all forms of exploitation." Further, Article 16 and Article 335 contained the provisions for making appointment to services and posts as well as provisions for promotion. Initially, 12.5 per cent and five per cent reservations were provided to SC and ST, and subsequently, it was increased to 15 per cent for SC and 7.5 per cent to ST. Against this backdrop, it is essential to examine the implementation of these provisions and see to what extent the educational interest of SC and ST communities has been protected by the nation as well as the extent of appointments were made in the university system of the country in the last 60 to 65 years.

According to the Higher Education in India at a glance, issued by the University Grants Commission (UGC) in February 2012; there were 564 universities, 33,023 colleges, 8.17 lakh teachers and 169.76 lakh students, in the year 2010-11 in India. This increase compared to the year 1950-51, is almost 20, 48, 35 and 43 fold respectively. These figures look very impressive. However, the present enrolment clearly shows that just 1.6 per cent of the total population of India accesses higher education. In terms of Gross Enrolment Ratio (GER), it works out to be almost 12 per cent. It may be noted that the precise GER is not known. According to the volume *Higher Education in India: Issues Related to Expansion, Inclusiveness, Quality and Finance,* based on the studies sponsored by the UGC (2009), GER was 10.84 per cent; and thereafter reported to be 13 to 15 per cent in documents circulated in official meetings and conferences. At one of the recent meetings of the Vice-Chancellors of Central Universities, UGC has reported the GER for higher education very close to twenty per cent. Even if, we accept GER for higher education in the range from fifteen to twenty per cent, it would still be quite low compared to the international average including those of some developing countries. However, the increase in enrolment over the preceding years for the last 20 years (1984-85 to 2005-10) remained between five and six per cent (Ved Prakash et al. 2011). In the same volume, published by UGC (Ved Prakash et al. 2011) it is mentioned that the precise level of GER and actual position would become clear after the findings of the All India Higher Education Survey being conducted by the National University of Educational Planning and Administration.

Although, the importance of education for the social and

economic development of the country was recognized, we could provide access to higher education to just 1.6 per cent population, even after more than 60 years of independence, and as a result GER remained lower compared to many countries. The GER ratio of Japan increased from nine per cent in 1960 to forty per cent by the mid-1990s. China which planned expansion of its higher education in 1998, could double its institutions of higher education from 1,022 to 2,263 and enhanced the GER from five to twenty-three pr cent within fifteen years. In South Korea, the increase was more dramatic, from five per cent in 1960 to over fifty per cent in the mid-1990s (Levin, 2010).

It is quite clear that higher education did not expand to the extent and the way it should have and remained, by design or default, confined to a small section of society, as was in the British period. It is known that the provision to make education as a fundamental right was successfully opposed by two members belonging to the higher castes from the South at the meeting of the Constituent Assembly held on April 22, 1947. Had this been accepted education would have become accessible to the underprivileged section of society and others, which would have resulted in the availability of human resource in large numbers. Probably, it would not be out of context, if mention is made of the Sargent plan. When India was at the threshold of independence, John Sargent then education commissioner to the Government of India had prepared a comprehensive plan in 1944, for post-war educational development in India. It was severely criticized by people including national leaders for proposing forty years for universalization of free and compulsory education for children in the age group 6-14 years, restricted admission to secondary education and higher education. However, even after 65 years of independence we were not able to provide primary education to 65 per cent of our children. The secondary and higher education remained mainly restricted to the upper castes and urban rich. The expansion of technical education was limited and mainly confined to IITs. It appeared that the members of higher castes, elites, urban rich and descendants of those who served the British faithfully, were involved in the making of policy and its implementation and made sure of the continuance of the British model of education in independent India. Through, education and knowledge, these people, as in the past, could control the society and all its institutions as well as governance and administration. Expectedly, higher education continued to be monopolized by the elite, making it, in turn, non-accessible to the underprivileged particularly SC and ST communities, despite various measures taken by the government in independent India.

Therefore, the factors responsible for exclusiveness of higher education need to be understood. Surprisingly, no reliable information on the enrolment of SC and ST students is available. Even the UGC which has its own statistical section to collect and prepare a database had used other sources like the National Sample Survey (NSS) to get GER of SC and ST students for its own publications (Ved Prakash et al. 2011). Sometimes, the details on enrolment of SC and ST students are completely ignored or avoided. An excellent example is an important publication of UGC entitled *Higher Education in India at a Glance*, published in February 2012, wherein no information is given on SC and ST communities.

According to NSS the sixty-first round (2004-05) and NSS sixty-fourth round (2007-08) GER for SC is reported to be 8.2 and 11.54 per cent respectively. In the case of ST, GER is shown to be 8.44 and 7.67 per cent according to the same NSS sixty-first round (2004-05) and NSS sixty-fourth round (2007-08) respectively. Within three years, GER increased by nearly three per cent in the case of SC and decreased by one per cent in the case of ST. As mentioned earlier, UGC has used the same data of NSS to show the rosy picture and ignored its own data. For example, the UGC Publication (2009) on Higher Education in India, reported GER for SC and ST as 6.52 and 6.57 per cent respectively for the year 2004-05.

The background paper prepared by the Ministry of Human Resource Development, Government of India for the first meeting of the National Monitoring Committee for Education of Scheduled Castes, Scheduled Tribes and Persons with Disabilities, held on June 27, 2011, in New Delhi showed 11.76 and 5.21 per cent representation of SCs and STs in enrolment in higher education. Further, the Department of Higher Education, Ministry of Human Resource Development, Government of India (2012) has released the first Provisional Report—the All India Survey on Higher

Education, according to which the percentage share of SC and ST students in total students' enrolment is shown as 10.2 and 4.4 per cent respectively for the year 2010-2011. Apart from the above, Selected Educational Statistics (SES), published annually by the Ministry of Human Resource Development, Government of India, and Population Census of India, published by Registrar, Census of India, Government of India are sources of data on enrolment in higher education in India. There were obvious variations in GER of higher education among different sources.

The official statistical system is known to play an important role in any policy making process especially in a large and diverse democratic country like ours. With the available information, policy makers could plan for the future of education. Despite the difference in GER, data from various sources seems to conceal more than reveal the facts. Therefore, understanding the exclusive nature of higher education needs to be scrutinized carefully and more critically. The GER for population sub-groups classified by gender, caste, religion and place of residence would be useful for the same.

The UGC-sponsored study provides insights into inter-group disparities in access to higher education. Srivastava and Sinha (2009), and Dubey (2009) determined, perheps for the first time, the GER for various groups, and brought out the differences in enrolment for the year 2004-05, between male and female, between SC, ST, OBC and others. Raju (2009) examined the male-female disparities in greater details. The findings of these above studies were summarized by Thorat (2009). Some of his observations are given below for the benefit of readers:

1. 'In 2004-05, GER for SCs, STs and OBCs was shown to be 6.3, 6.33 and 8.5 per cent, respectively, which was much lower compared to others (16.60 per cent). It was also seen that the GER for the SC/ST was almost three times lower compared to other remaining sections of society. Access to education is generally found to be lower for girls (9.11 per cent) than boys (12.42 per cent). The females belonging to the lower castes suffer more acutely in accessing higher education. In 2004-05, compared to the overall average of 9.11 per cent, GER among the females was 4.43, 4.76, 6.60

and 19.53 per cent for SC, ST, OBC and other females respectively. These observations indicated that the GER for among SC and ST females was about five times lower compared to others. In the case of OBC females, it was three times less'.

2. 'A significant difference was seen in enrolment rates among poor (2.21 per cent) and non-poor (12.36 per cent), which was almost twelve times lower for the poor. In the rural and urban areas, the GER for the poor was 1.40 and 4.0 per cent, respectively, which was quite low compared to 7.12 and 27.15 per cent for the non-poor, respectively. Within the poor households, the GER was the lowest among the poor households belonging to the SC and ST followed by OBC and others. The GER for the poor belonging to SC, ST, OBC and others was 1.84, 1.55, 2.30 and 3.58 per cent, respectively. In the rural areas, the GER was the lowest among the ST: 1.11 per cent, followed by 1.35, 1.13 and 1.66 per cent for SC, OBC and others respectively. In the urban areas, the GER for the urban poor was 3.86, 4.78, 5.16 and 7.0 per cent, for SC, ST, OBC and others respectively. Disparities in the GER are visible across occupational groups in the rural (3 per cent for non-farm wage labourers and 1.41 per cent for wage labourers) and the urban areas (3.26 per cent for casual labourers). Whether it is rural or urban areas, the GER for wage (casual) labourers was the lowest, particularly for the farm wage labourers. For the wage labourers, the GER was particularly low amongst the SC/ST compared with others. Against 1.41 per cent at overall level for the wage labourers in the rural areas, the GER was 0.67, 1.63, 1.16 and 1.93 per cent for ST, SC, OBC and other wage labourers, respectively. Thus, the enrolment rates were the lowest among the poor casual wage labourers households in the rural and urban areas; the rates were particularly low among the poor from the same group, and belonging to the SC/ST/OBCs'.
3. 'In case of ST, SC and OBC agriculture labourers the enrolment rates were 0.9, 0.1 and 0.93 per cent, respectively. Similarly the enrolment rates for the casual non-farm wage

> labourers in the rural areas stood at nil for both ST and SC, and 0.52 per cent for the OBC. In the urban areas, the enrolment rates for the poor casual labourers were reported to be 0.66, 2.62 and 3.92 per cent for the ST, SC and OBC, respectively' (for details see Thorat, 2009 and other articles therein).

It could be inferred from the above findings, that there is a need to go deep down beyond overall GER to understand the educational system and its social implications. Even after 69 years of independence, the regional, gender and social disparities in education still persist and are perhaps widening further. The upper castes, urban rich, and middle class groups have mainly been benefited from the expansion of higher education. The enrolment forecast for the socially disadvantaged groups reveals that the existing disparities in GER between SC/ST and the general category would continue. The forecast also indicates that while the current disparity will continue for the SCs, it is projected to increase further for STs. It is estimated that for SC and ST to catch up with the general category, 1.9 and 1.2 million additional enrolments of SC and ST are required (Duraisamy, 2009). Although, this forecast is for the Eleventh Five Year Plan period, the past experience suggests that the social disparities in higher education would continue in the coming years. The cause for continual social disparities might be found in the educational policies and their detrimental implementation, functioning of the universities, colleges and other academic institutes as well as lack of social responsibilities and social sensitivity of the people on the campuses.

Commissions, Committees and Education Policies

Since education, particularly higher education, is vital for the development of the nation, social and economic, the University Education Commission (UEC) was set up immediately after independence in 1948, under the chairmanship of Dr. Radhakrishanan, to suggest the reforms in higher education. Soon thereafter, it was realized that higher education cannot be built and expanded with quality without the solid foundation of secondary education. In view of this, the Secondary Education Commission (SEC) was constituted in 1950 with Dr. L. Mudaliar as its Chairman, also a member of UEC. Dr. Mudaliar was a link between both the Commissions. Despite these two commissions, the results were not as expected. The expansion of education was haphazard and was not complementary to each other.

To have an integrated approach for education in the country, then the Education Commission (EC) was set up in 1964 with Dr. D.S. Kothari as its Chairman, with a mandate to consider all aspects of education at all levels. The report is still considered to be a basic document even today for policy planning. It is important that the first National Education Policy was evolved in 1968 from this report, but could not be implemented effectively as the education was a state subject. Because of this, it was not possible for the central government to make mandatory or impose its policy on the state governments. Probably, to overcome such a difficulty, the Constitution of India was amended (forty-second) in 1976 to make education the joint responsibility of the Centre and the State. Subsequently, an attempt was made in 1979 to develop the education policy, but failed as it was not approved by the CABE. Later, a new National Education Policy (NPE 1986) was formulated in 1986 with a view to prepare students for the 21st century. For implementation of this new NPE 1986, the Plan of Action (POA, 1986) was immediately developed in 1986. After three-four years, the NPE 1986 was reviewed by the Committee under the chairmanship of Acharya Ramamurthy in 1990. On submission, its report was considered by the CABE, which, in turn, appointed another committee in 1991 under the chairmanship of N. Janardhan Reddy, to make recommendations for modification of NPE 1986. The Committee broadly endorsed the NPE with a few changes. This NPE 1986 (revised) as modified in 1992 (NPE 1992) was tabled in Parliament on May 7, 1992. The Parliament considered the same and suggested a complete revision of its POA. Accordingly, POA 1992 was evolved out of consensual processes involving twenty-two task forces.

Thus, in the first 45 years of independence, we have only appointed Commissions, Committees, prepared policies and their action plans. The net result was loss of precious time. As the era of globalization appeared, the rich and elite section of society found considerable profit in education, and to harvest and reap the same opened private institutes and colleges. They slowly exerted pressure on the government to withdraw from higher education and suggested to concentrate mainly on school education which was evident from the Ambani-Birla Report (2002). The corporate world wanted higher education be left for them. Then, the National Knowledge Commission (NKC) was established in 2005 followed by the Yash Pal Committee (2006). However, keeping the need of society in mind, both the NKC and Yash Pal Committee made several recommendations including the structural changes. Both the reports do not need further elaboration including the impact on the poor and Dalits, as their recommendation would not be implemented. Both Reports would be finally preserved in the archives and likely to serve as primary sources for the researchers and policymakers.

It may be noted that after 2009, a great deal of time and efforts were invested to set up the National Council of Higher Education and Research (NCHER) subsuming UGC and bringing another twelve educational councils under its umbrella. The respective Ministries successfully resisted the merger of their educational councils with NCHER. At the end, UGC and AICTE remained to be subsumed or merged with NCHER. Finally, it appeared, even that was not going to happen, and UGC and AICTE would remain undisturbed and likely to be strengthened further.

If this was to happen, then why was the futile exercise undertaken for five years? Consciously or unconsciously, we do not take any matter to a logical end.

In between, a process of granting Deemed to be University status to private colleges was accelerated; as a result there was a sudden rise in the number of Deemed to be universities, in a short span of time. This whole process had come under severe criticism. The granting of Deemed to be universities status was suddenly stopped in the year 2009 -10, and at the same time steps were taken to de-recognize many of them. Expectedly, the de-recognition was challenged and finally landed in the Supreme Court. Apart from this, for almost four to five years (during the period 2009 - 14), the government remained busy in drafting several bills related to educational reforms and introducing in the Parliament for their approval. We have to wait as some of these bills are still alive and see their impact on the Indian education system, if passed by Parliament. The government, during 2009-14, had adopted legal routes to reform education without many consultations, debates or discussions with stakeholders particularly academicians. However, there has been a general perception, wrongly or rightly, among the Dalits throughout the country that the succesive governments are focusing on the welfare of the corporate sector and became more insensitive than before, towards their educational needs.

It appears, we as a nation, continue to waste time and efforts in formulating educational policies one after another. It is evident from the UEC 1948, SEC 1950, EC 1964, NPE 1968, NPE 1986, POA 1986, Ramamurthy Committee 1990, Janardhan Reddy Committee 1991, NPE 1992, POA 1992, Ambani-Birla Report 2002, NKC 2005, Yashpal Committee 2006, several bills and regulations thereafter. By design or default, only an elite section of society and upper castes immensely benefited from such an educational chaos and kept others to starve, particularly SCs, STs and Denotified Tribes. In addition to these, surprisingly, the country has almost forgotten the needs and aspirations of the Denotified Tribes, which are large in numbers.

Recently, the government has appointed the UGC Review Committee (2014) under the chairmanship of Dr. Hari Gautam. The committee has examined the governance and administration of the UGC as well as its impact on the higher education of India. Dr. Gautam being a former chairman of UGC, he is aware of the strengths and weaknesses of this organization. The committee has made recommendations related to the structure and functions of the UGC as well as Indian higher education. Very soon, we are likely to see major organizational changes in the UGC setup and get a new education policy. One has to wait for the final outcomes. However, it would be interesting to obseve how the policy makers attend to the educational needs of the underprivileged section of society.

Expansion of Education

As mentioned earlier, because of relative numbers it appeared as if higher education expanded in an unprecedented manner after independence. However, the country which has more than a hundred crore population sends around 1.6 crore children to higher education. Its GER oscillates between thirteen and fifteen per cent, which is almost two times lower than the world average, three times lower than the countries in transition and five times lower than developed countries. The higher education, also in independent India, remained to be confined to a small section of society, and was non-accessible to most people as was during the British Raj. Expectedly, it caused an acute shortage of the human resources required for the development of the country. An inadequate and low quality research, as well as declining quality of education, adversely affected the process of knowledge generation. The education delinked from realities and remained unchanged with the changing time. The present educational system not only failed in providing accessibility to the large population but also in equity and equality of opportunities, resulting in social regional, geographical and gender disparities in education.

Thus, the spatial, temporal and social failures of the education system have thrown the country almost into a deep crisis in the time of globalization, which itself caused some adverse side effects. As a result, the country could not generate the required educated and skilled human resources. In the last sixty-five years, the country has produced a huge surplus of uneducated, unemployable and un-trained people, and instead of making them national assets, they have become a national liability.

With the assumption of an average annual growth rate of 7.25 per cent between 2010 and 2040, the GDP of India is estimated to reach US$ 32 trillion, higher than the GDP of the US (US$29 trillion) during the same period (Marchant, 2010). Further, the world is visualized as tripolar by 2040, that includes the US, China and India (Virmani, 2010). Apart from economic growth, India is also assumed to have a demographic advantage, as its population is expected to increase from 1.02 billion in 2001 to 1.7 billion in 2060. Because of these possibilities, the economists forecasted that India is likely to become a rich and strong nation.

Therefore, it is necessary to take measures to interlink, symbiotically, the economic growth and demographic advantage, and minimize various disparities to make India socially equal, economically developed and politically stable. In this context, one should remember that social democracy and economic democracy are the muscle fibres of political democracy. In the past, India missed an industrial revolution and paid a heavy price for the same. However, in the era of knowledge and knowledge society, India needs to have an educated and skilled population in large numbers to benefit from the demographic advantage. We may have to learn from Japan to use education as an instrument of social development and social change. China, which was lagging behind us, had revived and rejuvenated its education system in the late 1990s. As a result it went ahead of us in economic growth and development.

Although late, it appeared that the importance and significance of higher education for all was recognized. A target of 15 per cent GER was set in the Eleventh Five Year Plan. Rs. 46,000 crore were allocated for this plan which was nine to ten times higher than that of the earlier one. During the Eleventh Plan provision was made for setting up of around 1,464 new educational institutes comprising thirty Central Universities, eight IITs, seven IIMs, twenty NITs, two IISERs, two Institutes of Planning and Architecture, 374 model colleges and 1,000 polytechnics. The Eleventh Five Year Plan was rightly termed as 'Education Plan' and described it as the 'Second Wave' in the development of higher education. Apart from concomitant expansion with equity, the focus was on achieving quality and supporting reforms in higher education and promoting excellence.

This 'Second Wave' of higher education appeared to be a delayed response to globalization. Indeed, such expansion of higher education should have been initiated at least during the Eighth Five Year Plan itself, and then gradually expanded thereafter. Accordingly, the financial allocations should have been made and also increased gradually, considering the expenditure on education as an investment for the future of the country. However, Higher Education continued to be ignored during the Ninth and Tenth Five Year Plan periods. Further, the ban was also imposed on the recruitment in the Nineth Plan and continued for some time in the Tenth Plan, resulting in a shortage of teachers. During this period many senior teachers superannuated. The resultant vacancies were not filled, and left to relatively less experienced teachers to manage the university education. The depletion of experience and wisdom disturbed the academic ecosystem of campuses, which had gradually evolved and carefully nurtured. The non-recruitment of old as well as new teaching positions not only created the shortage of teachers in the universities, but also most adversely affected the interest of SC and ST communities as a large number of reserved posts and backlog posts remained unfilled. Some universities appointed the candidates belonging to the general category against the reserved posts, on an ad hoc basis, under the pretext that the teaching should not be affected. When an attempt was made to fill the reserved posts on a regular basis later on by SC and ST candidates, these ad hoc teachers from the general category resisted.

Meanwhile, the reservation for other backward classes (OBC) introduced in service in 1990, polarized the academic community on campuses. Indeed, it is a fact that the caste polarization always existed on campuses as well as, with some exceptions, in the minds of members belonging to the upper castes. However, it surfaced and became more visible after the OBC reservations. As an effect, the social sensitivity and social responsibility eroded to a great extent. The members belonging to SC and ST communities, particularly students, became soft targets and faced all kinds of humiliations and discriminations. The clusters of students were formed on caste lines. Benches in the classrooms, tables in the hostel mess, library and canteen were not shared with SC and ST students which indicated the hostility towards Dalit students. Such hostile conditions forced Dalit research scholars to change their guides. Some fought hostility and continued their research where they were. A few left research or left the central universities and found an alternative socially safe place in state universities or other academic institutes to pursue their research. Even the progressive teachers who supported social equality and raised their voice against the discrimination of Dalits were also not spared by the anti-reservation groups. The situation was not very different in state universities. Indeed, Dalit students experienced humiliations and discriminations right from school days.

Let us go back again to the 'second wave' of higher education. This latest expansion was like 'better late than never'. However, forty-three central universities have limited intake capacity which is indicative from the enrolment of just 1,51,975 students on March 31, 2010. The newly established seventeen central universities would take some time to be fully functional and to admit students in significant numbers. Some central universities have constituted and/or affiliated colleges, even without taking them into consideration, the total enrolment in the central universities would not go beyond three lakhs. Therefore, the central universities are going to make a limited contribution to the overall GER of the higher education of India, and in turn, in the harvesting of demographic dividends.

India is a country of diversity and it is necessary to see the social diversity on the campuses of central universities. Table 1 shows the enrolment of students in the central universities on March 31, 2010, and 2012.

Table 1: Enrolment of Students in Central Universities on March 2010 and 2012

Year	*Total*	*SC*	*ST*	*OBC*	*PH*
2010	151975 (100%)	17620 (11.59%)	10952 (7.2%)	22930 (15.09%)	1102 (03.73%)
2012	184741 (100%)	23163 (12.54%)	171986 (9.3%)	35140 (19.02%)	1707 (0.92%)

Source: Presentation of UGC at the Conference of Vice-Chancellors of Central Universities

The table clearly shows the dominant presence of students other than belonging to underprivileged sections of society. Out of the total enrolment, representation of SC, ST, OBC and PH is 11.59, 7.2, 15.09, and 0.73 per cent in the year 2010 and 12.54, 9.3, 19.02, and 0.92 per cent in 2012, respectively, which is lower than their share in the population.

According to the Census of 2011, SC and ST populations are 16.2 and 8.2 per cent. Figures in Table 1 are of admissions of SC and ST students and appear slightly better than a few years before. Considering the dropouts, an actual gap between students of upper castes and SC and ST is likely to be quite high. Therefore, the focus needs to be made on the retention of SC and ST students on the campuses. OBC is the largest social group and still their presence on the campuses of central universities is reported to be just 15.09

per cent for the year 2010 and 19.02 per cent for the year 2012. The recent twenty-seven per cent reservations to them provided in admissions is likely to increase their presence on the campuses. In case of differently-abled persons, their presence is just 0.73 per cent for the year 2010 and 0.92 per cent for the year 2012 against their share of three per cent. Under-representation of different social groups needs to be addressed to increase their presence on the campuses through enrolments. The diversities on campuses are known to contribute to academic excellence. These aspects have been discussed elsewhere, in this volume. The degree of diversity on college and university campuses is quite low. According to the UGC publication of 2011, on Higher Education in India, strategies and schemes during the Eleventh Plan Period (2007-2012) for universities and colleges, the high degree of inter-caste disparities existed at the national level.

The GER for SC, ST and OBC are 6.57, 6.52, and 8.77 per cent, respectively, which are markedly lower than others (GER 17.22 per cent). Although, recent calculations suggest a substantial overall increase in GER, the gap between disparities has not been significantly minimized. To minimize the educational disparity gaps and achieve a high degree of diversity on campuses, education needs to be spread uniformly in society. The Sachar Committee also suggested in its Report to achieve diversity on campuses including institutes run by the minorities.

Apart from an admission, it could be interesting to find out the situation of reservation particularly for SCs and STs in the teaching and non-teaching staff of central universities. The same is shown in Tables 2 and 3 for the years 2010 and 2012.

Table 2: Percentages of Reservations in Teaching Positions in Central Universities

Level	*SC*		*ST*		*OBC*		*PH*	
	2010	*2012*	*2010*	*2012*	*2010*	*2012*	*2010*	*2012*
Professor	1.05	0.79	0.49	0.89	NA	NA	0.33	0.20
Associate Professor	1.87	1.61	0.79	1.33	NA	NA	0.17	0.23
Assistant Professor	6.27	7.43	3.19	5.47	NA	4.51	0.41	0.72

Source: Presentation of the UGC at the Conference of the Vice-Chancellors of Central Universities

Table 3: Reservation in Non-Teaching Staff (in percentage) in Central Universities

Category	*Group A*		*Group B*		*Group C*		*Group D*	
	2010	*2012*	*2010*	*2012*	*2010*	*2012*	*2010*	*2012*
SC	8.81	9.33	6.69	9.17	7.10	13.77	18.23	NA
ST	3.58	7.82	2.41	7.22	4.19	6.98	3.58	NA
OBC	5.81	7.20	6.69	3.52	4.67	8.56	10.59	NA
PH	0.58	0.62	0.48	0.68	0.89	0.78	0.79	NA

Source: Presentation of the UGC at the Conference of the Vice-Chancellors of Central Universities

It can be seen that, at the level of Professor and Associate Professor, the presence of members of the SC and ST communities is insignificant. On average there is one per cent Professor and less than two per cent Associate Professors in each Central University. Even at the level of Assistant Professor, their presence in the faculty is quite low, and is just 7.43 and 5.47 per cent for SCs and STs, respectively, for the year 2012. No information is available for OBCs, except for Assistant Professor for the year 2012 and reported to be 4.51 per cent, far below the prescribed 27 per cent reservations. The situation is worse for the differently-abled persons. For the recruitments in administrative posts, it does not need the same academic eligibility as that of teachers. Because of this, the representation of various underprivileged sections of society in administration is expected to be very close to their share in population. However, Table 3 shows a wide gap between the general category and other category groups which have been provided reservations.

In short, it is amply evident that the central universities have not been implementing the reservation policy strictly. Indeed, it is known that some central universities were against the reservation policy particularly for teaching positions. These and other related aspects have been discussed in a separate chapter in detail. Thus, the Central University campuses continue to be almost academically exclusive in nature. The same might be true for state universities. The situation could be worse in private universities and Deemed to be Universities.

Like Central Universities, the Indian Institutes of Technology

(IITs) are centrally funded and supposed to adopt and follow the reservation policy of the Government of India. However, these institutes have been resisting the reservations under the pretext of autonomy and academic experience. These IITs established in the early 1960s, were given a mandate to develop technologies indigenously and make India self-sufficient. However, as mentioned elsewhere, these institutes failed to do so. On the contrary, these institutes who train skilled graduates prefer to go to Western countries and become part of the pool of skilled human resource of the host countries. These skilled human resource help host countries, like the US, in development of technology and its production, which in turn, India has been buying for the last several years. The technology is known to play a vital role in the progress of the nation. Unfortunately, the IITs are generating highly skilled human resource to meet the need of other countries. In addition, despite heavy financial investment and more academic freedom compared to the universities, IITs could not contribute in making India self-sufficient in indigenous technologies, and forced to import the same to meet its technological needs. Apart from experiencing diplomatic arm twists, by the developed countries, the imports cause loss of precious foreign exchange which puts pressure on the already constrained economy of the country. As the social returns from IITs are unexpectedly poor, the purpose for which these institutes were established was almost defeated.

According to N.R. Narayan Murthy, founder and chairman emeritus of Infosys, who addressed students and teachers in different academic institutes in Ahmedabad including IIT Gandhinagar, 'IITs and IIMs have merely become teaching institutes without paying much attention to research' (DNA, Ahmedabad, July 20, 2011), and very little research is being carried out in these institutes. According to him, in 2004, China produced 2,652 PhDs in Computer Science, and for the same year the figure was just twenty for India. He further mentioned that in 1967, at the Department of Electrical Engineering of IIT Kanpur, there were about sixty to seventy students registered for PhD, but today there are hardly five to six (*Times of India*, Ahmedabad, July 20, 2011). He continued to express the same views. It must be remembered that the IITs were always meant for training and research. This objective of research and training was emphasized in the IIT Act of 1961. However, IITs faltered on the research front (Gupta, 2011). The failure of IISC, Banglore, which was established one hundred and five years ago, to pay back to society made Narayan Murthy to question during its convocation ceremony on July 15, 2015 that, 'Have the institutes (in particular IISc and Indian Institute of Technology) over the sixty-plus years contributed to making our society and the world a better place? Is there one invention from India that has become a household name in the globe?' He then himself answered, 'The reality is that there is no such contribution from India in the last sixty years.' Further he went on to draw a comparison with the Massachusetts Institute of Technology, USA, where at least one hundred major inventions over the half century have changed the world (report in *The Hindu*, Thursday, July 16, 2015, p. 9). It appears that IITs have been teaching and training Indian students to do research and develop technologies for the USA and other countries.

However, interestingly, these IITs are still considered as centres of academic excellence. In the light of the above views and facts, it appears to be contradictory. It is unbelievable that the Institute could be academically excellent but at the same time could also be poor in terms of social returns. Or there is no link between academic excellence and social benefit, as it is, sometimes, between economic development and social development! With the exception of a few countries, it is seen that the economic growth has not reduced the poverty and instead widened the gap between the rich and poor. An excellent example is our own country where the rich became richer and the poor became poorer making India a rich country of poor people. In the Indian context, there is no relationship between academic excellence and social returns.

Despite their failure in the national duties, the faculty members and students of IITs consider themselves as the most talented with the highest degree of wisdom. Mostly, these teachers and students of IITs belong to the elite, urban rich and high castes of the country. Further, mostly these students and teachers are also descendants of the beneficiaries of British education, who helped the British to govern, administer and rule the country. As in the past, these elites and upper castes continued to control the governance and administration in independent India and did not allow education to percolate down and spread among the masses. Whenever the government had taken measures to expand education with equity, quality and equality to achieve inclusiveness, they resisted the same. Therefore, there was no surprise that students and teachers of IITs remained at the forefront of anti-reservation movements. The presence of SC and ST students on the campuses is considered to be a challenge to their social status and exclusiveness. Therefore, more than 65 years, after reservations were first introduced, classrooms in India's premier institutes continued to be hostile towards SC and ST students (Saxena Sobhna, *Sunday Times of India*, Ahmedabad, August 7, 2011, p. 9). Physical assaults, social boycott and deliberate failing are some of the features of caste discriminations. Sometimes the award of degrees is delayed. In one of the IITs, an award of PhD degree to a Dalit student was delayed for more than nine years. Unlike, universities, IITs are a closed system. The students cannot raise their voice and also cannot form a group or union and protest against caste discriminations. If protested individually or in a group SC and ST students are likely to be thrown out of the institutes under the pretext of academic discipline. Since, SC and ST students are unable to fight institutionalized hostility and indifference, some of them commit suicide.

Very recently (2015), in IIT Madras, the administration took action against Dalit students and their organization for protesting against discriminations. The hostile administration which suppressed the voice of Dalit students, has to retract back due to the continued struggle of Dalit students on the campus and nationwide protest.

With some degree of variation, indifference, humiliation and hostility are experienced by SC and ST students in almost all academic institutes of national importance like the All India Institute of Medical Sciences (AIIMS). Since 2007, more than twenty SC and ST students pursuing engineering and medical courses in such institutes have committed suicide. It is not surprising that the authorities had been quick to ascribe these sad acts to academic pressure leading to depression. Even after many suicides, it may be noted that there was no candle light protest at India Gate. There was also no protest march to the residence of Ministers and political leaders as well as Rashtrapati Bhawan. Further, no protests were seen from the section of civil society whose many members love birds and animals including street dogs, as well as no campaigns by TV channels which telecast live non-stop, days together, even the events like rescue operation of a buffalo stuck in a deep pit. Whenever, a student from an elite school in metro cities is caned or beaten by a teacher, these TV channels conduct debates at prime time. The persons including the top rung of governance come forward to issue statements to condemn such an 'inhuman' act and assure the country of taking preventive and curative measures. However, nothing happens on the loss of life of SC and ST students on campuses, except some ritualistic lip sympathy. It is not true that these students who committed suicide were not able to cope with academic pressure. Indeed it is the environment of these campuses with their entrenched casteism, that SC and ST students were not able to deal with (Kumar, *The Indian Express*, Ahmedabad, Wednesday, March 14, 2012).

The Committee (2007), chaired by Professor Sukhdeo Thorat, conducted an inquiry and found caste discrimination in AIIMS. Expectedly, the authorities of AIIMS termed the report as biased and refuted all the findings as false allegations. Indeed, refutation itself is indicative of their social insensitivity, feudal mind, upper caste arrogance and dishonesty. In one of the well-known medical colleges, thirty-five students belonging to SC and ST communities failed en masse, in one subject perhaps more than once. Dr. Bhalchandra Mungekar was appointed Commissioner of Enquiry by the National Commission for Scheduled Castes to probe this matter. The report unequivocally concluded that the college practised caste discrimination (Rahi Gaikwad 2012). A lot of information is available in the public domain about the caste discrimination on the campuses.

Wankhade (2013) has also shown and discussed the caste and social discrimination, and its nature, form and consequences in education. The study of Srinivasa Rao (2013) which used the perspective of Goffman (1963) on stigma to examine and interpret the experiences of SC and ST students in IITs, showed that the members belonging to the upper castes in IITs perhaps are predisposed to discriminate against the SC and ST students. The narration of their experiences is quite shocking. It must be remembered that caste discriminations are not only practised in the premier academic institutes like IITs and AIIMS, it is everywhere in other academic institutes including universities and colleges. At least many avenues are available in the universities and colleges for SC and ST students to voice their grievances. Being an open system, the incidence of suicides in the university system are relatively low compared to IITs, AIIMS and other academic institutes of national importance. The Universty of Hyderabad is an exception to this. In the last ten years more than ten students have committed suicides, including Rohit Vemula on January 17, 2016. He was a talented student. He had dreams. He, along with other students, was fighting against discrimination and asking for justice to Dalit students on campus. Rohit through his suicide exposed the ugly face of casteism on campuses. For the first time people from different walks of life and organizations from all over the country, raised the voice agaist this sorrowful incident and protested to get justice to Rohit. Dalit students of the University of Hyderabad have been very active on its campus and always fought for the cause of the community.The intolerant administration dominated by upper castes has suspended or expelled many Dalit students in the past. It is necessary to sensitize this privileged section of society and also make them understand that the inclusiveness and equity in education would contribute to a great extent to the progress of nation.

Unfortunately, as mentioned earlier to hide the discriminatory actions, the failures of SC and ST students in IITs, IIMs and other institutes of higher learning are attributed to factors like the inability to cope with high academic standards (Indiresen and Nigam 1993), non-cognitive handicap, cultural shock (Kripal et al. 1984), the incidence of psychological symptoms (Prakash 1995) and feeling of inferiority (Kripal and Gupta 1999). In this context it is pertinent to note that Indian doctors in UK appearing for knowledge and practical examinations, set by the Royal College of GPs, are routinely failing, despite having four attempts to take a chance. For the year 2012, the failure is 63 per cent (Indian Doctors in Britain Fail in Key Exams. *The Times of India*, Monday, December 24, 2012,

p. 13). It is well known that Indian doctors who go to the UK are mainly from urban-rich and upper caste communities. These failed doctors were expectedly angry and attributed their failure to racial discrimination. To get justice, the British Association of Physicians of Indian Origin (BAPIO) planned to take legal action against the British Medical Colleges, which set the examinations. It is quite contradictory, when urban-rich and upper caste students fail in UK, it is because of discrimination; but when SC and ST students fail in IITs, IIMs and other institutes of higher education, it is not discrimination.

Members of upper castes wanted the IITs and other national institutes of higher learning exclusively for themselves on the pretext of merit. Since, the admissions of SC, ST and OBC students cannot be stopped because of the reservation policy, which flows from the Constitution, they create a hostile condition on the campuses to make it difficult for SC, ST and OBC students to academically adopt and survive. The IITs and other institutes have also been successful to a great extent in resisting the appointments of SC and ST candidates in teaching posts. The presence of SC and ST teachers in these institutes is negligible.

Privatization and Professional Education

After independence of the country, members of SC and ST communities started accessing education. Although, faced with great difficulties and discriminations, SC and ST students could be seen in significant numbers on campuses, mainly because of the reservation policy as enshrined in the Constitution, and the post-matric scholarship. These underprivileged social groups became more visible, in the 1970s and 1980s on campuses. They consider, and rightly so, the reservations as compensation for the historic wrongs done to them for centuries. Therefore, they always fought and are fighting for the same. Apart from visibility on campuses, a large number of them became part of governance and administration. The demographic change on campuses and government services as well as awakening the SC and ST communities might have posed a threat to the social status of upper castes and their control over the institutions including education. To continue the secure status and control over society, the privatization of education was probably considered as one of the options. The gradual withdrawal of government from education and at the same time its encouragement to privatization of education could not be just coincidence.

Expectedly for the acceptability of privatization by the nation, the case was made and the impression was created that the public sector is not in a position to expand the capacity of its institutions to meet the rapid growth of demand of eligible graduates. On this pretext the government allowed private agencies liberally in the 1990s to establish institutes of higher education. The people who established private institutions are mainly upper castes, charge very high fees, beyond the capacity of the poor and underprivileged, the institutes are free from reservations, therefore, the private sector higher education became almost exclusively for the upper castes and by the upper castes only. It may be noted that the government also made drastic cuts in the budget for higher education and even advised the UGC to formulate a set of guidelines for establishing the private universities in the country (Ghosh, 2009).

Further, it has also put an indirect ban on opening of conventional colleges and universities. The government from the 1990s onwards probably was very keen to promote privatization, which is evident from the Ambani-Birla Report (2002). This report considered education as a very profitable market and asked the government to withdraw from higher education and leave that sector to corporate houses. Indeed in the name of privatization the corporate sector made the commercialization of higher education. The Ambani-Birla Report could be an outcome of the tacit understanding among upper caste people in governance and administration, the government itself and industrialists. Otherwise there was no reason for the government to plead openly for the privatization of higher education. Further while presenting the country paper at the UNESCO World Conference on Higher Education in Paris, in 1998; the representative of India justified the privatization of higher education and pleaded for the need of generating funds from the private sources. Expectedly, the government pushed the agenda of privatization of higher education, at the same time made higher education, particularly professional courses non-accessible, to SC and ST communities. It appeared to be a close link between the acceleration of privatization of higher education and acceptance of the Mandal Commission Report to provide twenty-seven per cent reservations in services for OBCs, in 1990.

Perhaps, the upper castes were worried about shrinking educational space due to reservations, not to get marginalized and keep privileged status and control, as was in the past, it was necessary for them to find alternatives and create new space; for continuance of dominance and control over education. They found in the form of privatization of education which would enable them to dominate and control the education sector, government institutions, government and in turn the Indian society.

There is nothing wrong in privatization of education *per se*. Our past experience showed that the colleges and universities in the private domain, with or without government aid, played a vital role in spreading education among the masses, contributed to social change and development. On the contrary, the aims and objectives of present-day privatization is completely different in its form and function. The colleges and universities established in the private sector are mainly owned by individuals, individual families or corporate houses. Banaras Hindu University was founded by Pandit Madan Mohan Malaviya, but he did not own it. Aligarh Muslim University was founded by Sir Syed Ahmad Khan, but he did not own it. Dr. B.R. Ambedkar founded the People's Education Society and established colleges, but he also did not own it. The same applies to DAV and Khalsa Colleges, and many other academic institutes in the country. There is no scope and also need to elaborate or discuss the issues such as how these present-day academic institutes in the private sector are managed and run. Everyone is aware of these aspects. It must be mentioned that unlike in India, the corporate sectors of Western countries fund education liberally. Major funding for scientific research, and technological inventions and innovations come from the corporate sectors. On the other hand, the Indian corporate sector which gets more than Rs. five lakh crore tax exemptions in various forms annually avoid supporting Indian education. The corporate sector makes meagre or no contribution to the scientific research and technological developments. It prefers to import technology, use it and earn a profit. Investing in research and development is perhaps considered as waste. Indeed, this sector could make contributions in the form of endowment through its 'corporate social responsibility.' Instead, some members of the corporate sector started their own academic institutes and universities. Apart from this, amazingly, 'when under developed Indian universities, short of funds, the Indian companies are investing in US universities such as Harvard, Cornell, Yale and Stanford which are already among the richest in the world. The total amount of Indian endowments that have been made to the Ivy League and elsewhere in the West stands over $ 120 million' (Jaffrelot, Christophe, 2015, Indian Direct Investment, *The Indian Express*, Monday, June 29, 2015, pp. 15).

The private sector focused on professional courses and ignored traditional courses in humanities, social sciences and basic natural sciences. After independence, slow at the beginning and then a steep increase could be seen particularly around the 1980s and thereafter in the number of institutes offering professional courses as well as enrolment of students. In 1947 there were one hundred and thirty-two institutes with 45,643 students on their role. In 2009, these numbers increased to 9,030 institutes and 3,16,833 students (Powar 2012). It was important that the increase of institutes offering professional courses observed to be quite high compared to social sciences, humanities and basic sciences. Significantly the focus was mainly on technical, medical and management education. Thirty-eight engineering colleges with around 2,000 students were in the year 1947. At present, engineering colleges are 3,393 with 14,85,894 students. A steep increase could be seen in terms of the number of Engineering Colleges and number of students when the private sector came in and started colleges. Many private colleges were established even in the remote part of rural areas with no infrastructure and other facilities, producing mostly unemployable graduates.

Because of the population of 1.2 billion and plethora of diseases, the medical research and teaching in India should have gone hand in hand and taken the lead in health sciences at global level. However, medical research did not become the priority, instead emphasis was given on teaching. As a result, increasingly more institutes teaching medical sciences were established. According to Powar (2012), at the time of independence, there were twenty-three medical institutes with around 25,000 students, which, in 2011, increased to 335 institutes, with 40,335 students, 289 dental colleges with about 12,000 students, and 1,458 nursing colleges with 83,000 students. In alternative systems of medicine there were 254 Ayurveda, 41 unani, 184 homeopathy, 9 siddha and 12 yoga colleges. Two factors, one the urban setting of medical colleges and second the poverty; became a steep barrier for the SC and ST communities to access medical education. They remained excluded.

Management emerged as a faculty in the early 1950s. In the year 2010-11, there were 3,150 colleges/institutes with enrolment of 0.28-0.30 million students. It can be noted that the institutes of management increased substantially after 1980 from 50 to 2,100 in the year 2010. It was expected, as during the 1980s, the government encouraged the privatization of higher education. Presently, management education is very popular and in demand. Therefore, within thirty years (1980-2010) more than two thousand management institutes came into existence compared to just fifty in the early thirty years of independence (1950-1980). Legal education has also become quite popular and many students are known to opt for legal studies in more than 900 colleges and university campuses, against one hundred and sixteen institutes of legal education with 9,098 students during 1946-47 (Basu, 1991). It comes to eight times increase, in around 65 years. Presently, the government is giving a lot of importance to teacher education, to overcome shortage of teachers at all the levels as well as for improvement in the quality of education. India has five million school teachers and nearly 0.7 million college teachers. According to information available in July 2011, 4,848 institutes and colleges were found to offer BEd programmes and 975 offer MEd programmes. The government is increasing colleges and universities to introduce courses on teachers' education and use of modern technologies in teaching. When the British left India, teachers' education was small in size with just 51 academic institutes.

According to the Higher Education in India at a Glance, February 2012 of UGC, the total enrolment of students was 169.76 lakh, out of which in terms of per cent, share of engineering and technology was 16.86 per cent, medicine 3.85 per cent, education 3.36 per cent, commerce and management 17.11 per cent and law 1.93 per cent. Importantly, the combined share of these five professional faculties in total enrolment comes to 43.11 per cent. Even ignoring the students enrolled in commerce courses, still the enrolment share of professional courses was more than 30 per cent. These facts indicated that a large number of students of India opt for professional courses.

According to the twelfth Five Year Plan Document on Higher Education, in the year 2011-12, there were 29,662 private institutions in the country which include 191 degree awarding institutes, 19,930 colleges, and 9,541 Diploma institutes. The professional courses are mainly located in these private institutes and colleges, private universities or Deemed to be universities. Out of the total professional colleges more than 90 per cent were private predominantly engineering colleges. In case of medical and health education more than 75 per cent colleges were in the private sector (Powar, 2012). The professional institutes hire staff mostly on contractual basis, academic programmes are largely undergraduate, and research is almost non-existent, with a few exceptions.

At present, India has more than a hundred private universities and their number is being continuously increased. Out of 130 the Deemed to be universities, 90 were self-financed. Around 20 to 30 lakh students study in these private institutes, which comes just to fifteen to eighteen per cent of total enrolment in the country. Presently, the possibility to get a job is quite high for graduates with degrees in professional subjects. Therefore, the students in large numbers rushed to join private institutes. However, the quality of education is poor in some of these private institutes, particularly which are located away from cities. Being private and self-financing, these institutes charge very high fees. It is 50 to 80 times higher than our public institutions. In countries like Japan, Korea and US it is eight to ten times higher than their public institutes. Only students belonging to upper castes, higher middle class, urban rich and elites can pay high fees and take advantage, by joining private institutes which maintain good standards. As a result, these private institutes are catering to the academic needs of almost exclusively of the people belonging to upper castes and rich sections of the society. On the other hand, because of the high cost of professional education the poor, SC and ST communities cannot think of taking admissions in good private institutes. In short, whether by default or by design, professional education is for a select few only and for the rich and higher castes.

Education in State Universities

Out of a total of 634 universities, state universities are 297 (47 per cent), established by the state governments. The state universities and colleges affiliated thereto mainly cater to the educational needs of the nation and could be considered as the backbone of higher education. Unfortunately, this sector has been neglected in terms of financial support, and at the same time subjected to external influence and pressure. Unlike the central university system, state universities, in the real sense, do not have autonomy in administration and governance, and academic freedom. In the recent past, at the central level, the government had realized the importance of higher education for the development of the nation and enhanced the budget nine to ten times higher in the Eleventh Five Year Plan compared to the earlier one, and also continued to take measures to increase an access to education with equity. However, at the state level, the government did not enhance financial allocations for their state universities. On the other hand, the state governments have withdrawn to a great extent from their educational responsibilities. The funds provided to state universities are inadequate, unpredictable and inflexible. Out of the total fund, 80 to 90 per cent goes for salaries of teachers and non-teaching staff and very little remains for maintenance and other purposes. For research, teachers have to depend on funding agencies, however, everyone does not get such help. It is known that the central funding agencies fund heavily the research of the few national institutions and central universities leaving very little to the teachers and researchers, large in numbers, from the state universities. Therefore, as mentioned above, in India science is not progressing and instead a few scientists are progressing. The same situation prevails in the humanities and social sciences. In one of the meetings, a Vice-Chancellor of the state university with a large number of enrolment and affiliated colleges mentioned that his university was given only Rs. 7 lakhs for the year 2013-14 as maintenance grant. The situation is almost the same for the other state universities throughout the country with some variations and few exceptions. The worst part of the state universities is that the vacant posts have remained unfilled for long. In many state universities the recruitment was not done for more than 15 years. Surprisingly, many states imposed a ban on recruitment, and perhaps still continued in some universities. To address the problem of shortage of teachers, the universities were permitted to appoint contract teachers, guest faculty and teaching assistants, either on a yearly basis or hourly basis on a meagre salary. In doing so, the colleges and universities are converted into coaching centres which in turn adversely affected not only the quality of education but the education system itself. The SC, ST and other underprivileged communities send their children mainly to such state universities and affiliated colleges for higher studies. For example, in the Government College, Kadapa, in the year 2010-11; out of the total enrolment of 1,858; students belonging to underprivileged groups including minorities were 1,464 (78.3 per cent). There were just 394 (21.7 per cent) of the open/general category. Programme-wise, in the BA, 89 per cent students were from an underprivileged background, whereas 11.96 per cent only from the open/general category. The situation was not very different in BSc and BCom programmes (Table 4). It was confirmed during the interaction with students and teachers that the students belonging to upper castes take admissions in the private colleges preferably in professional courses. At present in Andhra Pradesh, there are 316 Government Colleges, 179 aided colleges and 1,671 unaided colleges. These unaided colleges are in the private sector, run mostly professional courses. The situation is not very different in other states. Perhaps it is worse! This possibility is supported by the social profile of enrolment of the Sri Kalli Nageshwar Rao Gangaiah Government First Grade College, Gangavati, in the district of Koppal of Karnataka state; for the academic year 2014. Out of the total of 1,546 enrolled students, SC were 321 (20.76 per cent), ST 278 (17.98 per cent) and OBC 846 (54.72 per cent) and just 101 (06.53 per cent) general category students (Table 5). The enrolment of girls was very low compared to boys in this college. These numbers are quite disturbing. However, it appeared that government academic institutes are becoming almost exclusively for reserved category students, as the so-called upper caste community sending their children to private colleges and institutes which mainly run professional courses. This small number of general category students (06.53 per cent) studying in this government college belong to the economically weaker section. These two colleges are not exceptions and similar trends are found throughout the country. It is known that the private sector now accounts for 64 per cent of the total number of institutions and 59 per cent of the enrolment in the country as compared to 40 and 30 per cent respectively about a decade ago (Mishra Sobha and Pankaj Rajesh, 2012).

Table 4: Social Composition of Students in Government College, Kadapa, Andhra Pradesh in 2010-11

Category	*Programmes*		
	BA	*BSc*	*B.Com*
Open/General	61 (11.96%)	204 (26.32%)	129 (22.51%)
Backward Class	112 (21.96%)	262 (33.80%)	189 (32.98%)
Scheduled Caste	155 (30.39%)	221 (28.51%)	151 (26.35%)
Scheduled Tribe	16 (3.13%)	23 (2.96%)	09 (1.57%)
Minorities	166 (32.54%)	65 (8.38%)	95 (16.57%)
Total	510 (100%)	775 (100%)	573 (100%)

Source: Government College, Kadapa, AP, (2012); Report submitted to UGC for Autonomous Status

Further, in the state universities and affiliated colleges, the vacant posts reserved for SC and ST candidates are filled by appointing the candidates belonging to the general category, on ad hoc or temporary basis. Therefore, regular appointments of SC and ST candidates against these reserve posts are delayed under the pretext of non-availability of suitable candidates. Because of detrimental implementation of the reservation policy, SC and ST candidates remain unemployed even though they are available, eligible and suitable.

Table 5: Social Diversity in Enrolment in the Sri Kalli Nageshwar Rao Gangaiah Government First Grade College, Ganagvati, District Koppol (Karnataka) for the Year 2013-14

Category	*Male*	*Female*	*Total*
SC	272 (17.59%)	49 (03.17%)	321 (20.76%)
ST	248 (16.04%)	30 (01.93%)	278 (17.99%)
OBC	538 (34.80%)	308 (19.92%)	846 (54.72%)
General	45 (02.91%)	56 (03.62%)	101 (06.53%)
Grand Total	1103 (71.34%)	443 (28.65%)	1546 (100%)

Source: Self-Study Report (SSR) submitted to NAAC, Bangalore; for Re-accreditation of the college (2014).

The state governments and administration of state universities seemed to be inspired by the private institutions and private Deemed to be universities; and permitted to start self-financing courses in subjects like basic sciences, computer sciences and management. Although the fee charged for these courses is relatively lower than private institutes, but still not affordable to most of the SC and ST students. Some universities permit the admission with a certain number of admissions in self-finance mode and others through the normal route with low fees in the same subject making mixed classes, on the basis of payment of fees. With or without dual fees structure, the state governments and state universities by introducing self-financing programmes have converted public academic institutions into semi-private institutes. In the future, these state universities are expected to introduce more and more academic programmes in self-financing mode. The Chhatrapati Shahuji Maharaj University, Kanpur is perhaps an excellent example. According to its self-study report (2014) submitted to the NAAC, Bangalore for re-accreditation, this university runs around 60 PG academic programmes on its campus, apart from 42 PhD programmes. Out of these only 5 PG courses are funded by the government and around 55 are run in self-finance mode. Further, out of its more than 1,000 affiliated colleges just 61 are aided by the government and the remaining are self-financed, mainly running professional courses. Interestingly, this university at Kanpur is named after Chhatrapati Shahu Ji Maharaj, a king of Kolhapur, Maharashtra, who was a great social reformer and worked entirely in his life for the upliftment of the downtrodden and took a keen interest in their education. What a great contradiction! This trend of introducing and running courses in self-finance mode by state universities is becoming visible throughout the country, and likely to adversely affect the education system particularly the expansion of education with equity and equality.

The state university system is the real hope for SC and ST communities for their education. However, starting self-financing courses in the state universities would shrink the academic space for SC and ST students which would not only make it difficult for them to access higher education, but might throw them out of the education system sooner or later, if this trend continues. In addition, the self-financing courses are managed with teachers appointed on contract or temporary basis. The Chhatrapati Shahu Ji Maharaj University as mentioned above, runs sixty academic teaching programmes and 42 PhD programmes, has only 22 permanent teachers and on the other hand around 172 temporary teachers. On retirement of permanent teachers, the state government withdraws the financial support and asks the university to fill such vacancies, if required, and pay the salaries and provide other benefits to the newly appointed employees from its own resources. Similarly, Sri Kalli Nageshwar Rao Gangaiah Government First Grade College in Karnataka State also has just 20 permanent teachers but 87 temporary teachers to run the several UG and few PG courses. Such temporary and contract appointments generally do not come under the preview of the reservation policy; the institutions, colleges and universities are likely to have freedom to pick anybody of their choice for the appointments. In such circumstances, the probability of getting employment for SC and ST candidates would significantly reduce owing to caste biases and discrimination. Therefore, the self-finance courses started in the state universities are detrimental to the interest of the SC and ST communities.

Governance and Administration

The university system, particularly state universities are controlled by the small, but dominant section of the society through appointments of Vice-Chancellors, membership to statutory bodies and appointment to faculty positions. Table 5 clearly shows the exclusiveness in governance and administration of the universities. Although, the information in this table is for 210 universities and university level institutes, it provides the ground realities related to running the institutes of higher education in India. It could be seen that one hundred and fifty-four (95.65 per cent) positions of the Vice-Chancellors are occupied by members of the general category. However, the Vice-Chancellors belonging to the SC community are just seven (4.34 per cent) and none from the ST community. In case of Directors, 93 (93.94 per cent) belong to the general category, five (4.82 per cent) belong to the SC community and one (1.01 per cent) belong to the ST community. Almost all posts of Directors in the education system are equivalent to Vice-Chancellors of Universities. The posts of Heads of Departments (HOD) and Deans in the universities are key positions which practically control all the academic activities. From such support, the Vice-Chancellors derive their strength. Out of 3,525 HOD and Deans, the representation of SC and ST is 170 (4.82 per cent) and 55 (1.55 per cent) respectively. 3,301 (93.63 per cent) professors are from the general category. The post of the professor is the highest in the university system and every academician dreams to be one. However, realization of such a dream seems to be difficult for the aspiring junior faculty members of SC and ST communities as their representation is 327 (3.59 per cent) and 80 (0.88 per cent) respectively at the level of the professor, which is far below 8,694 (95.53 per cent) the general category. The representation of SC is somewhat better at the level of Lecturer now called Assistant Professor, as they are 2,157 (10.92 per cent) out the total of 19,771. In the case of ST the numbers stand at 691 (3.49 per cent) in the total.

There are 41 Central Universities in the country. Considering the share in population, among these 41 Vice-Chancellors more than six and three are expected to be from SC and ST communities respectively. However, at present, there are only two Vice-Chancellors belonging to SC communities. It may be mentioned that traditionally till date, the Vice-Chancellor of Babasaheb Bhimrao Ambedkar University (BBAU), Lucknow was always

Table 6: Vice-Chancellors, Directors, HoD/Deans and Lecturers in 210 Indian Universities and University Level Institutes (in position, 2007)

Posts	*General*	*SC*	*ST*	*Total*
Vice-Chancellors	154 (95.65%)	7 (4.34%)	0 (0%)	161 (100%)
Directors	93 (93.94%)	5 (4.82%)	1 (1.01%)	99 (100%)
HOD/Deans	3301 (93.63%)	170 (4.82%)	55 (1.55%)	3526 (100%)
Professors	8694 (95.53%)	327 (3.59%)	80 (0.88%)	9101 (100%)
Lecturers	16923 (85.59%)	2157 (10.92%)	691 (3.49%)	19771 (100%)

Source: University Grants Commission

appointed from SC/ST communities. However, for the first time, the government made a deviation and appointed the Vice-Chancellor of BBAU from the general category. As a result now, there is not a single Vice-Chancellor from the SC community in the old central universities. Both the Vice-Chancellors, mentioned above, and belonging to the SC community are in new central universities established in 2009. Indeed for first time, while appointing Vice-Chancellors in these newly established universities, the interest of all sections of society was considered and protected. Although, the exact number of ST Vice-Chancellors could not be ascertained, they are also perhaps under-represented in the central university system. If the North-East region is ignored, there is just one Vice-Chancellor from the ST community in the central university system. It may be mentioned that many Vice-Chancellors of the central universities which are located in the North-East region do not belong to ST communities. It is quite clear that SC and ST communities are ignored, while appointing the Vice-Chancellors in the central universities. Presently (2014–15), in the central universities there is just one ST Vice-Chancellor and none from the SC community.

Appreciably small in number, the representation of ST persons as Vice-Chancellor could be seen in the central universities. However, at the national level according to the Table 6, there was no ST person as Vice-Chancellor in 210 universities and university level institutions. This fact suggests that the data in the above Table 5 is mainly pertaining to the state universities. In the state universities, governments are known to influence the appointments of Vice-Chancellors, and while doing so, the interest and aspirations of SC and ST communities appeared to be ignored. It is evident from the low representation of SC and ST at the level of Vice-Chancellor or equivalent posts. The situation is almost the same for appointments at different positions and levels. Whether it is state or central universities or university level institutes, as mentioned above, SC and ST communities are ignored while appointing the Vice-Chancellors, Directors or other academic positions, and kept them away from governance and administration of higher education.

Medium of Instruction

The British arrived on the Indian coast in 1612, won the Battle of Plassey (1757) and ruled the country thereafter for one hundred and ninety years and finally left in 1947. During this long period, expectedly, English as a language deeply rooted in our soil, became the status symbol of an elite social group, medium of instruction from matriculation onwards and eventually spread among the educated masses. Meanwhile, it emerged as a link language of the world. In such a situation, India had an advantage and would have exploited its strong English base by adapting and implementing national language policy in such a way that our national as well as regional languages would have protected and flourished and at the same time, without harming the interest of these national and regional languages, English would have also continued in a planned manner, particularly in the field of education to make our entire human resource internationally competitive. India would have been immensely benefited in the area of globalization. We as a nation lost the opportunity to a great extent.

English was considered as a symbol of slavery by some Indian leaders. In the late 1950s and early 1960s, an agitation was launched and demanded the ban on the use of English in government offices as well as in private places. Consequently, English was banned and replaced by the regional language or mother tongue as a medium of teaching in the schools and then colleges and universities, particularly in state universities. The regional language or mother tongue as a medium of instruction was introduced in the state universities mainly which were away from the metro cities, particularly in small towns and cities. In some universities, including those located in cities, science subjects were permitted to be taught in English, with an option for students to write the examination in their mother tongue or regional language. As a result, the quality of education in such colleges and universities was irreversibly damaged. The poor quality of education made the students educationally handicapped and consequently unemployable. Such students, lakhs in number, come to the market of employment. Since they have a lack of the required skill and knowledge nobody hires them. Although, not a universal phenomenon, it is an open secret that the jobs could be sold, and bought by the rich. Therefore, one should have money to get an education as well as a job. Although it may not be always true but the fact is that the ethics in education are eroded to a great extent. Mostly the educated but unemployable youth are from the rural part of the country. They cannot go back to agriculture as their education makes them unfit to work in the fields. On the other hand, because of the language barrier, the talented students cannot migrate to other states and countries for a better future, and are forced to remain confined to their own region, wandering on roads in search of jobs, and for higher education. The teaching in the mother tongue is producing youths as a social and national liability. Interestingly, this huge waste of human resource is not seen by some English educated economists who remained busy in forecasting the bright future of India on the basis of the youthful demographic profile. It must be remembered that the victims of poor quality education and regional language medium mainly belong to the rural poor, SC and ST communities. It would be pertinent to mention that IIT Roorkee expelled 72 students, in July 2015, because of their poor performance in the first year examination, which was attributed to the lack of skill to communicate in English. Most of them had a background of non-English medium, either Hindi or of other regional languages. Out of these, ninety per cent belonged to SC, ST and OBC castes. Although, these students did well and scored average to high ranks in their respective categories in the joint entrance test (JEE), they failed in the first year examination. The success in the JEE itself proved, beyond doubt, the potential of reserved category students to study in IITs. However, the deficiency in English language has clipped their wings. A detailed story written by Usha Vishnu, in three parts, on this serious matter is carried by *The Indian Express*, dated August 5-7, 2015. Apart from other issues, the story revealed that the IITs from other places also gave marching orders to students due to 'bad academic performance'. During academic years 2006 to 12, IIT Bombay asked eight students, Delhi 86, Roorkee 278, Kharagpur six, Madras six, Guwahati 24 and Kanpur 403, to leave these premier institutes. The expulsion of these students confirmed that the success in premier academic institutes like IITs is determined by English language rather than talent and subject knowledge. It may be mentioned that long ago, Dr. Ambedkar emphasized the importance of English as a social leveller for the weak and vulnerable. Had there been easy access to English medium education, the socio-economic conditions of SC and ST communities would have been better than today.

Although, English was substituted by a regional language or mother tongue in academic institutes in the public sector, but it continued to flourish in missionary and private schools and colleges. The state universities in metros and other big cities did not discard English completely to protect the educational interests of upper castes and urban elites. The English educated elite social groups had a colonial legacy of metropolitan cities and towns of British India. These social groups while supporting the government on language policies and implementation of the regional language as the medium of instruction, encouraged the continuation of English medium schools, colleges and postgraduate studies in universities. Being a part of governance, administration and at other important positions and locations, this elite made policies and implemented the same, whose detrimental effects can be seen now.

The beneficiaries of British legacy and social hierarchy were well aware of the importance of English as a link language of the world; they saw to it that English medium education expanded with quality. This plan worked very well as these social groups grabbed all educational advantages. Surprisingly, the descendants of the *Angrezi Hatao* Movement in the 1960s and those who fought for the cause of regional languages send their children and wards to English medium academic institutes, in India or abroad. The Apex Court of India once described English as the flag bearer of knowledge economy and society. The upper caste educated section of society was aware of the importance of English education, and therefore mastered it. On the other hand, SC, ST and other underprivileged remained educationally handicapped, as they could not access English medium quality education.

As in the British Raj, in independent India, higher education continued to remain exclusively beneficial to a small section of society particularly people belonging to upper castes. Despite the provision of reservations, SC and ST remained marginalized in the sphere of education. The descendants of beneficiaries of British education, mainly belonged to upper castes and the urban rich did not allow education to be democratized, and kept educational institutes and education under their own control. In a planned manner, the reservations were implemented detrimentally in the public institutions, colleges and universities, making its beneficiaries as victims. After acceptance of the Mandal Commission Report and its implementation, the government privatized higher education in self-financing mode and at the same time slowly withdrew from education in the public sector, which shrunk the educational opportunities for SCs, STs, and the poor. The wrong policies and drastic cuts into financial support, adversely affected education and lowered its quality.

The changed circumstances forced the disadvantaged social groups to access low quality education in government or government-aided colleges and universities, making them unemployable. The mindset of higher castes and passive attitude of government, these social groups also did not benefit from the provision of reservations in recruitments in teaching and non-teaching posts. They were also inadequately represented in the governance and administration of higher education. Despite hostility, discrimination and humiliations on the campuses, detrimental implementation of reservation policies and shrinking educational space due to privatization of higher education, the underprivileged, particularly SC and ST have increasingly been accessing higher education.

REFERENCES

Abdul Kalam, A.P.J. (2002). *Ignited Mind*. Viking, New Delhi.

Abdul Kalam, A.P.J. and Singh, Srijan Pal (2011). *Target 3 Billion. PWRA: Innovating Solution Towards Sustainable Development*, Penguin Books, New Delhi.

Basu, A. (1991). Higher Education in Colonial India. In: *Higher Education in Indian Universities*, Moonis Raza (ed.), New Delhi, pp. 22-23.

Dubey, A. (2009). Determinants of Post-Higher Secondary Enrolment in Indian. In: *Higher Education in India. Issues Related to Expansion, Inclusiveness, Quality and Finance*, University Grants Commission, New Delh, pp. 139-198.

Duraisamy, P. (2009). Enrolment Forecast of Higher Education for Inclusive Growth in the Eleventh Five Year Plan. In: *Higher Education in India, Issues Related to Expansion, Inclusiveness, Quality and Finance*. University Grants Commission, New Delhi, pp. 27-50.

Gaikwad, Rahi (2012). How Casteist are Our Universities?, *The Hindu*, Wednesday, October 3.

Ghosh, Suresh Chandra (2001). *The History of Education in Ancient India*, Munshiram Manoharlal Publishers, New Delhi.

Ghosh, Suresh Chandra (2009). *The History of Education in Modern India*, Orient Blackswan, New Delhi, p. 228.

Goffman, E. (1963). *Stigma. Notes on the Management of a Spoiled Identity*, Penguin, London.

Gupta, Dipankar (2011). Fighting a Lonely Battle, *The Times of India*, Ahmedabad, Friday, June 3.

Indiresen, P.V. and Nigam, N.C. (1993). The Indian Institute of Technology, Excellence in Peril, In: *Higher Education Reforms in India: Experiences and Perspectives*, S. Chitnis and P.G. Altbach (eds.), Sage, New Delhi, pp. 334-364.

Jaffrelot, Christophe (2015). Indian Direct Investment, *The Indian Express*, Monday, June 29, p. 15.

Kadam, Shivajirao (2010). *Perspective on Governance of Higher Education*, Bharti Vidhyapeeth Deemed University Publication, Pune.

Kripal, V. (1976). Higher Education for Scheduled Castes and Scheduled Tribes, *Economics and Political Weekly*, 13(4-5), pp. 165-167.

Kripal, V. and Gupta, M.C. (1999). *Equality Through Reservation*, Rawat, Jaipur.

Kripal, V., Swamidasan, N. and Gupta, A. (1984). *The Adjusment of SC/ST students in IIT Bombay: A Report*, Bombay, IIT.

Kumar, Anoop (2012). The Death of Anil Meena, *The Indian Express*, Ahmedabad, Wednesday, March 14.

Levin, Richard (2010). Top of the Class. The Rise of Asia's Universities, *Foreign Affairs*, Vol. 89, No. 3, pp. 63-75.

Merchant, Minhaz (2010). New Triangle of Power, In an Emerging Tripolar World, Stewardship of India's Foreign Policy Needs Firmer Hands, *The Times of India*, Ahmedabad, May 1.

Mishra, Sobha and Pankaj, Rajesh (2012). Higher Education in India, Quest for Excellence, *FICCI Business Digest*, December, pp. 12-14.

Nambissan, Geetha B. and Srinivasa Rao, S. (2013). *Sociology of Education in India*, Oxford University Press, New Delhi.

Panikkar, K.N. and Nair, M. Bhaskaran (2012). *Globalization and Higher Education in India*, Pearson, New Delhi.

Powar, K.B. (2012). *Expanding Domains in India, Higher Education*, Association of Indian Universities, New Delhi, p. 63.

Prakash, Om (1993). Psychological Symptoms Amongst Untouchable Students of IITs: Challenge for the Technical Education Planners, *Journal of Educational Planning and Administration*, Vol. 7(2), pp. 165-180.

Raju, S. (2009). Gender Differentials in Access to Higher Education. In: *Higher Education in India, Issues Related to Expansion, Inclusiveness, Quality and Finance*, University Grants Commission, New Delhi, pp. 79-102.

Richter, J. (1908). *History of Missions in India*, Fleming Revell Company, New York.

Sankhdher, B.M. (1999). *Education System from 1857 to William Hunter's Commission 1882*, Deep & Deep Publications, New Delhi.

Saxena, Sobhna (2011). *Sunday Times of India*, Ahmedabad, August 7, p. 9.

Srinivasa Rao, S. (2013). Structural Exclusion in Everyday Institutional Life: Labeling of Stigmatized Groups in an IIT, In: *Sociology of Education*, Geetha B. Nambissan and S. Srinivasa Rao (eds.), Oxford University Press, New Delhi, pp. 199-223.

Srivastava, Ravi and Sinha, S. (2009). Inter-Social Groups Disparities in Access to Higher Education, In: *Higher Education in India, Issues Related to Expansion, Inclusiveness, Quality and Finance:* University Grants Commission, New Delhi, pp. 103-110.

Thorat, S.K. (2009). Emerging Issues in Higher Education Approaches and Strategy of Eleventh Plan, In: *Higher Education in India, Issues Related to Expansion, Inclusiveness, Quality and Finance*, University Grants Commission, New Delhi, pp. 1-26

Ved Prakash, Thyagarajan S.P., Qamar Furqan, Srivastava, Ravi and Sharma, A.K. (2011). Compiled and Edited, *Inclusive and Qualitative Expansion of Higher Education. Twelfth Five Year Plan, 2012-2017*, University Grants Commission, New Delhi.

Virmani, Arvind (2010). *From Unipolar to Tripolar World*, Academic Foundation, New Delhi.

Wankhade, G.G. (2013). Caste Discrimination: Nature, Forms, and Consequences in Education, In: *Sociology of Education*, Geetha B. Nambissan and S. Srinivasa Rao (eds.), Oxford University Press, New Delhi, pp. 182-198.

4

Implementation of Reservation Policy for the SC and ST in Colleges Affiliated to the University of Delhi

The University of Delhi was founded in 1922 by an Act of the Central Legislative Assembly. Initially incorporated as a unitary, teaching and residential University, it developed into a Federal University by an Act of Parliament in 1952. In 1981-82 the original Act of 1922 was amended to allow affiliation of colleges outside India. The University had a modest beginning with just three Colleges, two Faculties (Arts and Sciences) and about 750 students. At present there are 86 Postgraduate Departments, 82 Colleges, 14 Faculties, and 20 Specialized Centres. The university has nearly three lakh students on its rolls. The total number of teachers is around 8,000, while its administrative staff number is around 2,150 (University-appointed), and nearly 5000 (College-appointed). In an effort to cope with the enormous expansion, the University has opted for a new organizational pattern based on the multi-campus concept. The University of Delhi has shown exponential growth since its inception. It occupies a prominent place on the map of higher education.

With a long history and many achievements, the University of Delhi is one of the largest premier central universities of the country and is known for its high reputation in teaching and research with eminent scholars on its roll of faculty members. It enjoys special status among the central universities in terms of societal perception. The university through its academic activities has contributed immensely to nation building. One comes across many milestones in its path of academic progress. More importantly, the university has always remained at the forefront and protected the academic autonomy as well as interests of teaching and non-teaching employees of the Indian universities, particularly the Central Universities. Being located in the capital of India, it could influence the government policies and their implementation. Therefore, the University of Delhi represents an excellent model to understand the structure and function of the university system in India.

The University of Delhi and its many affiliated colleges receive a huge proportion of their funds in the form of grants from the UGC. Therefore, the University and its Colleges have to adopt and strictly follow different policies of the government including the reservations for SCs and STs. Untouchable communities suffered from discriminations and inequalities since ancient times due to the caste system which pushed them back in every sphere of life. On getting independence, the founding fathers of the nation to undo the historic wrongs made provision for reservation in the Constitution. This policy provides reservations in legislations, services and education for their social upliftment. The UGC as a part of government endeavours to fulfil the allotted quota of reservation of fifteen per cent for the SC and 7.5 per cent for the ST enshrined in the Constitution under Article 335, has constituted a Standing Committee on SC and ST to monitor the implementation of the reservation policy in Indian universities. Through this monitoring committee, UGC interacts with colleges and universities including the University of Delhi and reviews the implementation of reservations and suggests measures to be taken for its effectiveness. Being the intellectual hub, the University of Delhi is expected to be more responsive, responsible and sensitive towards the social cause, such as the reservation policy. Therefore, the implementation of this policy is likely to be more effective, in the University of Delhi which has highly talented and enlightened faculty members on its roll. As these intellectuals could understand the need and benefits of the reservation policy, they are expected to contribute to its successful implementation and desired outcomes. Against this background, an attempt has been made to evaluate the present status of the reservation policy in recruitments in teaching and non-teaching positions in the fifty colleges of the University of Delhi..

Contrary to expectations, the present study showed that the University of Delhi has failed to honour and implement the constitutional provisions of reservation which aimed to uplift the SCs and STs socio-economically. Further, it also found that the SCs and STs have been made victims rather than beneficiaries because of detrimental implementation of the reservation policy by the University and its affiliated colleges.

Representation of SC and ST in Teaching Positions

More than eighty colleges affiliated to the University of Delhi, around fifty-three colleges get a maintenance grant from the UGC. It is mandatory, at least, for these fifty-three colleges, which get financial aid from the UGC, to provide the reservations to the extent of fifteen and 7.5 per cent for the SCs and STs respectively in teaching and non-teaching positions. Therefore, the present study is mainly confined to these grant-in-aid colleges. The colleges receiving grants are required to furnish the information to the UGC from time to time about the implementation of reservations. The author has compiled and processed the data from such information. Table 1 shows the representation of SC and ST in teaching positions in fifty colleges of Delhi. For the other remaining three colleges, either data is not available, or they do not follow the reservation policy of the Government of India on some or other pretext including minority status.

Table 1: Number of SC and ST Teachers in 50 Colleges Affiliated to the University of Delhi as on March 22, 2005

General	*Scheduled Caste*		*Scheduled Tribe*		*Vacant*	*Total*
	Filled	*Shortfall*	*Filled*	*Shortfall*		
4019	147(2.8%)	588.3(12.2%)	17(0.3%)	350.4(7.2%)	720	4902

Source: Data compiled and processed by the author from the information furnished by the colleges to UGC.

There are 4,903 teaching positions in all these 50 colleges. Out of these, 4,019 positions are occupied by the teachers belonging to the general category. However, there are just 147 and 17 teachers belong to the SC and ST categories respectively in these colleges. In terms of percentage, it is 2.8 per cent for the SC and 0.3 per cent for the ST. The shortfall in teaching positions is 588 and 350 for the SCs and STs respectively. It is amazing that, out of a total strength of 4,019 teachers belonging to the general category are 2,964 Readers (now called Associate Professor) while there are just five, who belong to the SC category (out of their filled strength of 147) and none from the ST category (out of their filled strength of 17). This is perhaps an excellent example of untouchability practised by the academicians.

Considering the total strength of 4,903 teachers in 50 colleges, SC teachers per college are expected to be around 15. However, nearly ten colleges do not have a single teacher of the SC category. The case of the STs is even worse. About 36 colleges have no ST teacher. Importantly, some of these colleges have faculty strength of more than one hundred.

It may be mentioned that the University of Delhi has adopted the roster system only in 1996 for teaching positions resulting in a shortfall of 588 and 350 positions for the SC and ST categories respectively. Therefore, this huge shortfall is attributed to the late adoption of the roster system for the implementation of the Reservation Policy. Amazingly, the university managed its recruitments without the roster! This is an act of negligence and lapses and no one seemed to notice. Not even UGC. Had the colleges ensured due compliance of the orders of reservation issued by the Government of India from time to time, the present shortfall could not have arisen. Non-implementation of reservations in faculty recruitments for such a long time reflects the mindset of educated people in this institute of higher learning.

The present Reservation Policy is an outcome of the Poona Pact between Mahatma Gandhi and Dr. B.R. Ambedkar in 1932. As the University of Delhi was established in 1922, it is 10 years older than the Reservation Policy itself. In the eighty-three years of its long life, the University of Delhi might have admitted a reasonably large number of SC and ST students and on successful completion of the courses might have also awarded degrees to them. In the event of this, it was possible for the colleges, to attract and appoint some of them as teachers. By not appointing a few from them, the university and colleges have exhibited in open their biases and done injustice to the SC and ST communities all along this long period. This act of the University and colleges is indicative of caste discrimination on the campuses. Most of the colleges are governed and administered by the people belonging to so-called upper castes. They always assume that the SCs and STs lack scholarly acumen and in turn declare them not fit for teachership. Such deliberate attempts implant the idea in the minds of the general public that the candidates belonging to SC and ST communities are not meritorious. Such a mindset could even be seen among the subject experts in many selection committees.

The SC and ST had not asked for the reservations and were compelled to accept the same (Kumar, 2005). Indeed, they had been fighting for social equality. Further, implementation of reservation remained in the hands of non-SCs and STs and therefore, the success and failure of the Reservation Policy was determined by them.

As mentioned earlier, the Reservation Policy came into existence in 1932. It was notified for the first time in 1943, thus taking a total of eleven years to commence. Further, the Reservation Policy became operative from 1950 onwards, after making provision in the Constitution. Interestingly, the University of Delhi took 42 years, as it adopted the roster system for the implementation of the Reservation Policy in the teaching positions in 1996. Although, the concerns were expressed from different quarters from time to time, but that did not perturb the University authorities.

The Parliamentary Committee on the welfare of the SCs and STs (2001-02), had taken serious note and asked the University the reasons for the delay in filling the positions reserved for SC and ST. Further, while disposing of the PIL (Case No. 2590/99) on July 9, 2001, the Honourable Delhi High Court directed the authorities of Delhi University to take immediate steps to fill the vacancies in the light of the Resolution No. 241 of the University of Delhi and the Office Memorandum dated July 2, 1997 issued by the Government of India, Ministry of Personnel, Public Grievances and Pensions, Department of Personnel and Training. These and other facts were suggestive of the non-sensitivity of the University and its colleges towards the socially sensitive issues. It would not be out of context to mention that the British were more sincere in the matters concerning implementation of reservations. Let us take an example of the Indian Civil Service (ICS). The reservations were provided for Indians in the ICS. In 1920, 33 per cent of ICS posts were reserved for Indians, and they were to increase it by 1.5 per cent every subsequent year (Montagu-Chelmsford Report 1918, Talukder, 1998). In ten years, the quantum of reservations reached 48 (Singh, 1962). The composition of ICS in 1942 (out of 1,056) was as follows: Europeans 448, Hindus 363, Muslims 109, Indian Christian 23, Anglo-Indians 9, Parsis 9, Sikhs 11, Scheduled Castes (then called untouchables) 1, and other 43 (Ambedkar, 1991). Thus, the British were able to fill more than 52 positions of ICS with Indians within 22 years. It may also be mentioned that Muslims were under-represented in the service. To address their grievances, many Muslim candidates (68 per cent of total Muslim ICS officers) were recruited to the ICS through nomination during the period from 1925 to 1943, in accordance with an undertaking given by Sir Alexander Muddiman in the Council of States on March 2, 1925.

This undertaking, subsequently referred to as 'the Muddiman Pledge', served in effect to reserve the posts for Muslims. Of the 87 Muslims who had entered the ICS during the above period, 29 were successful at the examination. The remaining 58 were nominated from the candidates who were unsuccessful at the examination, in order to redress the communal inequalities (Potter, 1996). On the other hand, in independent India, the SCs and STs were denied and kept away from reservation benefits by their own people.

The non-availability of SC and ST candidates is one of the reasons given for non-filling of reserved vacancies. This argument has been put forward not only by the University of Delhi, but also many other universities, institutes and organizations. However, the ground reality is different. For example, JNU is one of the leading universities known for its high standards of teaching and research. The students get admission to JNU through a cut throat competitive examination and could be considered as the cream of society. JNU is able to attract good students and maintain high standards mainly because of its highly talented and socially sensitive faculty (with exceptions). As far as the SC and ST teachers are concerned, many of them have been appointed against unreserved vacancies at all the three levels including Professors.

This act of JNU, i.e. going beyond the Reservation Policy for appointment of the SC and ST to faculty positions confirms of the availability of qualified and talented SC and ST candidates in the academic field.

It was found that in the Delhi University colleges, reserved vacancies/positions are also not filled on the ground of non-suitability of the SC and ST candidates. It is assumed that the SC and ST candidates are not meritorious and rejected, even though they possess the essential and desirable qualifications and required knowledge. The elimination of SC and ST candidates helps the colleges to appoint their own candidates as ad hoc or temporary teachers against these unfilled reserved positions. At the same time, the recruitment process for reserved vacancies is also kept active to show that efforts are being made to find suitable candidates belonging to SC and ST communities. Therefore, the vacancies are advertised, selection committee meetings are held (many times after an enormous delay), and the SC and ST candidates are subsequently rejected after the interviews. This rejection makes it possible for the college authorities to provide further extension(s) to the already appointed ad hoc/temporary teachers. This cycle could be repeated till the ad hoc or temporary teachers get absorbed at the same or at other places. On getting recruited, these teachers become relatively more senior and eligible for other benefits. The fairly large number of ad hoc and temporary teachers working in Delhi colleges seems to be closely linked to the so-called 'non-suitability' of the SC and ST candidates. It is understood that due to a lot of protest and pressure, the university reluctantly stopped appointing non-reserved candidates against the reserved vacancies. However, before doing so, the large number of non-reserved category teachers were already recruited.

The students who wish to be teachers should have qualified the National Eligibility Test (NET). Since, a limited number of students clear the NET examination, there is a gap between NET qualified candidates and requirement of colleges and universities. Further, there is also a scarcity of candidates with NET in few subjects. The shortage is more in the case of SC and ST candidates. It is difficult to get the SC and ST candidates with NET in certain subjects like Chemistry, Commerce, English, Mathematics and

Physics. The scarcity becomes a very useful weapon to implement the Reservation Policy detrimentally. It is evident from some of the advertisements. The posts are reserved in subjects such as those mentioned above in which SC and ST candidates are not available. It enables the colleges to delay or avoid the entry of SC and ST candidates and at the same time appoint their own candidates against these vacancies as ad hoc, temporary or guest lecturers.

Delhi colleges maintain reservation rosters at the department level instead of cadre-wise*. Further, it is an open secret that nobody wants the SC and ST candidates in their departments. Therefore, while reserving the vacancy/position, like football, it is goes from one department to another. In some universities, individuals or deparments have approached the courts to resist reservation in particular subjects. The reservation roster registers also reached courts for verification. Since the reservations are mandatory and cannot be avoided; the subjects are carefully chosen and reserved. Therefore, it is no surprise that the posts are reserved in subjects like Urdu, Arabic, Persian and other subjects mentioned above.

According to the present post-based system of roster, the first reserve point comes at the seventh position. Therefore, all efforts are made to keep the total strength of the teachers in departments at the maximum of six. This fact is more visible in the newly established departments at the College and University level. Therefore, the sixth point in the roster is like a magic number which works as a water tight barrier to stop the entry of SC and ST candidates to the departments. This number has been successfully used against the interests of the SC and ST. In the post-based rosters there are many such numbers (reservation points). The seventh and thirteen points are reserved for the SC and ST respectively. It means that practically there cannot be a single ST teacher in a department with less than thirteen teachers. The entry of second SC teachers can be blocked by maintaining the strength of the teachers less than thirteen in a department. When a new department is established at least an SCs can have some hope but not for ST to get the job of a lecturer.

SC/ST in Non-Teaching Staff

Non-teaching staff is essential for the smooth running of any college. The non-academic staff could be classified into four groups: A, B, C, and D. Educational qualifications required for these different groups vary from the seventh standard to graduation. The colleges are not expected to face much difficulty in finding the SC and ST candidates for appointment to the non-teaching positions. Table 2 shows the strength of non-teaching staff belonging to the SC and ST in fifty colleges of the University of Delhi. The representation of SC and ST in non-teaching staff is shockingly low. The University started maintaining the roster since 1974 and 1989 for Group C and D, and Group A and B respectively. Their non-adoption of the roster system simultaneously for all these posts raises several questions and doubts about their sincerity in implementating the reservation policy. As mentioned earlier, the University of Delhi opened the roster only in 1996 for recruitment of teaching positions. It appeared that this university remained carefully careless towards the reservation policy and its implementation.

Table 2: Number of SC and ST Non-Teaching Employees in 50 Colleges Affiliated to the University of Delhi as on March 22, 2005

Group	*General*	*Scheduled Caste*		*Scheduled Tribe*		*Vacant*	*Total*
		Filled	*Shortfall*	*Filled*	*Shortfall*		
A	70	1 (1.1%)	12.5 (13.9%)	0	7 (7.5%)	19	90
B	206	3 (0.80%)	34.0 (14.2%)	0	18.5 (7.5%)	37	246
C	1277	160 (10%)	78.3 (5%)	6 (0.30%)	113.2 (7.1%)	146	1589
D	1166	358 (18.9%)	—	18 (0.43%)	115.4 (7.07%)	362	1904

Source: Data compiled and processed by the author from the information furnished by the colleges to UGC.

There is just one person in Group A and three in Group B who belong to the SC category; and shockingly none from ST against ninety and 246 total posts. Group C posts need matriculation. Delhi colleges could find only one hundred and sixty SC and six ST candidates, when the total strength of this group is 1,589. In terms of percentage it is ten per cent and 0.30 per cent for the SC and the ST respectively. There are 18.9 per cent SC in Group D. Some of the duties of Group D service are mainly performed by the people belonging to the SC. Moreover, they are easily available around the colleges. Therefore, it is expected to have a relatively higher representation of SC in Group D. It is amazing that out of 1,904 employees in Group D, STs are just eighteen. Taking all groups together, the total non-teaching staff in fifty colleges is around 3,829. Of this, ST employees are twenty-four. It is quite clear that there is a wide gap between 22.5 per cent share of the SC and ST in population and their actual number in colleges. The wide gap when there was a high probability of getting the suitable SC and ST candidates for non-teaching jobs refutes their theory of 'non-availability' and 'non-suitability' of SC and ST candidates for appointment as teachers in the colleges, and supports the possibility of non-academic reasons for the shortfall and back log of reserved positions in both teaching and non-teaching cadres.

It is on record that the UGC, Parliamentary Committee on the Welfare of SC and ST, National Commission for SC and ST and the Ministry of Human Resource Development have been writing and reminding through the UGC from time to time to implement the Reservation Policy in the Universities. However, the University has conveniently ignored the directives from various Government Organizations/Agencies, and delayed the implementation of the Reservation Policy. The Liaison Officer is to be nominated to ensure due compliance of the orders of the government on reservation, issued from time to time in favour of the SCs and the STs, to ensure timely appointments, prompt disposal of the grievances of the employees of these classes, and to scrutinize and consolidate the statistical data. With a few exceptions, most of the colleges did not appoint the Liaison Officer till March 22, 2005. Perhaps, the colleges wanted a free hand and no checks while dealing with matters related to the Reservation Policy.

Of the twenty-nine colleges, other than the fifty-three mentioned earlier, get the grants directly either from the Central Government (Ministry of Human Resource Development) or the Delhi Government. They are also expected to follow the Reservation

Policy for SC and ST. Although, these twenty-nine colleges were not considered in the present study, the picture of implementation of the Reservation Policy is likely to be not very different. At least two colleges of Delhi University do not follow the Reservation Policy for the SC and ST. These colleges claim to be minority institutes under Article 30 of the Constitution. It is the same constitution, which has also given the privileges to the socially deprived who suffered for centuries. Therefore, constitutionally speaking, the minorities and SC and ST communities have some similarities and common interest. Is it not the duty of these minorities and minority institutes to help and protect the interests of the socially handicapped people? Indeed, it is their moral and social duty. However, on the contrary, the minority institutes are directly or indirectly serving the interests of a few elites who exploit the society for their own benefit. The minorities should see their rights and those of SCs and STs as complementing rather than conflicting.

SC and ST in the University

The impression has been created that the university always informed and pursued the colleges from time to time to strictly implement the Reservation Policy. Whatever the reasons, it did not yield the desirable results and the reserved posts remained largely unfilled. It is possible that the university may have its limitations to compel the colleges to strictly follow the Reservation Policy. With this background, it would be pertinent to look at the implementation of the Reservation Policy in the University of Delhi itself. Table 3 shows the number of teaching and non-teaching staff belonging to the SC and ST categories in the year 2003-2004.

There are fifteen Lecturers, two Readers, and one Professor of the SC category in the University departments. It may be mentioned that the UGC has accepted the reservation policy at the level of Lecturers only and not for Professors and Readers in the Central Universities.** The University of Delhi has done fairly well in filling the Lecturers positions for the SC to the extent of more than eleven per cent against the prescribed fifteen per cent. However, it is lagging behind the reservation target of 7.5 per cent in the case of ST. In a total strength of one hundred and thirty Lecturers, only

Table 3: Number of SC and ST Teaching and Non-Teaching Employees in the University of Delhi in the Year 2003-2004

Service Personnel	*General*	*Scheduled Caste*		*Scheduled Tribe*	
		Filled	*Shortfall*	*Filled*	*Shortfall*
Faculty					
Professors	271	1(0.38%)	39	1 (0.36) %	19
Readers	225	2(0.88%)	32	0 (0.00) %	17
Lecturers	130	15(11.5%)	5	2 (1.53) %	8
Non-Teaching					
Group A	133	6(4.51%)	13	3(2.25%)	-
Group B	515	26(4.51%)	51	3(2.25%)	36
Group C	1079	109(10.10%	53	1(0.19%)	80
Group D	1068	303(31.89%)	—	16(1.58%)	64

Source: Data compiled and processed by the author from the information furnished by the colleges to UGC.

two belong to ST. Representation of both the SCs and STs in posts of Professors and Readers is poor. The same is the case of non-teaching staff. As the implementation of reservations in the University of Delhi would be dealt along with other Central Universities elsewhere separately, not discussed here in detail. However, the University of Delhi may have to make more efforts to increase the representation of SC and ST in its own departments, as the overall picture has not changed even after eight to nine years. Representation of SC at the level of Professor, Associate and Assistant Professor was 0.00, 0.15 and 6.22 per cent respectively in 2012. The strength of Assistant Professors came down to 6.22 per cent (in 2012) from 11.5 per cent in 2003-04. The university had one Professor in 2003-04 but none in the year 2012. In the case of ST at the level of Professor, Associate and Assistant Professor it was 0.00, 0.15 and 1.88 per cent respectively. Thus, the representation decreased in the case of SC between the years 2003-04 and 2012. The marginal gain at the level of Associate Professor and Assistant Professor could be seen in the case of ST, whereas loss at the level of Professor. Although, UGC is responsible for the implementation of the Reservation Policy and its monitoring in the Indian universities, it has not taken much interest and indirectly gave a free hand to the University of Delhi in this matter.

Conclusion

It is quite clear, that the colleges affiliated to the University of Delhi, which get maintenance grant from the UGC, have not implemented the Reservation Policy for the SC and ST in letter and spirit. The delay in the adoption of the roster showed their lack of interest in its implementation. The delay in the adoption of the roster seems to be a well-planned strategy to avoid the reservation. The colleges have carefully bypassed the reservation process on the pretext of non-availability and non-suitability of the SC and ST candidates. The resulting shortfall of SC and ST posts enabled the colleges to appoint their own candidates as an ad hoc or temporary teachers against the unfilled reserved posts. The Ministry of Human Resource Development, the National Commission for SC and ST and the UGC monitor the implementation of the Reservation Policy, even their guidelines and directives issued from time to time appeared to be deliberately ignored. Further, the concern shown by the Parliamentary Committee on the Welfare of SC and ST (2001-2002), directive of the Delhi High Court (Civil Writ Petition No. 259 of 1999) and Memorandum submitted to the President of India (July 19, 2002) also did not yield desirable results. Article 15 of the Constitution which prohibits discrimination on the ground of caste and Article 16 which guarantees the equality of opportunity in employment seems to be non-existent for these colleges. The aforementioned facts perhaps are reflective of the widespread prejudice against the SC and ST in the University of Delhi and its affiliated colleges. With a few exceptions, the situation may not be very different in other central universities. The studies on similar lines in centrally funded universities may perhaps reveal more surprises.

From the above study, it could be inferred that the shrinkage of opportunities in state and public sector organizations and detrimental implementation of reservations would make SCs and STs as victims rather than the beneficiaries. Large sections of the society consider the reservations as the root cause of increasing unemployment and the suffering of 'meritorious' students belonging to the general category. The present findings prove otherwise. The government has to take immediate steps to implement the reservations satisfactorily in its own sectors. Otherwise, it will look like a pretender while pursuing the private sector to provide reservations for the SC and ST.

NOTES

* The University of Delhi has now adopted the reservation roster cadre-wise from 2013.

** University of Delhi has adopted reservation at the level of Associate Professor (then Reader) and Professor only in 2013.

REFERENCES

Dr. Babasaheb Ambedkar: Writing and Speeches (1991), Vol. 10, Government of Maharashtra, p. 418.

Kumar, Vivek (2005). Understanding the Politics of Reservations, *Economic and Political Weekly*, Vol. XL, No. 9, p. 803.

Montagu-Chelmsford Report (1918), Para 317.

Potter, David C. (1996). *India's Political Administrators: From ICS to IAS*, Oxford University Press, pp. 90-91.

Singh, S.N. (1962). *The Secretary of State for India and His Council 1858 to 1919*, Munshiram Manoharlal Publishers, New Delhi, p. 102

Talukder, S.R. (1998). *Indian Civil Service Examination and the Savarna Merit*, Blumoon Books, New Delhi, p. 22.

5

Reservation for SC and ST in Central Universities: Is it Lack of Will or Efforts?

The Scheduled Castes belong to the social group which was formerly known as untouchables. In the past, being at the bottom of the caste hierarchy, they were supposed to serve society without any claim on returns. Indeed, they were treated as social slaves with only duties and no rights. They were made to believe and accept that graded inequalities based on the caste system have a divine sanction and one's place in the social hierarchy is predetermined by the *karma* in earlier life. However, denial of access to material, cultural and spiritual resources as well as deprivation of dignity, selfhood, and rights resulted in their dehumanization and humiliation, which went on for centuries and continued well into the modern period. The toils and tears of the Scheduled Tribes were not very different from the SCs. STs were completely isolated, neglected, and exploited. Their oppression has been going on since the past several thousand years. With some degree of variation in mode and magnitude, both the SCs and STs continued to suffer from social disabilities even today.

On achieving independence, the nation took the conscious decision to undo the social and historic wrongs and provide social justice to SCs and STs. Therefore, provisions were made in the Indian Constitution, adopted by us on January 26, 1950, could be seen in the Articles such as: 14, 15, 16, 17, 46 and 335. The steps undertaken in pursuance of these constitutional provisions for the SC and ST could be categorized as protective, developmental, and preferential. Providing the reservations in employment is one of the important preferential provisions.

According to Section 2(f) and Section 3 of the University Grants Commission Act, 1956, there are three types of Universities in India, i.e. Central Universities, State Universities, and Deemed to be Universities. In the exercise of the powers vested under Section 20(1) of the above Act, UGC is under directions from the government to ensure effective implementation of the reservation policy in the university system except in minority institutions under Article 30(1) of the Constitution. Therefore, the UGC issues guidelines, from time to time, regarding adequate representation of teaching, non-teaching staff and students. The instructions issued by the government are statutory in nature, as per the judgment of the Hon'ble Supreme Court in case of *Indira Sahney vs. Union of India and Others* (AIR 1993 SC 447), since these instructions are issued for the purpose of implementation of constitutional [Article 16(4)] provisions.

The people who are involved in teaching and running the universities are highly educated. Being enlightened, they can see the future of the country through the window of the past, and accordingly set the national goals, and expected to make the necessary preparations in the present, to achieve the same, through their teaching, writing and research. They create knowledge and generate human resource required for making policies and their implementation, governance, administration, research and development, technology and industry, and in turn influence the minds of the people and future of the nation. Several welfare schemes and programmes of the government emerge from their academic pursuits and creativity. The scholarship makes them recognize the significance of social equality and measures taken to achieve the same. Therefore, being responsive and responsible citizens, they are likely to contribute towards the successful implementation of reservations in the university system. However, not much information is available on the status of reservations particularly on recruitments in the universities.

With this backdrop, an attempt has been made to examine the implementation of reservations in recruitments to teaching and non-teaching positions in the Central Universities.

Representation of SC and ST in Faculty Positions

There are twenty Central Universities in India (Table 1).** Out of these, 18 universities are funded by the UGC. The other two are Indira Gandhi National Open University, New Delhi, and Central Agricultural University, Imphal. The former is directly funded by the Ministry of Human Resource Development and the latter by the Ministry of Agriculture respectively. The present study is focused on 18 universities, which get both development (Plan) and maintenance (non-Plan) grants from the UGC.

Table 1: List of Central Universities

S.No.	*University*	*S.No.*	*University*
01.	Aligarh Muslim University	11.	Tezpur University
02.	Banaras Hindu University	12.	Nagaland University
03.	Delhi University	13.	Mizoram University
04.	Hyderabad University	14.	BBA University
05.	Jamia Millia Islamia	15.	MGA Hindi University
06.	Jawaharlal Nehru University	16.	MAN Urdu University
07.	North Eastern Hill University	17.	University of Allahabad
08.	Pondicherry University	18.	Manipur University
09.	Vishva Bharati University	19.*	Indira Gandhi National Open University
10.	Assam University	20.*	Central Agricultural University

*Universities at S. Nos. 19 and 20 are not included in the present study.

In these eighteen central universities, the total sanctioned teaching posts are 8,765 consisting of 1,430 Professors, 2,592 Readers, and 4,189 Lecturers. However, the existing strength of the faculty members is 6,588, leaving 1,177 total posts vacant. Out of the present strength of 6,588; Professors constitute 1,276, Readers 1,935, and Lecturers 2,272. Therefore, presently 1,54, 657 and 1,917 posts of Professors, Readers, and Lecturers respectively are lying vacant in the Central Universities. When thousands and thousands of youths armed with degrees are wandering on the roads in search of jobs and many of those already in service waiting for promotions, it is quite disturbing to see the posts lying vacant in such large

** This number is increased to 41

numbers. There might be academic and even non-academic constraints of universities, but failure to fill the vacancies is likely to adversely affect the professed national agenda of empowerment of the underprivileged, marginalized and deprived sections of the society particularly the SC and ST communities.

The representation of SC and ST communities in teaching posts in the Central Universities is shown in Table 2. Out of the sanctioned 1,430 posts of Professors, 1,248 have been occupied by the general category faculty members. However, there are only eleven and seventeen Professors belong to the SCs and STs respectively. Statistically, it comes to less than one Professor of SC and ST each per university. Only five universities have a Professor(s) who belongs to the SC community. Thus, there is no Professor who belongs to the SC on the rolls of thirteen universities. The universities without SC Professors include Banaras Hindu University (BHU), Pondicherry University, Jamia Millia Islamia (JMI), North Eastern-Hill University (NEHU), and Allahabad University. The Delhi University (DU), one of the oldest with faculty strength of 1,086, has just one Professor of from the SC community.

Table 2: Representation of SC and ST in Teaching Posts in Central Universities as on March 31, 2006

Post	*Scheduled Caste*		*Scheduled Tribe*		*General*	*Vacant*	*Total Sanctioned Posts*
	Filled	*Shortfall*	*Filled*	*Shortfall*			
Professor	11 (0.77%)	204 (14.23%)	17 (1.18%)	91 (6.32%)	124 (87.27%)	8154 (10.77%)	1430 (100%)
Reader	29 (1.11%)	360 (13.89%)	31 (1.19%)	169 (6.31%)	1875 (72.34%)	657 (25.35%)	2592 (100%)
SG/SL	37 (5.78%)	59 (9.22%)	40 (6.25%)	8 (1.25%)	640	-	-
Lecturer	192 (4.58%)	436 (10.42%)	148 (3.53%)	166 (3.97%)	1932 (46.60%)	1917 (45.75%)	4189 (100%)
Others*	11 (1.58%)	72 (13.02%)	2 (0.36%)	40 (7.14%)	452 (78%)	-	554 (100%)

Source: Data compiled and processed by the author from the information furnished by the Central Universities to the UGC. Others* as a category is not well defined and seems to include posts like part-time teachers.

Vishwa Bharati University with a total number of 655 teachers also has only one SC Professor. The other universities such as the University of Hyderabad, JNU, and Assam University have two, three and four SC Professors respectively. In terms of percentage, eleven out of the total strength of 1,430 Professors comes to be 0.77 per cent for the SC with the shortfall of 204 (14.23 per cent) posts. It is amazing that the shortfall of 204 posts for the SC is higher than the available 154 vacant posts. In the case of ST, their percentage of representation in the post of Professor is also quite low (1.18 per cent), creating a shortfall of ninety-one posts. The combined shortfall of posts for the SC and ST Professors is very close to 300. It could be mentioned that out of the seventeen Professors who belong to the ST, twelve are in only two universities and that too from the North-Eastern regions of the country. From the remaining five Professors of ST, three are in JNU and one each in DU and Vishwa Bharati University. Surprisingly, thirteen Central Universities do not have even a single Professor from the ST community.

The total sanctioned posts of Reader in Central Universities are 2,592 of which 1,875, twenty-nine and thirty-one are occupied by the General, SC, and ST communities respectively (Table 2). The remaining 657 posts are lying vacant. This poor representation of the SC (1.11 per cent) and ST (1.19 per cent) communities resulted in the shortfall of 360 (13.89 per cent) and 169 (6.31 per cent) posts, respectively. Six central universities including NEHU, Mizoram, and Manipur Universities, do not have a single Reader from the SC community. At least three universities namely, NEHU, Mizoram, and Manipur, being located predominantly in the tribal belt, were expected to try and attract more SC candidates from all over the country. More than 50 per cent of the total strength of existing posts of Reader (twenty-nine) belong to the SC community comes from Vishva Bharati (seven), Hyderabad (six), and BHU (four). As mentioned earlier, all together, Readers belonging to the ST community are thirty-one i.e., two more than the SC. However, they are not spread evenly among the universities. More than two-third Readers of the ST community are just in two Universities, i.e. six in Nagaland University and nine in Mizoram University. Out of the remaining six, JNU has three and Tezpur, and Vishwa Bharati have one each. Interestingly twelve Universities do not have on its roll a single Reader who belongs to the ST. Most surprisingly NEHU, Assam, and Manipur universities, which are located in the North-Eastern region, have no Reader in the ST category.

There is no provision of reservations at the level of Professor and Reader in the Central Universities.* This pretext was always used to justify the lower presentation of the SCs and STs at the level of Professor and Reader. It means that whenever and wherever the reservation policy is applicable, the SCs and STs are given due representation as prescribed in the guidelines of the government. Since in the Central Universities, presently, the reservation in teaching is given only at the level of Lecturer, it will be interesting to see its implementation in recruitment at the level of Lecturer. Indeed it is expected to be quite satisfactory. The fifteen per cent for the SC and 7.5 per cent for ST reservation is applicable. It could be noted that no restriction of percentage is prescibed for filling the backlog vacancies of the SC and ST. The representation of the SC and ST candidates in central universities in teaching at the level of Lecturer could be seen in Table 2. It is 4.58 per cent for SC and 3.53 per cent for ST, quite below the prescribed minimum 15 and 7.5 per cent respectively. The total sanctioned posts of Lecturers are 4,189. There should have been 629 and 314 Lecturers of the SC and ST categories respectively in the Central Universities. Instead, the SCs are 192 and STs 148. There is still a shortfall of 436 posts for the SCs and 166 posts for the STs. On the other hand, 1,932 posts of lecturers have been occupied by general category candidates. 1,917 posts are still lying vacant. At least four universities do not have any Lecturer from the SC community. Similarly, in three universities no Lecturer from the ST community is available. Further, more than one Lecturer belonging to the ST (out of 148) are in universities which are located in the North-East region, indicative of their poor represention in other central universities. It is interesting to see the increased percentage of vacant posts if we go from Professor to Lecturer level. It is almost doubled from one level to the next. At present, 45.75 per cent posts of Lecturers

* Reservation is provided at the level of Reader (now Associate Professor) and Professor from 2006.

are lying vacant. Keeping almost fifty per cent posts of Lecturers vacant is probably nothing but avoidance of the implementation of the reservation policy.

Reservation in Non-Teaching Positions

One of the important functions of the University is to impart knowledge and provide training to students and in turn convert them into human resources, for participation in nation building. The University is also supposed to generate new knowledge and contribute to the advancement of existing ones. For such activities, the university needs highly educated, talented, and skilled teachers with a high degree of wisdom. The universities have a mindset that the SC and ST candidates lack these required traits and justify the low representation of the SC and ST in teaching posts due to their non-availability and non-suitability. Although, the non-availability and non-suitability of the SC and ST candidates needs to be critically examined, a similar problem may not be faced by the universities to appoint the SC and ST for non-teaching positions, as the required qualifications for non-teaching jobs are not the same as of teachers. Highly educated persons are not required even for the Grade A positions. Hence, the representation of the SC and ST is expected to be significantly high in non-teaching posts.

Contrary to expectation, the current representation of SC (6.13 per cent) and ST (5.25 per cent) in non-teaching posts is quite low (Table 3). There are only seventy-seven SC officers in Grade A posts in all eighteen universities out of the 1,257 total sanctioned posts. As per the fifteen per cent share, there should have been 189 Grade A officers belonging to the SC community. To achieve the target, backlog/shortfall of 112 posts needs to be cleared. Relatively, the situation of the STs with 66 Grade A officers, is slightly better than the SCs. However, out of these fifty Grade A officers belonging to the ST are in universities which are situated in the North-East region of the country. The presence of STs is comparatively poor in other universities. Surprisingly, there is no Grade A SC officers in six universities and ST officers in eight universities.

The total sanctioned Grade B posts in Central Universities are around 1,800. Instead of 402, only 144 reserved posts consisting of 110 SC and thirty-four ST have been filled in the Central

Table 3: Representation of SC and ST in Non-Teaching Posts in Central Universities as on March 31, 2006

Post/Grade	*Scheduled Caste*		*Scheduled Tribe*		*General*	*Vacant*	*Total Sanctioned Posts*
	Filled	*Shortfall*	*Filled*	*Shortfall*			
A	77 (6.13%)	112 (8.87%)	66 (5.25%)	28 (2.25%)	784 (62.37%)	330 (26.25%)	1257
B	110 (6.15%)	158 (8.85%)	34 (1.91%)	100 (5.59%)	1398 (78.23%)	245 (13.71%)	1787 (100%)
C	5.79 (5.11%)	1122 (9.89%)	456 (4.02%)	394 (3.48%)	8328 (73.43%)	1978 (17.44%)	11341 (100%)
D	2364 (19.03%)	-500 (- 4.03%)	520 (4.18%)	412 (3.32%)	7882 (63.44%)	1658 (13.35%)	12424 (100%)

Source: Data compiled and processed by the author from the information furnished by the Central Universities to the UGC.

Universities. In terms of percentage it comes to 6.15 per cent for SC and 1.19 per cent for ST. The shortfall of Grade B posts for the SCs is 158 and one hundred for the STs. Not even a single person belonging to the SC and ST communities are serving in Grade B posts in four and six universities respectively. As expected, the maximum number of ST persons (twenty-two) working in Grade B are in the select group of universities, and that too again from the North-East region of the country. Surprisingly, the presence of the SC and ST even in the Grade C posts is just 5.11 and 4.02 per cent, respectively. On the contrary, 73.43 per cent posts have been occupied by the general category persons. Shockingly, 1,122 posts reserved for the SC and 394 posts reserved for the ST are lying (or kept) vacant. Only 579 persons of the SC community and 456 persons of the ST community out of the total sanctioned 11,341 posts are in Grade C. As mentioned earlier (Kale, 2006), some of the duties of Grade D service are mainly performed by the people from the SC community. Moreover, they are easily available as these jobs are menial and supposed to be below human dignity. Therefore, it is not surprising to see higher representation of the SCs in Grade D services. However, out of the 12,424 employees in Grade D service, ST constitutes only 520 (4.18 per cent). It may be observed that around 300 persons belonging to the ST are serving in six universities of the North-East region. In the other remaining twelve universities, the STs in Grade D number 230 out of the total 11,629 sanctioned posts. In percentage, it comes to 1.9 per cent. Indeed there should have been 872 ST personnel in Grade D services in these 12 universities. Hence, there is a long road ahead for the ST to travel.

Table 4: Representation of OBC in Non-Teaching Positions in Central Universities as on March 31, 2006

Grade	*Sanctioned Posts*	*Existing Posts*	*OBC*
A	1257	927	19 (1.51%)
B	1787	1542	13 (0.72%)
C	11341	9363	111 (0.98%)
D	12424	10766	148 (1.19%)

Source: Data compiled and processed by the author from the information furnished by the Central Universities to the UGC.

It is difficult to believe the non-availability of suitable candidates as the reason for less per cent of the SC and ST persons than prescribed 22.5 per cent for them in teaching and non-teaching posts in the Central Universities. Further, the non-suitability of the SC and ST candidates appears to be a 'suitable' lie, deliberately designed to deny them their due. This possibility is evident from the very low presence of OBC in non-teaching posts. The data in Table 4 shows that nineteen (1.51 per cent), thirteen (0.72 per cent), one hundred and eleven (0.98 per cent) and one hundred and forty-eight (1.19 per cent) OBC are in Grade A, B, C and D services respectively. On an average, it is just around one per cent against the prescribed twenty-seven per cent reserved for them. The presence of OBC in large numbers in the state universities but not in the Central Universities is indicative of a deliberate act to avoid implementation of reservations. Although, the differently-abled [a.k.a physically challenged (PH)] persons do not represent a particular social group, even they are not spared by the Central Universities. Their representation is less than 0.5 per cent (Table 5). The PH and their status in Central Universities will be dealt with separately in detail elsewhere. It would be interesting to see how different social groups within the PH category are treated in recruitments. However, their low representation also supports the fact of avoidance of reservation meant for them by the Central Universities, is a deliberate act.

Table 5: Representation of PH in Teaching and Non-Teaching Positions in Central Universities on March 31, 2006

Post/Grade	*Sanctioned Posts*	*Existing Posts*	*PH*
Teaching Staff			
Professor	1430	1276	4 (0.28%)
Reader	2592	1935	13 (0.50%)
SG/SL	-	640	2 (0.31%)
Lecturer	4189	2272	19 (0.45%)
Non-Teaching Staff			
A	1257	927	2 (0.16%)
B	1787	1542	16 (0.89%)
C	11341	9363	62 (0.55%)
D	12424	10766	53 (0.43%)

Source: Data compiled and processed by the author from the information furnished by the Central Universities to the UGC.

It may not be out of context to underline the fact that the geographical spread of Central Universities is distinctly uneven (Table 6).* Out of the twenty central universities, eight are in the Northern region, seven are in the North-East region, while three are in the South and one each in the East and West regions. Thus,

Table 6: Region-wise Spread of Central Universities

	North	*North-East*	*South*	*East*	*West*	*Total*
Universities	8	7	3	1	1	20
Teaching Staff	6228 (71.05%)	1226 (13.98%)	578 (6.59%)	655 (7.47%)	78 (0.88%)	8765 (100%)
Non-Teaching Staff	20470 (76.41%)	2489 (9.28%)	2048 (7.64%)	1715 (6.39%)	77 (0.28%)	26799 (100%)

Source: Data compiled and processed by the author from the information furnished by the Central Universities to UGC. Data related to strength of the teaching and non-teaching staff is for 18 Central Universities.

* After the establishment of the new 14 Central Universities in the year 2009, there is at least one Central University in each state, except Goa.

fifteen universities in two clusters are mostly located in the two regions of the country. Since, one university in West has strength of six teaching and fifty-seven non-teaching staff, its academic impact is minimal. Another university in the South is fairly new and relatively small in size. Both have been ignored in the discussions. The total faculty strength in all the eighteen central universities is 8,765. Out of this, 6,228 and 1,226 are in the universities located in the North and North-East region respectively. This number is three times higher than the total faculty strength of the South (578), East (655) and West (78) taken together. The situation is also similarly uneven in the case of non-teaching staff. Out of the total strength of 26,809 non-teaching staff members, more than 20,000 staff members work in the universities of the North region. It is also three times more compared to the entire strength of all the remaining universities of other regions. Thus, 71.05 and 76.41 per cent teaching and non-teaching staff respectively, are serving in the universities located in North India. The extent of implementation of reservation is also not uniform. The implementation of reservation is slightly better in the Southern region universities compared to the North. As mentioned earlier, reservation in teaching posts is applicable only at the level of Lecturer. The percentage of SC and ST teachers at the level of Lecturer in the universities in the North Region is 3.74 and 1.20 per cent respectively which is quite low if seen against the prescribed percentage, i.e. fifteen per cent for the SC and 7.5 per cent for the ST. Even in the total existing strength of Lecturers the representation of SCs is 6.48 and 2.08 per cent for the ST. In non-teaching staff of universities in the North region, SCs constitute 4.51 per cent and STs 0.56 per cent which is again quite low compared to universities in the Southern region of the country (Table 7). A systematic study needs to be undertaken to explore the reasons for the differences in response between the North and South regions of the country towards the reservation policy for the SC and ST and its implementation.

UGC, Central Government (MHRD) and Reservations

The data shown in Tables 2 and 3 are indicative of quite low representation of the SC and ST in both the teaching and non-

Table 7: Region-wise Representation of SC and ST in Sanctioned Staff in Central Universities

Category	*North*	*North-East*	*South*	*East*	*West*
Lecturers					
Total Strength	2910	962	223	323	6
SC	109 (3.74%)	42 (4.36%)	19 (8.52%)	21 (6.50%)	0 (0%)
ST	35 (1.20%)	98 (10.18%)	8 (3.58%)	5 (1.5%)	0 (0%)
Non-Teaching Staff					
Total Strength	10177	1697	1082	837	57
SC	459 (4.51%)	64 (3.77%)	142 (13.12%)	89 (10.6%)	2 (3.84%)
ST	57 (0.56%)	451 (26.57%)	24 (2.21%)	20 (0.23%)	0 (0%)

Source: Data compiled and processed by the author from the information furnished by the Central Universities to UGC. The non-teaching staff belonging to Grade D is excluded from the data.

teaching posts, than the prescribed fifteen per cent for SC and 7.5 per cent for ST. The Central Government (Ministry of Human Resource Development, Department of Secondary and Higher Education) took serious note of the matter, and held the UGC responsible for the same. In Office Order No. F. No. 6-30/2005.U.5 dated December 6, 2005, it clearly stated that the UGC had failed to ensure effective implementation of the Reservation Policy in respect of the SC and ST in the Central Universities and grant-in-aid institutions which are Deemed to be Universities. The Central Government perhaps for the first time has accepted the failure of its statutory organization in the implementation of the reservation policy. Otherwise, most of the time, some or the other reason or explanation was provided for the strikingly lower representation of SC and ST. Significantly, the government has directed the UGC through its above Office Order 'to ensure effective implementation of the reservation policy in the Central Universities and those institutes Deemed to be Universities receiving aid from the public funds.'

Among the powers and functions mentioned in Sections 12-19 of the University Grants Commission Act, 1956, the UGC is supposed to advise the government on the matter related to higher education. At the same time, as per Section 20(1) of the UGC Act, 1956, it is under direction from the Central Government on the question of policy relating to national purposes. Thus, both the UGC and MHRD have symbiotic relations. In the light of this fact, efforts made in the past by UGC and the Central Government in implementing the reservation policy would be examined.

Although, the Government of India set up an interim UGC by resolution and began to function from the last week of December 1953, it came into existence through an Act of Parliament in November 1956. India became a Republic on January 26, 1950 by adopting a new Constitution, in which reservations for the SC and ST were incorporated. Therefore, the government should have directed and the UGC should have adopted the reservation policy at least from 1956, if not from 1953. On the contrary, the UGC kept reiterating that no reservations should be made available to SC and ST for appointments particularly to the posts of teachers in Universities and Colleges (Sharma, 2003). However, after twenty-two years of its coming into existence, for the first time, the UGC at its meeting held on July 14-15, 1975 agreed in principle to provide reservations to the SC and ST for recruitments to the posts of Lecturers [D.O. No. F.1-46/75(CP) August 26-29, 1975], with condition not to operate reservations on a roster system and also not to carry forward reserved posts. The Committee of Vice-Chancellors of Central Universities gave recommendations for the implementation of reservations [No. F.1-46(CP), dated September 8-10, 1976], which were not in consonance with the letters and spirit of the reservation policy. However, the UGC accepted the same and insisted on not operating the roster system, and not to carry forward the reserved posts from a year-to-year basis [D.O.No. F.7-3/83(SCT), dated April 19-30, 1983]. By doing so, the UGC almost gave a free hand to the Universities to implement the reservations the way they wanted. It gave indirect encouragement to implement the reservations detrimentally. It was, for example, evident from the fact that out of 220 appointments of Lecturers in the Banaras Hindu University during the years 1984, 1985, and 1986 none belonged to SC/ST [Recommendation Serial No. 29 (para 4.75) of the Parliamentary Committee of the Welfare of the Scheduled

Castes/Scheduled Tribes as contained in their 43rd Report (1988-89) (8 Lok Sabha)]. Apart from the will and efforts, the absence of the roster system was the main reason cited for not filling the reserved posts. The above referred Parliamentary Committee took serious note of 'the injustice done to the SC and ST, in the absence of the practice to carry forward the reserved posts' in the university system. During the evidence, the Parliamentary Committee found that the suggestions made by the UGC to deal with this problem, were protracted and time consuming. Therefore, the Committee recommended that the practice of carrying forward the posts reserved for the SC and ST should be introduced immediately in all the central universities so that candidates belonging to the SC/ST get their due in appointments. Accordingly, the UGC at its meeting held on July 30-31, 1990, considered the recommendations of the Parliamentary Committee as well as instructions from the Government of India (D.O. letter No. F.7-1/89-U.5 dated July 18, 1990, Department of Education, Ministry of Human Resource Development) and agreed to introduce the practice of carry forward of posts. However, while communicating its decision for implementation in all the universities [No. F.1-18/89(SCT) dated October 8, 1990] the UGC sent a contradictory message. In a communication of UGC it was stated that, 'carry forward of posts does not mean non-filling of such posts. It simply means that if an SC/ST candidate is not available in a particular recruitment year, the post may be filled by a general category candidate and in subsequent years efforts should be made to fill the carry forward vacancy along with other vacancies that may arise.' When the post meant for the SC/ST is filled by a general category candidate, then there is no vacancy to be carried forward. Further, without the roster, the vacancy cannot be carried forward. Such contradictory decisions might have enabled the Central Universities to avoid the filling up of reserved posts.

It must be mentioned that the Parliamentary Committee in its 42nd Report, asked the UGC to make it obligatory for all the Universities receiving grants-in-aid to adopt and implement all the orders/instructions issued by the Government of India from time to time regarding reservations for the SC and ST [Referred in UGC Letter No. F.1-46/75(CP) dated May 18, 1976]. Prior to this, the

Commission for SC and ST also pleaded with the UGC for reservations in teaching departments in Universities/Colleges [Referred in the same UGC letter No. F.1-46/75(CP) dated May 18, 1976]. Amazingly, instead of ensuring effective implementation of the reservation policy as enshrined in the Constitution, the UGC approached the Ministry of Education & Social Welfare with the request to seek a legal view on whether it should be made obligatory for all the universities to adopt and implement all the orders/ instructions issued by the Government of India regarding reservations, as well as whether the UGC can issue such a directive to the universities [No. F.1-46/75(CP) dated May 18, 1976]. In response, the Ministry promptly took 'the necessary action' and conveyed to the UGC that its Act of 1956, does not provide any punitive power, it cannot issue directives or withhold grants to the universities on the ground of non-compliance with the guidelines/orders/instructions on reservations to the SC and ST (No. F.16-34/76-LU, dated August 12, 1976). The same views were once again reiterated by the Ministry on August 30, 1976 in a separate letter (D.O. No. F.16-34/76-LU). This advice of the Ministry tied the hands of the UGC and at the same time gave a free hand to the universities not to follow reservations in teaching posts. The UGC and the Ministry seemed to have forgotten that reservations actually flow from the Constitution. Although, nothing is above the Constitution, both the UGC and the Ministry of Education and Social Welfare tried to use Acts, Statutes, Rules, Regulations, etc., to build barriers to stop the flow of reservations. Thus, the Ministry of Education & Social Welfare has also contributed to a great extent and is responsible consequently for the failure of the UGC in the effective implementation of the reservation policy.

From time to time, the UGC received representations with a request to extend the reservations in the direct recruitment at the level of Readers and Professors for the SC and ST candidates [D.O. No. F.1-46/75(CP) dated August 26-29, 1975; No. F.6-4/82(SCT) dated August 23, 1982; D.O. No. F.7-3/83(SCT) dated April 19, 1983; D.O. No. F.1-15/97(SCT) dated March 24, 1998, etc.]. The UGC also received communication from the National Commission for the SC and ST with a similar request [UGC letter D.O. No. F.1-15/ 97(SCT) dated March 24, 1998]. However, the UGC kept reiterating its position to allow reservation for the SC and ST at the level of Lecturer only. The UGC argued that the pool from which the Readers and Professors are recruited is that of Lecturers and took a line that providing reservation more than once would not be appropriate [D.O.F.1-15/97 (SCT) dated March 24, 1998]. Since a cadre is generally construed as the number of posts in a particular grade from the reservation point of view, Lecturers, Readers, and Professors are three different cadres. Therefore, the perception of the UGC was a violative of the reservation policy and was absolutely detrimental to the interest of the SC and ST communities. The UGC also did not provide reservations for the SC and ST in the Merit Promotion Scheme/Career Advancement Scheme [D.O. No. F.1-6/89(SCT) dated July 30, 1989]. Instead it is designed in such a way that the reservations for the SC and ST communities cannot be extended.

The UGC appeared to become proactive regarding to reservations in the 1990s for some time and then from the year 2002 onwards. It was quite visible from some of the steps the UGC had taken. The UGC had informed the universities and institutes about the complete ban on de-reservation of vacancies reserved for the SC and ST, carry forward the same to the subsequent recruitment year, not to fill these vacancies by recruiting general candidates under any circumstances and keep the reserved posts vacant till these are filled by the candidates belonging to the SC and ST communities [No. F.1-18/89(SCT) dated October 7, 1992]. In the case of non-teaching posts, the universities were asked to follow scrupulously the Government of India instructions as contained in the 'Brochure on Reservations for SC and ST in Services', extend the reservation up to the level of Deputy Registrar, club the equivalent/ corresponding posts including that of the Registrar for the purpose of reservations and to apply reservations to teaching posts similar to the Government of India instructions to teaching posts for providing reservations in Class-I posts [No. F.1-18/89(SCT) dated July 21, 1993]. The Universities were also asked to include a Representative of the SC/ST Category, as a member in the selection committees for recruitments of reserved posts or a candidate from the SC/ST category appearing for general posts [No. F.1-1/95(SCT) dated August 7, 1995] as well as to issue a special notification to fill the backlog posts at the earliest [D.O. No. F.1-6/90(SCT) dated June 28, 1996]. The UGC directed the Universities and Deemed to be Universities to appoint a Liaison Officer to monitor the implementation of reservation policy [No. F.1-16/97(SCT) dated October 7, 1997]. However, unfortunately the UGC left it to the discretion of each university to make reservations either discipline-wise, department-wise, or subject-wise for implementation of the Reservation Policy [No. F.1-8/96(SCT) dated October 16, 1996]. Indeed, the roster is supposed to be prepared cadre-wise. The Reservation roster is an aid to determine the entitlement of quantum of posts reserved for the SC and ST. As mentioned earlier, the cadre is a group in which all the posts are in a particular grade. Accordingly, in teaching posts there could be three cadres, i.e. the Lecturers, Readers, and Professors. The discipline, department, and subject cannot be considered as cadre for purpose of implementation of reservations. The decision of the UGC gave ample scope to the universities and colleges to avoid reservation for the SC/ST. Many universities and colleges ignored the advice of the UGC to appoint the Liaison Officer to avoid the monitoring of reservations. By not appointing the Liaison Officer, some universities and colleges ensured non-compliance with the orders of the UGC on reservations. Expectedly, the outcome was most unsatisfactory. According to the UGC itself, the representation of SC and ST were much below the desired level as per the Government of India orders [No. F.1-5/2004(SCT) dated April 2004 and No. F.1-10/2005 (SCT) dated May 28, 2005]. In view of this fact, as mentioned earlier, the Government of India directed the UGC 'to ensure effective implementation of the reservation policy for the SC and ST' (F.No.6-30/2005-U.5 dated December 6, 2005). The government (MHRD) blamed the UGC for the failure of implementation of the reservation policy, conveniently forgetting its own contribution to the same.

In response to the communication No. 6-30/2005-U.5 dated December 6, 2005 from the MHRD, the Registrars of all the universities and deemed to be universities were invited to the meeting of the UGC Standing Committee on the SC/ST held on January 19, 2006. They were asked to identify all the SC and ST vacancies in the teaching and non-teaching posts and to take immediate action to fill the backlog before March 31, 2006. Tables 2 and 3 show the status of representation of the SC and ST in teaching and non-teaching posts as on March 31, 2006, which in itself is self-explanatory. It is perhaps a classic example of the failure and lack of both the will as well as efforts. Meanwhile, the UGC finalized the guidelines for the strict observance of the Reservation Policy of the government in universities, deemed to be universities, colleges and other grant-in-aid institutions, and centres as prepared by its Standing Committee on the SC/ST. Among other things, now reservations have been provided up to the level of Readers and Professors in the new guidelines issued to the universities by the UGC. The impact of new guidelines is still to be seen and assessed.

It could be recalled that the Prime Minister had announced that all the backlog of vacancies under the government as well as autonomous and statutory bodies were to be filled by the December 31, 2005. In view of this, the government was continuously monitoring the progress of the implementation of the reservation policy for the SC/ST. When the review was undertaken, the progress in this regard in various Central Universities was found to be unsatisfactory. It was noticed that, in particular, the Delhi University, the Vishwa Bharati at Shantiniketan, the BHU, and the Pondicherry University had failed to fill the reserved vacancies. The University of Allahabad was also found to be one of the defaulters. The government did not find any valid reason for not filling the vacancies particularly in respect of the various categories of non-teaching posts. Resultantly, the MHRD asked the UGC to take appropriate action against institutions violating the national policy on reservations for the SC and ST. The UGC was also asked not to release the financial assistance without obtaining a clarification from each university, to the effect that every vacancy in respect of posts under direct recruitment/promotion by way of backlog reserved for the SC and ST have been duly advertised and filled (D.O. No. 6-30/2005-U.5 dated May 9, 2006). Accordingly, the UGC at its meeting held on June 11, 2006, resolved to implement the order of MHRD [D.O.F.1-8/2006 (SCT) dated June 23, 2006]. It would be quite interesting to see the results and the follow-up action taken by the UGC and MHRD.

It is a matter of pleasure, seen from the view of empowerment of the SC and ST that the Government of India (MHRD), changed its perception after more than twenty-nine years and asked the UGC to withhold the grant of defaulter Universities and Institutes. The UGC also readily agreed to implement this order of the government. If this trend is continued, the SC and ST communities hope to secure some space in the university system. It would not be out of context to refer to the appointments to posts of Vice-Chancellors in the central universities. There are twenty central universities. There should have been at least three to four Vice-Chancellors belonging to SC/ST communities. There is no dearth of talent and knowledge in the SC and ST communities. The MHRD should think of harvesting the same, for nation-building through the system of higher education. Appointment of a few persons belonging to the SC and/or ST communities as Vice-Chancellors would contribute to the acceleration of empowerment of these weaker sections of society. It would also enhance the degree of democratization of higher education resulting in very high social returns.

Universities and Implementation of Reservations

The existence of many castes makes Indian society heterogeneous in nature. The social structure made up of hierarchical castes is rigid in which their relative positions are fixed and cannot be changed. Any alteration in its rigidity and relative positions of castes is not tolerated and is considered to be a challenge to the status and privileges particularly of people belonging to higher castes. In India, people are politically equal but socially unequal. To fulfil the constitutional promises, whenever the government undertakes measures for advancement and empowerment of weaker sections of the society, the so-called higher castes perceive it as their personal loss, uprootment, and displacement with no possibility of rehabilitation, ultimately leading to their social downfall. Further, with some exceptions, the caste system makes the upper and middle castes prejudiced and biased against the SC and ST communities. Therefore, the policies and schemes introduced by the government for the welfare of the SC and ST are met with resistance and it, therefore, becomes difficult to implement them effectively. The policy related to reservations for the SC and

ST in teaching and non-teaching posts should be the rule, rather than the exception, that it has become.

The success and failure of any policy depends on the way it has been or is implemented. The present reservation policy for the SC and ST has been implemented by the Central Universities. Therefore, these universities could be held mainly responsible for its failure. Perhaps, the lack of efforts and will on the part of the central universities has made the reservation policy almost a educational disaster. The universities should have been proactive, instead, they probably planned the stonewalling of the implementation of the reservation policy. The recent study on implementation of the reservation policy in the Delhi University and its 50 affiliated colleges (Kale, 2006) supports this assertion. Indeed, reservation is not a post-independence phenomenon. Reservations were also provided to Indians/Indian communities in British India. However, the British were more honest and sincere than us (the so-called Indians) in implementing the same. The reservations provided for the SC and ST are a constitutional obligation. Everyone should honour and respect the Constitution which was prepared, presented, and adopted by us. Unfortunately, it is assumed by some people that talent is the copyright of the so-called upper castes. It is also assumed that members of the SC and ST communities have no merit. With this mindset it has always been claimed that no candidates who belong to SC and ST are either available or suitable for appointments to teaching and non-teaching positions. And when qualified candidates are actually available, they are falsely branded as unsuitable for the jobs.

Apart from this, the aforementioned study also provides sufficient grounds to believe that the central universities through manipulations have not implemented reservations particularly in recruitments to the teaching posts. The universities kept on delaying/postponing the adoption of the roster system. The JNU could be perhaps an exception to some extent as it always remained proactive for weaker sections of the society including the SC and ST. It would be pertinent to see its experience. The Executive Council of JNU vide its resolution No. 5.18/EC dated April 20, 1983 resolved that it would endeavour to fill at least one post at the level of Assistant Professor with the SC/ST candidates in each centre by the end of the Sixth Plan period. As a result, as on September 1, 1993, there were eleven teachers (five Associate Professors and six Assistant Professors) belonging to the SC and ST communities. Since, the absence of the roster system and of carry forward, not making much headway, the JNU decided to introduce the school-wise roster for appointment of teaching posts as on March 7, 1994. The JNU was the first among the central universities to introduce the roster system for the teaching posts. In addition to the regular mechanism of advertisement, JNU had set up the Search Committee for each school to identify suitable candidates. At present (as on October 2006), there are twenty-nine SC/ST Assistant Professors in JNU. Although, no reservations are available, above the level of Assistant Professor (i.e. Lecturer) six Associate Professors and six Professors of SC/ST are on the rolls of JNU. Quite a few Assistant Professors belonging to the SC/ST category were selected against the unreserved vacancies. This fact suggests that for successful/effective implementation of the reservation policy, the roster needs to be accompanied by will and effort.

The Constitution Bench of the Hon'ble Supreme Court in case of *R.K. Sabharwal* vs *State of Punjab* as well as *J.C. Mallick* vs *Ministry of Railways* had held that, 'the reservations of jobs for the backward classes/SC/ST/OBC should apply to posts and not to vacancies;' and 'with a view to bringing the policy of reservation in line with the law laid down by the Supreme Court', the government asked the universities to replace the vacancy-based roster by post-based roster from July 2, 1997. Therefore, most of the universities might have directly opted for the post-based roster system around that period. In view of the above, it became quite clear that the central universities which are autonomous organizations indirectly under the control of the Government of India, took more than fifty years after independence to reconcile with the concept of reservations constitutionally provided for the SC and ST particularly in the recruitment of teachers. First, the delay in introduction of the vacancy-based roster and then shifting to post-based roster, adversely affected the interests of the SC and ST. An excellent example was that of the fifty colleges affiliated to the University of Delhi. The representation of the SC and ST at the level of Lecturer in these colleges was 2.8 and 0.3 per cent respectively (as on March 31, 2003).

Although, the present discussion centred around the reservations in teaching, the realities were also quite similar in the case of reservations in recruitment to the non-teaching posts. Let us take the example of the University of Delhi and the Jawaharlal Nehru University. The University of Delhi introduced the roster system for implementation of reservations for SC and ST in non-teaching posts in the year 1974 and 1989 for Group C and D posts and Group A and B respectively. The Jawaharlal Nehru University adopted rosters in the year 1975 and 1978 for the Group C and D post and Group A and B posts respectively. Although, the information is not available about other central universities, the reality is likely to be the same with some degree of variation. However, the acceptance of the roster system in a protracted manner, particularly in the case of the University of Delhi, confirm the fact that the central universities in general, from the very beginning, were keen not to implement reservations for the SC and ST. Further, it is also confirmed that the central universities only under pressure and only in a non-avoidable situation accepted the reservations and took some steps only due to compulsion to implement them. It is evident from the present recruitment drive. Many teaching and non-teaching posts are being advertised and filled, as a result of the letter (D.O.No. 6-30/2005-U.5 dated May 9, 2006) written by the MHRD to the UGC informing 'not to release the financial assistance under the Plan funds for the second quarter, without obtaining a certification from each Central University to the effect that every vacancy in respect of the posts under direct recruitment/promotion by way of backlog reserved for the SC and ST have been duly advertised and filled.'

It must be remembered that the roster determines the share of different categories in the quota of reservations, but cannot ensure the filling of the reserved vacancies. Further, the 'carry forward' clause gives ample scope not to fill the reserved posts. For example, the posts are reserved according to the roster points but in the subjects such as mathematics, commerce, Persian, and Arabic in which it is difficult to get eligible candidates even from the general category. As a result, reserved posts remain unfilled and could be delayed further by re-advertising repeatedly. On the pretext of non-availability and non-suitability of the SC and ST candidates, the reserved vacancies are carried forward only to appoint the candidates belonging to the unreserved category on an ad hoc or temporary basis against the reserved vacancies. The ad-hoc appointment of general category candidates against the reserved vacancies is not allowed now. Earlier, the roster was operated as a 'running account' which created a large backlog of reserved posts. Therefore, the prescribed representation for the SC and ST was never achieved, although the roster system was accepted in the 1970s for teaching and non-teaching posts. This was also one of the main reasons for the presence of ad hoc teachers in large numbers in some universities. The way the roster was handled, the universities could achieve twin goals. They could claim that the roster system was accepted and implemented the reservation policy very late and at the same time made no SC/ST appointments and carried forward the same vacancies only to get them accumulated. Since, presently the roster is to be operated on the principle of replacement and the Government of India has taken some measures to fill the reserve posts as well as backlog posts, the situation is likely to change.

Keeping these and other aspects in mind, the UGC has prepared new guidelines for the strict implementation of the Reservation Policy for the SC/ST in the government in Universities, Deemed to be Universities, Colleges and other Grant-in-Aid Institutes, and Centres. The copy of the same has recently been sent to all concerned [No. F.1-5/2006(SCT) dated August 25, 2006]. The UGC has directed all the universities to adopt these guidelines by appropriate resolutions through their respective governing bodies/ Executive Councils/ Syndicate/Senate, etc., to ensure effective implementation.

Among others, in the new guidelines, the reservation policy is now 'applicable to all teaching posts such as the posts of Lecturers, Readers, Professors or by whatever other nomenclature the posts are known, and to all posts of non-teaching staff.' The instructions by the Government of India for grouping of posts should be resorted to wherever applicable. The 'practice of creating department-wise cadres, which tends to create single posts or cadres with artificially reduced number of posts in order to avoid reservation is strictly forbidden'. It is also mentioned in the new guidelines, that the Universities should initiate action so as to 'effect the necessary amendments to their Acts/Statutes for the statutory support for reservation in admissions, appointments to teaching and non-teaching posts, and representation of the SC/ST in their bodies like Syndicate/Executive Council/Academic Council/ Selection Committees, etc.' The details of coverage and applicability of reservation, extent of reservation, procedure to be followed in matters of reservation for teaching as well as non-teaching staff, procedure to be followed in matters of reservations for admissions, inclusion of reservation-related issues in a separate chapter of the annual report, admission to hostels, admission to staff houses, liaison officer to monitor the implementation of reservations, provision of the SC/ST cell to process grievances of SC/ST, advisory committee to review the implementation of reservations, etc., are provided in the new guidelines.

These guidelines of the UGC, particularly providing the reservation at the level of Associate Professor and Professor, were bitterly opposed by the most of central universities, including the JNU, the hub of most progressive intelectuals of the country. Although, the JNU adopted the reservations for the above mentioned posts in 2008, the large number of faculty members belonging to the general category, with few exceptions, derailed the implementation by using various means. However, the plan of derailment could not be sustained for long and collapsed due to the force of unity of teachers belonged to the SC, ST and OBC communities on the compus, which also compelled the administration to extend the reservation at the level of Associate Professor and Professor. The experience at the other Universities was almost the same. The University of Delhi adopted the reservation for these posts in the year 2013. The delay of five and seven years by the JNU and DU respectively, in extending the reservation to the post of Associate Professor and Professor, after the insuance of guidelines by the UGC, reflected the hegemonic mindset of those who govern and administer the central universities. Practically, the SC and ST communities were provided the reservations at the senior position of teaching 60-65 years after the independence.

Legal Hurdles and Reservations

In general, an advanced section of Indian society has some special traits. They are aware of their own rights and benefits; but only duties of others. Indeed, the social and economic advancement of these sections of the society has a cumulative effect that has been achieved at the cost of the SC and ST. Whenever the measures are taken to undo the historic and social wrongs, they revolt and even show disrespect to the constitution and constitutional functionaries. All kinds of hurdles, barriers, and ploys are used to bypass the implementation of reservations for the SC and ST. The legal path is one such hurdle, which has been used with great success. The public interest litigations were filed in courts which strengthened the hands of the universities to delay or to stop implementation of reservation policies. It is difficult to cover all the aspects in detail. However, a few incidents will be discussed in brief, in support of the aforementioned cruelty.

The Hon'ble Supreme Court in the case of *Indira Swahney & Others vs Union of India & Others* (AIR 1993 SC 447) ruled that reservations of appointments or posts under Article 16(4) of the Constitution are confined to initial appointments and cannot extend in the matter of promotions. This ruling completely blocked the promotional avenues and in turn the social and economic advancement of the SC and ST as envisaged in the Constitution of India. To overcome this legal difficulty and to continue providing reservations in promotions, the Parliament passed the Constitutional Amendment 77 Act, 1995 adding Clause (4A) in Article 16:

> (4A) Nothing in this Article shall prevent the state from making any provision for reservation in matters of promotion to any class or classes of posts in the services under the State in favour of Scheduled Castes and Scheduled Tribes which, in the opinion of the State are not adequately represented in the services under the State.

It may be mentioned that in 1963, the Hon'ble Supreme Court had ruled that total reservations cannot exceed 50 per cent in any year. Subsequently, in Indira Sawhney's case (1992), the Honourable Supreme Court also ruled that total reservations in a given year including carried forward reservations, should in no case exceed the prescribed limit of 50 per cent. Resultantly, the 'Backlog vacancies' could not be filled nor could any 'Special Recruitment Drive' be launched to fill such vacancies. This adversely affected the interest of the SC and ST communities. As a result, a large number of SC and ST people were kept away from enjoying the benefits of reservations. To overcome this difficulty, the Parliament again passed the 81 Constitutional Amendment Act, 2000 adding the Clause (4B) after Clause (4A) in Article 16:

> (4B) Nothing in this Article shall prevent the State from considering any unfilled vacancies of a year which are reserved for being filled in that year in accordance with any provision for reservation made under Clause (4) or Clause (4A) as a separate class of vacancies to be filled in any succeeding year or years and such class of vacancies shall not be considered together with the vacancies of the year in which they are being filled for determining the ceiling of fifty per cent reservation on the total number of vacancies of that year.

The government remained proactive and made two more Constitutional amendments. It added the provison to Article 335 in 2000 through the Constitutional 82 Amendment, permitting it to make provisions for the SC/ST for: (a) relaxation in qualifying marks; (b) lowering standards of evaluation for promotions. Further, in 2001, the 85th Amendment of the Constitution was carried out to undo the 1999 Supreme Court ruling which said even if SC/ST were given 'accelerated promotions' by quota they will not get 'Consequential Seniority'. It took almost thirty-seven years to restore the privileges of SC and ST. During this long period the SC and ST remained deprived of recruitment benefits.

Although, the recent judgment (in the month of August 2005) in *Inamdar vs State of Maharashtra & Others* is not directly relevant to reservations in the recruitment, but is worth mentioning. The Hon'ble Supreme Court abolished the state quotas in private unaided professional colleges. Such ruling can influence the minds of the general population and those who are supposed to implement the various reservation policies in spirit and letter. Perhaps to assure the socially and economically backward people about their privileges, the Parliament passed the 93rd Constitutional Amendment Act, 2005 in December 2005, by inserting the Clause (5) in Article 15 of the Constitution.

In addition to these, *R.K. Sabharwal vs State of Punjab* (AIR 1993 SC 447) and *J.C. Mallick vs Ministry of Railways* are another two legal cases that need mention. The earlier vacancy-based rosters had been prescribed in order to implement the reservations in recruitments for the SC and ST. The application of reservation on the basis of these rosters was called into question before the Court. As mentioned earlier, the Constitution Bench of the Supreme Court, in the case of *R.K. Sabharwal vs State of Panjab* as well as *J.C. Mallick vs Ministry of Railways* has held that the reservation of jobs for the backward classes SC/ST/OBC, should apply to posts and not to vacancies. With a view to bring the policy of reservations in line with the law laid down by the Supreme Court, 200-point, 40-point and 120-point vacancy-based rosters were also replaced by post-based rosters. Similarly rosters were also prepared to replace the 100-point rosters in respect of local recruitment to Group C and D posts on the basis of the same principle [O.M.No. 36012/2/96-Estt.(Res.) dated July 2, 1997, Dept. of Per. & Trg., GOI].

Apart from these, the Court also 'held that the vacancy-based rosters can operate only till such time as the representation of persons belonging to the reserved categories in a cadre, reaches the prescribed percentage of reservation'. However, the vacancy-based roster were quickly shifted to post-based rosters before reaching the prescribed percentage of reservations and were operated to the detriment of the interests of the SC and ST communities.

According to the present post-based roster, 7, 15, 20 ... points and 14, 28, 40 ... points are reserved for the SC and ST respectively. On the other hand, in old vacancy-based rosters 1, 4, ... points and 7, ... points were reserved for the SC and ST respectively. With this change, deliberate efforts are/were made by the Universities and Colleges to keep the total strength of posts in particular departments or artificially reduce the strength of cadre, to avoid the recruitment of persons belonging to the SC and ST communities. This could be seen particularly in newly established departments. In a department with strength of 13 posts, there can only be one SC candidate and not even a single ST candidate. There was a hope for both the SC and ST in the vacancy-based roster system. The present post-based roster system could be manipulated so as to effectively delay and/or avoid the recruitment of the SC and ST candidates.

The reservations were again placed in the vortex of legality by challenging the four Constitutional Amendments, i.e. 77 (1995), 81 (2000), 82 (2000), and 85 (2001). The Five-Judge Constitution Bench comprising Chief Justice Y.K. Sabharwal and Justices K.G. Balakrishnan, S.H. Kapadia, C.K. Thakkar and P.K. Balasubramanyan examined the relevant provisions made in Articles 16(1), 16(4), 16(4A), and 16(4B) of the Constitution. The Five-Judge Bench of the Supreme Court gave the verdict on October 19, 2006, and upheld the validity of constitution amendments related to reservations in recruitments and promotions but has suggested impracticable conditions for their implementation. The Bench ordered: the exclusion of the 'creamy layer' among the SC and ST from the ambit of reservations; no state can exceed 50 per cent quota in jobs; vacancies of reserved category posts have to be filled in time; such vacancies cannot be carried forward indefinitely; for new castes to be included in quota; data about its backwardness and inadequate representation in government jobs has to be provided, and the government has to show that the quota does not affect governance. The verdict seemed to be more concerned about the success of surgery rather than the actual state or well-being of the patient. This verdict is going to have far-reaching consequences particularly for extending the 'creamy layer' criterion from OBC to SC/ST and thereby putting SC/ST at par with socially and economically backward classes. The caste and its social disabilities, and not economic accomplishment determine the SC/ST status. The OBC did not suffer from the stigma of untouchability, isolation, and exploitation. Therefore, it is wrong to consider them together for reservation purposes. However, it appears that the present judgment paved the way for abolition of reservations. The legal battle would not end here. The past experience suggests, that the government or Parliament may intervene in this matter. Any action taken by the government in this regard is likely to be challenged again in the Supreme Court. A new round of legal battle may start soon. However, at the end, the losers would be the beneficiaries of the reservations.

Minority Institutes and Reservations

The minority institutes referred to in Clause (1) of Article 30 of the Constitution are exempted from the provisions of reservations. To get immunity from the reservation policy, some sections of society have been trying to get their institutes recognized or established as minority institutes. It is known that some of the institutes run by the minority communities are not exclusively for the minorities. In such institutes, when the presence of non-minority community persons does not affect or dilute the minority character, then how can the representation of the SC and ST in admissions and recruitments in these institutes affect or dilute their minority character? An exemption from the provision of reservation seemed to be interpreted as not to appoint SC and ST candidates particularly to the teaching posts. One gets such an impression from the example of Aligarh Muslim University (AMU). The total sanctioned teaching posts in AMU are 1,593 and out of the existing strength of 1,512 teachers there is only one teacher who belongs to the SC community. None are from the ST category. The situation of non-teaching staff recruitment is also not very different. Out of the 183 and 238 sanctioned posts, there is 1 Grade A and 2 Grade B officials respectively belonging to the SC, while again none are from the ST. Further, eleven SC and four ST persons are working in Grade C posts. The strength of Grade C cadre is 2,456. The minorities and minority institutes should see their rights and those of SC/ST as complementing rather than conflicting. The need of the hour is to help each other, grow together, and branch out to flourish. It is pertinent to mention that some of the minority communities are affluent and advanced, occupying prominent positions in the society. At least this section of minorities should come forward and open the doors of their institutes for the SC and ST, both in admissions and recruitments, and in turn contribute to the nation-building process through empowering the SC and ST communities.

Conclusions

The endless suffering of the SC and ST from the social disabilities for centuries together has moved the nation to take a conscious decision, to undo the social and historic wrong doings. With an aim to achieve social equality, the provisions such as protective, developmental, and preferential were made for them in the Indian Constitution. Reservation in employment is one of the examples of preferential provisions. The universities are our conscience keepers. However, these temples of learning have failed to effectively implement the policies on reservations for the SC and ST in recruitments. The pretext of non-availability and non-suitability of SC and ST candidates is used to prevent their appointments particularly in teaching posts. Although, highly educated people are not required for non-teaching posts including Grade A, the representation of the SC and ST was found to be abysmally low. It could be inferred that the Central Universities were mainly responsible for non-implementation of the reservation policy. The delay as well as acceptance of the roster in a protracted manner by the universities also adversely affected the interest of the SC and ST. The UGC has also not made enough efforts to pursue the Central Universities in this regard. There is evidence that the government has also contributed to some extent in the failure. It is quite clear that the government, UGC and the universities do not work in a coordinated manner. However, the situation has now changed. The government and UGC are proactive for reservations and taking measures to ensure its effective implementation. Although, Clause (1) of Article 30 of the Constitution shuts the doors of minority institutes for the SC/ST, it was suggested that the minorities and minority institutes should see their rights and those of the SC/ST as complementing rather than conflicting. The legal hurdles delayed the implementation of reservations. In the context of creamy layer, it must be mentioned that the poor representation of the SC and ST in Central Universities is like very little milk in a large container. In such a scenario where is the scope to skim cream from such a small quantity? If you heat it to obtain the creamy layer it would dry up, burn, and turn into ashes. Resultantly, there would neither be milk nor cream.

REFERENCES

Kale, R.K. (2006). Implementation of Reservation Policy for SC/ST in the Colleges Affiliated to the University of Delhi, *University News*, A Weekly Journal of Higher Education (AIU), Vol. 44, No. 04, pp. 1-10.

Sharma, Kavita A. (2003). *50 Years of University Grants Commission*, A Publication of University Grants Commission, New Delhi, p. 119.

6

Enrolling or Rolling Out: SC and ST Students in Central Universities

The present education system was introduced by the British with the purpose to prepare the manpower to help them to administer our country which was under their control and not for social reformation or development. Expectedly, the expansion of education was slow and a select few benefited. On achieving independence in 1947, India inherited a very small and highly un-democratized education system. The literary rate was just 14 per cent and enrolment at the elementary level was around thirty per cent. Only one-third of children (of the relevant age group) were attending school. There were about 19 universities, 496 colleges and 2.4 lakh students (less than one per cent of the relevant age group). Because of the caste system and prevailing social disparities, the SCs and STs remained deprived of education in British India. On the other hand, the rich, elites and upper castes, particularly Brahmins grabbed the opportunities to become educated and in turn its main beneficiary. This educational differentiation contributed to the already existing social disparities.

After independence, measures were taken immediately by policy makers to expand education far and wide. Several Commissions and Committees had been set up from time to time. Some of them are University Education Commission (1948), Secondary Education Commission (1952), Education Commission (1966), Teacher Education Commission (1985), National Knowledge Commission (2005) and Yash Pal Committee (2006) to mention a few. The first National Policy Resolution on Education was adopted in 1968 on the Education Commission (1966) Report, which could not be fully implemented for several reasons. After bringing education on the concurrent list through the constitutional amendment in 1976, an attempt was made to develop a National Policy during 1979. Even this could not materialize due to non-approval by the Central Advisory Board of Education (CABE). In 1985, the then Ministry of Education took the initiative to develop a databased document of critical analysis in the field of education entitled, 'Challenge of Education' in two volumes; and after nation-wide debate and discussions the New Educational Policy (NEP) on education was formulated and subsequently passed by the Parliament in 1986, ensuring particularly 'access and quality to all' in education. For effective implementation, a detailed Plan of Action (POA 1986) was developed after deliberations on NEP (1986) by twenty-three task forces. NPE (1986) was reviewed in 1990 but in between there was a change in government. Again, in 1991, NPE (1986) was reviewed by a CABE Committee and submitted its report in 1992 which is referred as NPE (1992). In this report, it was noted that while very little of NPE (1986) required formulation, the Programme of Action (POA 1986) needed considerable revision. Accordingly, the POA (1992) was evolved through the similar consensual processes adopted earlier. We spent a lot of time and efforts in committee rooms and seminar halls on discussing and drafting policies. However, that did not change the nature of class rooms and laboratories. Most importantly, education remained undemocratic. It is important that the revised POA (1992) highlighted among other things, education and justice in education for disadvantaged groups of society, particularly, SCs and STs. The Knowledge Commission in its Report to the Nation 2006 had mentioned that the disparities in educational attainments are intimately linked to caste and social groups. The Yash Pal Committee (2006) also highlighted disparities and shortcomings of the present system. Indeed, way back in 1964, the Kothari Commission found the socio-educational distance between high and low 'large, tending to widen' and being made more complicated by the 'undemocratic institution of caste'. Recent findings of the High Level Committee (2006), popularly known as the Sachar Committee, indirectly reflected the need to spread education in SC and ST communities. At least, while making policies, the concerned were made about the educational needs of SCs and STs. Ambani-Birla Report (2000), prepared by 'new age', industrialists asked the Government to concentrate on the primary and secondary education and leave higher education to private initiative. The Report considered higher education as an instruments of generation of wealth and ignored the social responsibility, making higher education non-accessible to poor, particularly SC and ST communities.

SCs and STs are most oppressed and socio-economically backward communities of Indian society. The SCs, formerly called untouchables, were held in social slavery and servitude for centuries. They experienced all forms of discrimination, untouchability and social exclusion emanating from the caste system. On the other hand, marginalization and deprivation of ST was a result of their geographical and spatial isolation. According to the 2001 Census of India, the SCs and STs are about 16.2 and 8.2 per cent respectively in the total population which together comes close to twenty-five crore. This population of SC and ST is almost equal to the population of USA, double the population of Japan, three times of Germany and four times of UK. This huge population which remained in a sub-human status for many centuries, could not be ignored while planning the development of the nation, after its independence. Probably with this in mind, numbers of provisions, including the reservation in admissions in academic institutes, were incorporated in the constitution of independent India. After more than sixty-five years, SC and ST communities should have benefited to a great extent from the provision of reservation in the colleges and universities and other educational institutes. However, information on the status of SC and ST in higher education is either scanty, incomplete or scattered (Kale, 2005). Sometimes, the information on SC and ST is avoided or ignored while compiling the same. For example, the UGC publication (of year 2002) on 'University Development in India: Basic Facts and Figures (1995-96 to 2000-2001)' provides data on universities, university level institutes and colleges in the country. Surprisingly, there is nothing in this volume of printed A4 size 234 pages, not even a single entry on SC and ST. Indeed educational attainments of SC and ST have been completely blacked out.

Therefore, there is a need to get the information, from various sourses, related to enrolment of SC and ST to detrmine the extent of social inclusiveness in the higher education system. In pursuance of the same, an attempt has been made to understand the educational status of SC and ST students in Central Universities as a case study and in turn to probe the permeability and spread of higher education in these communities.

Findings of the present study may have some significance as all the successive governments of independent India claimed to be concerned about the social backwardness of SC and ST communities and tried to uplift them through education.

SC Students in Central Universities

Out of twenty central universities,* eighteen universities are directly funded by the UGC (Kale, 2006a). The present study is mainly confined to these UGC funded universities. The level-wise enrolment of SC students is given in Table 1. The total strength of

Table 1. Students' Enrolment in Central Universities as on March 31, 2005

Level	*Enrolment*	*SC Students*	*ST Students*
Under graduate (UG)	55352 (100%)	3600 (06.50%)	1091 (01.91%)
Post graduate (PG)	35650 (100%)	3322 (09.31%)	4000 (11.22%)
M Phil/M Tech.	1249 (100%)	209 (16.73%)	50 (4.00%)
Ph D	12215 (100%)	956 (07.82%)	476 (03.89%)
Certificate/ Diploma	13988 (100%)	813 (05.81%)	105 (0.75%)
Total	118454 (100%)	8900 (07.51%)	5722 (04.83%)

Source: Data compiled and processed by the author from the information furnished by 18 Central Universities to the UGC. Data for two Universities, namely, Manipur and Allahabad is for the year 2006.

* This number is now increased to 41.

the students in eighteen central universities is 1,18,454. Their level-wise enrolment is: Undergraduates (UG) 55,352; postgraduates (PG) 35,650; MPhil/MTech 1,249; PhD 12,215 and certificate/diploma courses 13,988. The number of students registered for UG courses should have been more. It appears some of the universities have not provided the information related to the strength of students enrolled in their affiliated colleges. In case of SC students, they are 8,900 in number which comes to 7.51 per cent compared to total intake. It is lower than the national level of enrolment, i.e. 9.7 per cent (Ravi Srivastava, 2007). As mentioned earlier, SC constitutes about 16.2 per cent of the total population (*Census of India 2001*) of the country; the 7.51 per cent enrolment of SC students is almost fifty per cent lower than the prescribed fifteen per cent reservation. Since, the spread of education among SC community is slow compared to other sections of the society, the present one per cent rate of increase of their enrolment (Srinivas Rao, 2002; Kale, 2005), is need to be accelerated. It may be noted that general category students enrolment enhanced at the rate of 8.3 per cent, whereas their enrolment in technical education enhanced at the rate of 12.4 per cent annually (Srivastava, 2007).

At different levels, enrolment of SC students is 3,600 in UG; 3,322 in PG; 209 in MPhil/MTech, 956 in PhD and 813 in certificate/diploma courses. In terms of per cent it is 6.5, 9.31, 16.73, 7.82 and 5.81 per cent respectively. It appears that representation of SC students increases from UG to MPhil/MTech Courses and then suddenly declines at PhD level. The certificates and diplomas known to have importance and significance as add-on courses. However, these courses were not popular among the SC students as enrolment is around five per cent. It may be possible that the certificate/diploma courses are not easily accessible to them for some or other reasons. Interestingly, in the MPhil/MTech programme the enrolment of SC students is 16.73 per cent which is quite high and even exceeds the prescribed fifteen per cent reservation for them. It is difficult to understand the reason for higher enrolment, for the MPhil/MTech programme. However, it suggests a high interest of SC and ST students for research. It is possible that they are not allowed to go for a direct PhD programme or forced to discontinue further study after completion of the MPhil.

It is known that the teachers belonging to higher castes avoid taking SC and ST students for the PhD. Therefore, a small number of SC students in the PhD programme is not a surprise.

In general, 35,650 enrolment in PG and 12,215 enrolment in PhD are suggestive of the possibility that 34.26 per cent students prefer to go from the PG to PhD programme in the central universities. For the year 2002-03, at all India level 2,85,873 students were enrolled for the PG programme and 62,213 in the PhD programme (www.ugc.ac.in). A rough estimate suggested that only 7.3 per cent postgraduate students are attracted to research. Thus, a significant number of students (34.26 per cent) carry out research in central universities compared to other universities (7.3 per cent). The Central University campuses appear to provide a better academic climate for general category students, but not for SC students

It may be mentioned that the students belonging to the reserve category face many difficulties to get admission in the PhD programme in Departments/Universities where the reservation policy for admission is not strictly followed. With a few exceptions, SC students are reluctantly accepted/taken by the teachers and sometimes not guided properly which makes them frustrated and isolated. In the universities where admissions for the PhD programme is through competitive examinations, SC students do not get the subject/topic of their choice for research, and also pushed towards the teachers who are progressive and sympathetic to their cause resulting in the formation of a cluster of reserve category of students around such teachers. Sometimes, SC students continue to remain in a hostile academic climate till the completion of their research work. In the light of this, it is quite remarkable that even such unfavourable conditions almost one third of SC students (28.78 per cent) of PG prefer to go for PhD. It is indicated from 3,322 and 956 SC students in PG and PhD respectively. In the event of encouragement, equal opportunity and non-discrimination, more SC students might join for research as the chance to get a job is quite high with the highest academic degree.

For the UG and PG programme, two universities have no SC students on their roll. In the other two universities, the SC students at PG levels are less than one per cent, and between two and four per cent SC students are enrolled in the other three universities. It is quite important that four universities have enrolled SC students more than the prescribed fifteen per cent in their PG courses. These are University of Hyderabad (18.22 per cent), Pondicherry University (19.57 per cent), Vishva Bharati (17.11 per cent) and BBA (40.45 per cent). University of Delhi, Jamia Millia Islamia and Jawaharlal Nehru University are located in the capital city of the country and the enrolment of SC students in PG courses of these universities is 7.32, 9.83 and 12.27 per cent respectively.

Surprisingly, not a single student who belongs to the SC community was found registered for the PhD programme in six central universities. Further, there were three universities in which less than two per cent SC students were enrolled for PhD. Thus, almost nine central universities were not accessible for SC students to carry out the research work. From the remaining, mainly five central universities have been catering to SC students as their enrolment for PhD was found to be more than twelve per cent. It is quite clear that some of the central universities are not implementing reservation policies in letter and spirit. The University of Hyderabad, JNU, Pondicherry University and BBA University are making an effort to honour the mandate given by the Constitution. In these universities the enrolment of SC students is relatively high at both PG and PhD level, and is very close to the prescribed fifteen per cent reservations in admissions. In case of other universities there was a wide gap between the PG and PhD level enrolment of SC students. For example, the gap was 9.60 per cent for Jamia Millia Islamia (9.85 per cent PG and 0.23 per cent PhD enrolment), 7.02 per cent for Banaras Hindu University (13.53 per cent PG and 6.51 per cent PhD enrolment), and 4.39 per cent for Delhi University (7.32 per cent PG and 2.93 per cent PhD enrolment). Unexpectedly, the enrolment of SC students in Delhi University has been relatively low at both PG and PhD levels.

As mentioned earlier, a few Central Universities including JNU and the University of Hyderabad are making efforts to provide opportunities for SC students to join the Ph D programme. JNU and the University of Hyderabad are known for academic excellence. Both were recognized by the UGC as the universities with potential for excellence. Further, 'JNU is the only University from India that has found a place in the global ranking of universities or institutions of higher learning' (IITs and IIMs are also in the list but are not part of the University systems of India). JNU conducts the entrance examination in more than sixty-eight centres countrywide and two overseas centres. In the second phase the University conducts the viva-voce examination of successful candidates to find their potential to pursue research. Through such cut-throat competition, large numbers of SC students get into JNU. Getting admission for PhD in the University of Hyderabad is also not easy. Thus, the relatively high number of SC students in JNU and University of Hyderabad confirms the availability of SC students for the PhD programme. In addition, although, the presence SC students in large numbers are on these campuses, the quality of education has not gone down. It suggests that giving admission to SC students does not adversely affect the quality of education. Therefore, there seems to be something seriously wrong with universities where none or very few students belong to the SC community are pursuing the PhD programme.

ST Students in Central Universities

In eighteen central universities, 5,722 ST students are studying in different courses. Compared to the total enrolment, they are just 4.83 per cent which is less by 2.73 per cent and 3.37 per cent compared to the prescribed 7.5 per cent reservation and to their population (8.2 per cent) respectively. As far as their enrolment at different levels is concerned, it is: 1.91 per cent for undergraduates, 11.22 per cent for postgraduates, four per cent for MPhil /MTech, 3.89 per cent for PhD and 0.75 per cent for certificate and diploma courses. The representation of ST students in admissions for undergraduate and certificate/diploma courses is unexpectedly very low.

On the other hand, they are large in number (11.22 per cent) in the PG programme of study which exceeds even their share of 8.2 per cent in population. On completion of postgraduate courses many ST students are expected to join the MPhil /PhD programme. However, their enrolment in the MPhil (four per cent) and PhD (3.89 per cent) is quite low. With sufficient number of fellowships for research with a sizeable amount available, many ST students are likely to apply for research in the central universities. Although, reservation is in jobs, an avoidance of filling of reserve posts with PG qualifications would also make ST students available for the PhD programme (Kale, 2006a; 2006b). Therefore, it is difficult to understand the low percentage of ST students in research programmes.

It may be mentioned that the teaching of PG courses is face-to-face group teaching in the classrooms. Teachers do not mind teaching large numbers of students in groups with or without knowing their social background. On the other hand, MPhil /PhD is a personalized teaching and guidance. Interaction at an individual level, for SC and ST communities may not be liked by some teachers. Further, many teachers who belong to higher castes think of SC and ST students as non-teachable and non-meritorious and considered to be a liability. In many universities, the teachers select research scholars and register under them for PhD. It is an open secret that some teachers avoid taking SC and ST students for research. It was brought to the notice of the present author that several teachers discourage the students to be registered under them for PhD the moment they came to know that the students are aspirant for the Rajiv Gandhi Fellowship. Apart from this, an experience of discrimination and humiliation during the PG programme might also be discouraging SC and ST students to join the PhD programmes of study. Probably, there is need to identify academic and non-academic reasons which keep SC and ST students away from the PhD programme in some of the central universities.

It may not be out of context to refer to D.O. Letter No. F. 1-7/ 98-U.5 dated August 18, 1999, from the Government of India, Ministry of Human Resource Development, Department of Education seeking comments of the UGC on the fourth report for the period 1996-97 and 1997-98 of the National Commission for SC/ST. In response, the UGC considered the matter regarding reservation of seats in MPhil and PhD for SCs and STs in faculties/ departments in universities and colleges, and decided to abolish reservation for SCs and STs in admission to these two academic programmes and informed accordingly to the Ministry with copy to the Registrars of universities [D.O. Letter No. F. 1-6/98(SCT) dated March 15, 2000]. This caused a lot of unrest among SC and

ST students throughout the country. The agitated SC/ST students pressurized and pushed the ministry to a corner, and compelled it to reconsider the matter. Sensing the trouble, the UGC took a U-turn, changed the decision and withdrew the aforesaid letter D.O.No. F.1-6/98(SCT) of March 15, 2000 with immediate effect; and conveyed the same to the Ministry vide D.O. Letter No. 1-6/98(SCT) dated April 8-10, 2000 with copy to the Registrars of all Central/Deemed to be Universities receiving hundred per cent grants, as a part of damage control. However, it revealed the mindset of some people who were supposed to protect and implement the constitutional provisions for SC and ST. Such an anti-reservation mindset of statutory bodies of government may encourage the universities to implement the reservation policy detrimentally.

Let us come back to the postgraduate programme again. Mizoram is the only university in the North-Eastern region which has a hundred per cent ST students at the PG level. Nagaland and North Eastern Hills are the other two universities where around eighty per cent students belong to the ST community. A high enrolment of ST students at PG levels in these three Universities is mainly responsible for their overall 11.22 per cent in central universities. Manipur University and Tezpur University have 21.87 and 9.38 per cent ST students in PG courses respectively. Ten central universities other than JNU (8.48 per cent), Hyderabad University (13.33 per cent) and Jamia Millia Islamia (6.13 per cent); have four per cent or even less ST students pursuing their studies in PG courses. Being away from the tribal region, JNU, Hyderabad University and Jamia Millia Islamia are able to attract and enrol a substantial number of ST students. However, this is not the same case with other universities and need to be understood. Like JNU and Jamia Millia Islamia, Delhi University is also in Delhi, the capital of the country but surprisingly has just 3.43 per cent ST students on its role for PG programmes.

At least in three central universities not a single ST student is registered for the PhD. Further, there are two universities which have just one per cent and three universities which have even less than one per cent ST students pursuing research. The enrolment of ST students is expected to be high in all the universities located in the North Eastern region of the country. However, only Mizoram University (92.06 per cent), and Nagaland University (76.23 per cent) have high enrolment of ST students. Manipur University with 11.86 per cent enrolment is the third highest. Other universities in this region have around four per cent or less ST students in research. North Eastern Hill University has 83.73 per cent ST students in the PG programme of study but surprisingly only 4.36 per cent in the PhD programme. In terms of absolute number, it is just sixteen out of 321 PhD students. The objectives of the NEHU as mentioned in its Act is 'to disseminate the advance knowledge by providing instructional and research facilities in such branches of learning as it may deem fit; to pay special attention to the improvement of the social and economic conditions and welfare of the people of the hill areas of the North-Eastern region and in particular, their intellectual, academic and cultural advancement'. Is NEHU not deviating from its own objectives?

As mentioned earlier, a relatively high percentage of ST students could be seen in Jamia Millia Islamia (6.13 per cent) and University of Hyderabad (13.33 per cent) for the PG programme of study. However, they are very few in PhD in both these Universities, i.e. 0.41 per cent in Jamia Millia Islamia and 2.58 per cent in the University of Hyderabad. Where have all these ST students who completed their PG studies disappeared? Why could these Universities not retain ST students for the PhD programme? The answers, if found, probably surprise everyone. It may be mentioned that JNU is perhaps the only university which is doing better and protecting the interest of ST students in admission at all the levels. It strictly follows the reservation policy in admission even at the level of PhD and is able to attract ST students in large numbers (6.25 per cent in the year 2005 and 7.46 per cent in the year 2006). JNU is also the only central university where the highest number of SC (362) and ST (178) students are doing PhD. Unbelievably, in six central universities, ST students registered for PhD are in single digit. Efforts need to be made to provide access to SC and ST students to the PhD programme of study in many central universities.

Table 2. Existing System of Reservation for SC/ST in Some Central Universities

S.No.	*University*	*Extent of Reservation (%)*
01.	Nagaland University	50
02.	Mizoram University	50
03.	North Eastern Hill University	50
04.	BBA University	50
05.	Manipur University	33

Special Provision of Reservations

The special provision of reservation has been made for SC/ST in central universities in the North-East region and Babasaheb Bhimrao Ambedkar University, Lucknow (Table 2). The existing provision of reservation for SC/ST in Nagaland, Mizoram, North-Eastern Hill and Babasaheb Bhimrao Ambedkar Universities is to the extent of fifty per cent. Manipur University provides 33 per cent reservation for SC/ST (two per cent for SC and thirty per cent for ST). As a result, the actual available reservation for SC/ST in Central Universities goes beyond the prescribed 22.5 per cent (15 per cent for SC and 7.5 per cent for ST) due to a special provision in the five above mentioned universities.

Data shown in Table 1 clearly indicated that overall enrolment of SC/ST students in eighteen central universities is 12.34 per cent which is almost fifty per cent less than the prescribed reservations (22.5 per cent) for these communities. If we consider the special provision for fifty per cent reservations for SC/ST in four universities and thirty three per cent in another one, this gap/shortfall would be more than fifty per cent. Thus there is a high deficit of SC/ST students in higher education in central universities system which comes under UGC and MHRD. With the exception of one or two universities, other central universities have failed to implement the reservation policy for SC/ST effectively in admission. The measures need to be taken immediately to minimize this deficit, as a part of social justice, generation of human resources and development of the nation.

SC and ST Students in Minority Institutes

Minority Educational Institute is defined as an 'Institute established and administered by minorities under Clause (1) of Article 30 of

Constitution and so declared by an Act of Parliament or by the Central Government or declared as Minority Institute under the National Commission for Minority Education Institute Act 2004'. The minority institutes do not follow the reservation of the Government of India or the respective state governments, for SC and ST. AMU is an excellent example of a minority institute as being old and one of the largest central universities with a total enrolment of 20,547 students to understand the enrolment of SC and ST students in minority institutes. It has always been claimed that AMU has never denied admission to SC and ST students as and when they approach. If true, then it is quite unexpected that only 172 students belonging to SC and ST communities are studying in AMU, i.e. just 0.84 per cent. At different levels of study programmes the presence of SC and ST students in number is: at UG level eighty (0.78 per cent), at PG level thirty-one (0.99 per cent), at PhD level fifty-five (3.59 per cent) and at certificate/ diploma level six (0.11 per cent). The details on enrolment in AMU given in Table 3 are self-explanatory. It may be remembered that the unprivileged, particularly SC, are large in number in Aligarh district and its surroundings. They are relatively rich compared to their counterparts in some of the regions of the country. Moreover, there is awareness among the SC of this region about higher education. In Uttar Pradesh, the SC population (21.1 per cent) is more than the Muslim population (18.5 per cent). As far as the literacy rate is concerned it is almost the same (46.27 per cent for SC and 47.79 per cent for Muslims) (*Census of India, 2001,* Registrar General of India). Therefore, at least, some reasonable number of students at least belonging to SC should have been in AMU.

Table 3. Students Enrolment in Aligarh Muslim University as on March 31, 2005

Level/Programme	*Students Enrolment*		
	SC	*ST*	*Total Enrolment*
UG	76	04	10314
PG	23	08	3131
PhD	54	01	1534
Certificate/Diploma	NIL	06	5568
Grand Total	153	19	20547

Source: University Grants Commission

In this context it is important to note one of the recommendations of the PM's High Level Committee on Social, Economic and Education Status of the Muslim Community of India (Justice Rajinder Sachar Committee Report, 2006). The Committee has stated in its report that 'there is an urgent need to enhance diversity on educational campuses'. It has also recommended that the 'UGC should be encouraged to evolve a system where part of the allocation to colleges and universities is linked to the diversity in the student population. Even private colleges, including those run by minorities and which have affiliation with universities or recognized by the state bodies can be provided additional funds if they have diverse population' (Para 3.1, Chapter 12, p. 245). Therefore, it is perhaps the right time for minority institutes to recognize the significance of the inclusiveness as well as the diversity on the campus. Otherwise the constitutional provision meant to safeguard the interest of vulnerable groups (minorities) itself might be perceived as an instrument for the oppression of more vulnerable groups (i.e. SC and ST). This should not be allowed to happen. The constitutional provisions for minorities and SC/ST as well as OBC, as mentioned earlier, should be considered as complementary and not as conflicting.

It appears the mindset of Minority Institutions is changing and slowly realizing their social responsibilities. For example, St. Stephen's College in Delhi has offered twenty per cent seats to SC/ST students from the academic year 2007-08, and the remainig eighty per cent would be divided equally among Christian and general category students (Anuradha Mukherjee, 2007). When implemented, it would be historic events and likely to show the path to other minority institutions. It may be mentioned that there is already a 'Supreme Court ruling which allows up to 50 per cent seats in minority institutions to be set aside for members of the same minority community which runs the institutions'. There is no legal problem but of a conscience and duty towards the society. Jamia Millia attracts students belonging to underprivileged sections of society.

Diversity on Campus

India is a country of diversity. However, Indian diversity has intrinsically been exclusive in nature. To keep the dominance and complete control on society, Brahmanism did not allow diversity with present meaning to flourish in any sphere of life including higher education. Therefore, the recommendation of the Prime Minister's High Level Committee to enhance the diversity on the educational campus including minority institutes has a great significance (Justice Rajinder Sachar Committee Report, 2006). Since, the education system in India is still dominated by people from upper castes, for their own benefits, there is a lack of diversity to a great extent in the student population on most of the campuses. Perhaps JNU is one of the few universities which was able to achieve and maintain diversity in the student population on campus and hence discussed briefly.

It is important that the students from all over India join the JNU (presently from thirty-five states/union territories) with different socio-economic, linguistic and religious backgrounds. The social and gender profile of JNU students in respect of the year 2005-06 is shown in Tables 4 and 5. Out of 5,264 students, 669, 370 and 140 belong to SCs, STs and Differently-abled groups respectively. Further, out of the total (5,264) strength of students, 1,862 girls are on the rolls of JNU. About 241 students from more than thirty different countries are also on the campus.

Table 4. Social Profile of JNU Students in 2005-06

S.No.	*Social Group*	*Strength of Students*
01.	Scheduled Caste	669
02.	Scheduled Tribe	370
03.	Physically Challenged	104
04.	Foreign Nationals	241
05.	Others	3880

Source: Jawaharlal Nehru University 36th Annual Report (2005-06)

Table 5. Gender Profile of JNU Students in 2005-06

Gender	*Strength*
Female	1862
Male	3402
Total	5264

Source: Jawaharlal Nehru University 36th Annual Report (2005-06)

JNU provides 22.5 per cent reservations for SC and ST students (fifteen per cent for SC and 7.5 per cent for ST) as well as three per cent for the Differently-abled. Over and above the intake fixed for each programme, fifteen per cent of seats are also reserved for foreign nationals. Out of this quota of fifteen per cent, up to 7.5 per cent seats are kept aside for those appearing in the entrance examination and the remaining 7.5 per cent for candidates applying from abroad whose cases are considered *in absentia* (the ratio is interchangeable, if necessary). In pursuance of the first schedule of the University Act, an attempt have been made to get students, in adequate number, from abroad especially SAARC and other developing countries. Internationalization of education is important as, on completion of studies those would be our cultural ambassadors.

Strict following of the reservation policy of the Government of India enabled JNU to attract students belonging to the disadvantaged section of society in large numbers every year (Table 6). Although no reservation in admission is available for OBC students.* Before the year 2006, JNU followed its own affirmative policy. Deprivation points (ten points for women candidates and five points for men candidates) are provided to OBC candidates [excluding the creamy layer as mentioned in Column three of the Schedule to the Government of India, Department of Personnel & Training O.M. No. 36012/22-93 Estt(SCT) dated September 8, 1993] and as per the OBC list drawn by the Government of India and also excluding Income Tax payers. Apart from this, all candidates (including OBC) who hail from Quartile-1 Districts and Quartile-2

Table 6. Diversity in Student Population on JNU Campus

S.No.	*Category*	*Enrolment*		
		2003	*2004*	*2005*
01	SC/ST	24.48%	23.73%	24.13%
02	PH	2.59%	2.87%	2.48%
03	OBC	19.00%	18.30%	21.02%

Source: JNU Annual Reports

* 27% reservation is provided in admissions for OBC from the year 2006.

Districts are also awarded five and three points respectively. The Quartile is a measure of regional backwardness. It is understood that the classification of districts in quartiles was made on the basis of the work of Prof. G.S. Bhalla, one of the founding faculty members of the university. Further, all Kashmiri migrants as well as widows/wards of Defence Personnel who made supreme sacrifices or got disabled during the war or peace time, awarded five deprivation points. These details are reproduced from the prospectus of JNU, for the benefit of readers. Many students have been benefited from the reservations and affirmative action of JNU. For example, of 1,426 students admitted in the year 2005-6; 13.8 per cent SC, 10.33 per cent ST and 21.02 per cent OBC students enrolled in different courses. As far as gender is concerned, 892 were boys and 534 girls. Importantly, the candidates admitted to various academic programmes from one hundred and thirty-one Indian universities/institutes/boards. Of the total (1,426), 633 students belonged to the lower and middle income group and income of their parents was below Rs. 6,000 per month and the remaining 739 belonged to the higher income group and their parents' income was more than Rs. 6,000 per month. Although 524 students come from a rural background and 902 from urban, with ratio close to 1:2, just 417 studied in Public Schools and the other 1009 in municipal and non-public schools (JNU Thirty-Sixth Annual Report 2005-06).

The above facts confirm the high degree of diversity in students' population on the campus of JNU. It is possible that this diversity probably contributed to a great extent to the enhancement of academic standards. Otherwise, JNU would not have been in the list of the global ranking of universities or institutions of higher learning.

Some people claim that the reservations lower the academic standards. JNU is the answer for them. More than forty per cent of its students belonged to reserved categories, if scheduled castes, scheduled tribes and other backward classes are taken together. With such a high number of resereved category students, JNU should have become worse in academic standards. However, it did not happen. The standard of education is neither lowered nor has JNU collapsed. On the other hand, it achieved academic excellence, enriched and sustained the same. Therefore, the success of JNU is evidence to show that the reservations were not detrimental to quality or standard of education. Instead, the socio-economic backgrounds of reserved category students enrich education and contribute to achieve academic exellence. JNU provides an opportunity and the right climate on the campus. Other institutions of higher learning particularly, central universities and minority institutions may wish to have a close look at diversity on campus and the success story of JNU.

Role of UGC

The central government issues instructions from time to time for implementing the Reservation Policy for SCs and STs. UGC being an autonomous statutory organization is under directions from the government to strictly implement the said instructions by all grant-in-aid institutions. Accordingly, the UGC has been directing all the Universities, Deemed to be Universities, colleges, and other grant-in-aid or research institutions and centres to adopt the Reservation Policy of the Government of India and also writing and reminding from time to time to implement the same effectively.

Probably for the first time, the UGC wrote to all the Universities [Letter No. F.1-159/72(CD) dated January 1, 1973] inviting their attention to the Government of India, Ministry of Education letter No. F.4-65/71-U.2 dated October 11, 1971 regarding the reservation in admission for Scheduled Castes and Scheduled Tribes and informing therein that twenty per cent seats were reserved for them and also given a concession of five per cent marks in the minimum percentage of marks required for admission to any course. In addition, as the twenty per cent seats earmarked for them were found to remain unfilled, institutes were asked for further relaxation in the marks to them, 'in order of merit inter-se amongst themselves so that all the reserved seats are filled by the candidates belonging to these categories'. It was evident from the correspondence [for example, letter No. F.1-35/77(CP) dated November 13, 1978] that UGC had pursued this matter of reservations in admission, with the universities from the year 1973 onwards. No instructions from UGC to the universities could be seen before the year 1973. If it were true, then it appears that for 20 years from the establishment of UGC (1953), the reservations for SC and ST in admissions were not followed by the central universities.

In 1982, the position in respect of reservations in admissions and appointment for Scheduled Castes and Scheduled Tribes was reviewed by the Ministry of Education in the context of their percentages in population of the country, and was decided to provide reservation to the extent of fifteen per cent for SCs and 7.5 per cent for STs in admission to various courses of studies and appointments [Letter No. F. 6-4/82(SCT) dated August 23, 1982]. The UGC went on reminding and requesting the universities [for example, D.O. letter No. F.1-2/89 (SCT) of June 1989] about complete fulfilment of reservations for SCs and STs in admissions. Meanwhile, in order to ensure the effective implementation of the reservations in every faculty/departments of each university/college in the country, detailed guidelines were prepared by the UGC and issued to all the Vice-Chancellors including those of Central Universities vide D.O. Letter No. F.1-6/89(SCT) dated July 30, 1989. Besides, a clarification regarding inter-transferability of seats among SCs and STs had also been issued vide D.O. Letter No. F.1-6/89(SCT) dated March 18, 1972 and Letter No. F.1-4/97(SCT) dated December 12, 1998.

The above mentioned guidelines were for implementation from academic year 1989-90 onwards [D.O. Letter No. F. 1-6/89(SCT) dated July 30, 1989]. These guidelines provided detailed procedures to be followed by the universities. Among many things in these guidelines, the Vice-Chancellor, as the head of the university family, was supposed to take full responsibility for ensuring the implementation of reservations in admission. For fulfilling his responsibility the Vice-Chancellor was asked to make any internal arrangement as he deemed fit. The Universities were directed to set up an Advisory Committee under the Chairmanship of the Vice-Chancellor to assist the matters related to reservation as well as other educational programmes for SC and ST students.

The Universities were required to furnish a complete and comprehensive report and statistical data indicating representation of SC and ST students in admission, scholarships and fellowships [D.O. No. F.8-1/95 (SCT) August 1, 1995] with a copy to Special Commissioner for Scheduled Castes and Scheduled Tribes. The

UGC asked for such information from time to time to monitor the pace of implementation of the reservation policy. However, it was observed that in spite of efforts made by the UGC, the enrolment of the SC and ST students is much below the desired level. Out of deep concern, the UGC wrote to all the Vice-Chancellors that UGC would be grateful, if the Vice-Chancellor could kindly look into the matter personally and ensure that the Government of India and UGC guidelines in respect of reservation policy were followed scrupulously and a compliance report with full data in prescribed performa be sent to the Commission [Letter No. F.1-10/2005 (SCT) dated May 28, 2005]. The message from UGC to universities was loud and clear.

UGC introduced the scheme to establish the SC/ST cells in universities to ensure effective implementation and monitoring the reservation policy for SCs and STs (Kale, 2005). Most importantly, at the UGC level there has been the Standing Committee on SC/ST to oversee the implementation of reservation in the university sector. There has also been the Monitoring Committee to discuss the problems in implementing the policy. Through the region-wise meetings/workshops the committee reviews the functioning of SC/ST cells, interacts with the universities to understand the problems faced by them and suggests remedies. Thus, the UGC has been keeping a close watch on implementation of the reservation policy in the universities and also taking all possible measures to ensure the same.

In case of SC and ST students the need of the hostel is imperative, specially, on account of unfortunate traditional conservative social attitudes. It is difficult for students from these communities to get private accommodation. Even if available, most of them would not be in a position to hire the same because of their poor background. Perhaps, keeping this in mind, the UGC decided to reserve twenty per cent seats for SC and ST students in Hostels [Letter No. F.1-86/76(CP) dated April 18, 1977] and subsequently the same was reviewed and enhanced to 22.5 per cent (fifteen per cent for SC and 7.5 per cent for ST) [Letter No. F.6-4/82(SCT) dated August 23, 1982]. As a follow up action, UGC had been writing to the universities with request to ensure the seats for SC and ST students in the Hostels [For example, see Letter No. F. 6-22/82(SCT) dated November 29, 1982 and D.O. Letter No. F. 1-7/90(SCT) dated December 4, 1990]. Further, the UGC also clarified that the unfilled seats in the hostels should be allotted only to the candidates belonging to SC or ST, by adopting the principle of interchangeability between these two categories [Letter No. F. 1-7/90(SCT) dated July 1993].

The UGC at its meeting held on October 26, 1988 considered the recommendations/suggestions of the Committee on Prevention of Atrocities on Scheduled Castes and Scheduled Tribes consisting of SC/ST Members of Parliament constituted under the direction of the Prime Minister and decided among other things, that the hostel rent may not be charged from the students belonging to SC and ST communities and can be adjusted against the grants paid by the respective agencies [D.O. No. F.1-3/89 (SCT), June 5, 1991]. These measures taken by the UGC were expected to enhance the enrolment of SC and ST students in the Central Universities. However that did not happen.

In between, the Central Government, Ministry of Human Resource Development (Department of Secondary & Higher Education) reviewed the implementation of the reservation policy in the matters of admissions as well as recruitment to the teaching and non-teaching posts in the universities and grantee institutions which are deemed to be Universities, in the light of Article 46 of the Constitution and seemed to be quite unhappy about the situation. It was quite clear from the O.O. No. F.6-30/2005 U-5 dated December 6, 2005, that the UGC was held responsible for the failure and was directed to 'ensure effective implementation of the reservation policy in the universities'.

Probably, with this backdrop, UGC with the help of the Standing Committee on SC/ST reviewed and examined the existing guidelines and circulars issued from time to time and prepared fresh 'guidelines for strict implementation of Reservation Policy of the Government in universities, colleges and other Grant-in-aid Institutions' and Centres [Letter No. F.1-5/2006(SCT) dated August 25, 2006]. From now onwards, the UGC is likely to take action against the Universities which may fail in effective implementation of the Reservation Policy. Considering the past experience, it would be interesting to see whether UGC could take action against defaulters! Let us wait and watch.

Conclusions

Enrolment of SC and ST students in central universities is quite low compared to their share in population as well as compared to national level enrolment in higher education. Presence of SC students in UG and PG programmes of studies is satisfactory in a few universities like JNU, Hyderabad, Pondicherry, Vishwa Bharati and BBA Universities. The Universities other than the above need to make some efforts to attract more SC students. Surprisingly, in six Central Universities not even a single SC student has been registered in the PhD programme. There are three other universities with less than two per cent SC students in the PhD programme. These facts indicate that about nine central universities are practically out of bound for SC research scholars. From the remaining, mainly five central universities have been protecting the interest of SC students and encouraging them to join the PhD programme, as it is evident from their enrolment of more than twelve per cent. These disparities in terms of low enrolment in the PhD programme make it clear that some universities either do not follow the reservation policy in admissions or implement the same detrimentally. It may be mentioned that the enrolment of SC students is relatively high at both PG and PhD level and very close to the prescribed fifteen per cent reservation in JNU, Hyderabad, Pondicherry and BBA Universities. In case of other universities such as Jamia Millia Islamia, BHU, enrolment is somewhat better at PG level but quite poor at the PhD programme of study. Unexpectedly, the presence of SC students at PG as well as PhD level has been relatively low in the University of Delhi.

On an average enrolment of ST students is 4.83 per cent in the Central Universities which is quite low. However, at the PG level it is 11.22 per cent which might be due to the high enrolment of ST students in Mizoram, Nagaland, North-East Hills and Manipur Universities. In ten Universities other than JNU, Hyderabad University and Jamia Millia Islamia there are just four per cent or even less ST students in PG courses. Like JNU (8.48 per cent) and Jamia Millia Islamia (6.13 per cent), Delhi University is in the capital of Delhi, but has only 3.43 per cent ST students on its role for the PG programme. With the exception of Mizoram and Nagaland Universities the situation with regard to registration of ST students in the PhD programme is quite unsatisfactory. Although Manipur University and NEHU are located in the North-East region, enrolment of ST students for the PhD programme is unexpectedly low. Surprisingly, NEHU with more than eighty-three per cent ST students in PG courses, has just around four per cent in the PhD programme. Almost the same case applies to Jamia Millia Islamia and the University of Hyderabad. The enrolment of ST students in PG programmes is relatively better in the two Universities mentioned but poor in the PhD programmes. JNU is perhaps the only University where the representation of ST students is satisfactory both in the PG and PhD programmes. Unbelievably, at least in three central universities no ST student is registered for PhD and in the other six universities they are only one per cent or less.

Even with the special provision of fifty per cent reservation for SC and ST in four universities and thirty-three per cent in another one, there is a high deficit of SC and ST students concerned in central universities which come under the control of UGC and MHRD. With an exception of one or two, it could be inferred that the central universities have failed to implement the reservation policy for SC/ST effectively in admissions.

Article 30(1) of the Constitution immunizes the Minority Institutions against reservation policy for SC/ST. However, it is evident from the report on St. Stephens' College (appeared in the *Hindustan Times* dated June 8, 2007) that the social responsibilities and social realities are influencing slowly the change in the mindset of minority institutions. It is a positive sign and would help in evaporating the perception that constitutional provisions meant to safeguard the interest of minorities is used as an instrument for the oppression of SC and ST communities. In the fast changing world, there is urgent need to help each other and grow together and flourish. This possibility could be realized by enhancing the diversity on educational campuses including minority institutions.

Unlike in recruitments, the UGC appeared to be relatively more proactive and made some efforts and pursued the Central Universities for 'effective implementation of the Reservation Policy for SC/ST in admission'. However, the low enrolment suggested that many Central Universities were not keen to safeguard the interest of SC and ST communities. The UGC seemed to remain passive and did not take action against the defaulter universities. From the time of inception, the primary beneficiary of education has been a small section of the society. With some degree of variation, the same trend seemed to be continued.

REFERENCES

Jawaharlal Nehru University. *Annual Reports* for the year 2002-03 to 2005-06.

Kale, R.K. (2005). Special Schemes of UGC for Empowerment of SC/ST, *University News*, A Weekly Journal of Higher Education, Association of Indian Universities, New Delhi, Vol. 43, No. 47, pp. 45-54.

Kale, R.K. (2006a). Reservation for SC and ST in Central Universities: Is it a Failure of Will or Efforts? *University News*, A Weekly Journal of Higher Education, Association of Indian Universities, Vol. 44, No. 48, pp. 92-105.

Kale, R.K. (2006b). Implementation of Reservation Policy for SC/ST in the Colleges affiliated to the University of Delhi, *University News*, A Weekly Journal of Higher Education, Association of Indian Universities, Vol. 44, No. 4, pp. 1-10.

Mukherjee, Anuradha (2007). Stephen's May Yield Finally; Plans SC/ST Quota, *Hindustan Times*, Friday, June 8, New Delhi.

National Policy on Education (1968). Ministry of Education, Government of India, New Delhi.

National Policy on Education (1986). Ministry of Education, Government of India, New Delhi.

National Policy on Education (with modifications undertaken in 1992). Department of Education, Ministry of Human Resource Development, Government of India, New Delhi.

Programme of Action (1986). Department of Education, Ministry of Human Resource Development, Government of India, New Delhi.

Rao, S. Srinivasa (2002). Equality in Higher Education: The Imparting Affirmative Action Policies in India. In: *Higher Education in Diverse Democracies*, Beckhman, Edgar (ed.), Association of American Universities and Colleges, Washington DC, pp. 41-46.

Report of National Knowledge Commission (2006). Government of India, New Delhi.

Report of the CABE Committee on Education Policy (1992). Ministry of Human Resource Development, Government of India, New Delhi.

Report of the Committee of Review of National Policy on Education 1986, Department of Education, Ministry of Human Resource Development,

Government of India, New Delhi, 1990.

Report on Social, Economic and Educational Status of the Muslim Community of India (2006). Cabinet Secretariat, Government of India.

Report of National Knowledge Commission (2006). Government of India, New Delhi.

Srivastava, Ravi (2007). Meeting Social Goals or Neoliberal Reform, *Economic and Political Weekly*, March 10, 2007, pp. 812-815.

University Development in India: Basic Facts and Figures (2002). University Grants Commission, New Delhi.

7

Diversity on Campuses: JNU Shows the Way

On March 9, 2005, the Prime Minister of India had constituted the committee, under the chairmanship of Justice Rajindir Sachar, to find out the social and economic conditions as well as status of education of the Muslim community of the country. Among other things, this high level committee, known as the Sachar Committee, has examined whether the Muslims, in India, have had an equal opportunity to harvest the benefit of development, and compared their conditions with different socio-religious sections of the society. In the report, submitted on November 17, 2006, the Committee has strongly suggested the framing of policies to mitigate their relative deprivation as part of inclusive development and bring the community into the mainstream of society. The Sachar Committee has accorded a high degree of importance to the diversity and suggested to achieve the same at all places of living and working as well as academic institutes even those run by the minority communities. Further, it suggested to develop a mechanism for providing the equity and equal opportunity to make our society inclusive; and implement in such a way that the diversity could be achieved and discrimination could be eliminated at the same time.

Since, the significance of education as an instrument of social change and economic progress has been well recognized and accepted, it should be made accessible to everyone. However, differential and undemocratic spread of education remained beneficial to the few socially select and economically elite, while being detrimental to the interests of the rest. The Sachar Committee Report that provided information on the pathetic educational condition of the Muslim community might be the result of the same. Further, therein, a high per cent of 'deficit' in higher education has been reported for the Muslim community. As part of the corrective measures for welfare, the Sachar Committee has made several recommmendations. In addution, the committee has suggested that the UGC should take measures and make a provision to link the providing of funds to colleges and universities to the diversity of students' population. This provision should be extended to the academic institutes and colleges, affiliated to the universities or recognized by the government bodies, including those established and run by the minority communities, and given additional grants proportionally to their degree of diversity among the students' population. The UGC has been advised to be proactive and take measures to sensitize colleges, universities and other academic institutes and make them understand the significance of diversity on their campuses. In course of time, for the Muslim community the space on academic campuses has shrunk. According to the report, various measures are required to be undertaken for promoting diversity, so that all sections of the society including deprived groups based on caste, race, gender, religion, disability, and regional variations get their due share in higher education.

It must be noted that no formal mechanism is currently available to enhance the diversity on the campuses. Further, the Sachar Committee is not in favour of the measures such as, the reservation or the quota system for minorities to achieve diversity in student population in the colleges and universities. In such a situation, it is necessary to look around and learn from the experiences of some of the institutions of higher learning like JNU, which has made some efforts in this direction. Perhaps, JNU is the only institution of higher learning which could considerably overcome the social exclusiveness usually observed in the Indian education system, and achieve diversity and sustain the same on its campus. Therefore, initiatives taken by JNU to enhance diversity on campus are examined and discussed below. The experience of JNU may be useful to other colleges and universities and help them to develop an affirmative policy and also to implement the reservations effectively, which in turn may contribute to the enhancement of diversity on their campuses.

Establishment of JNU

The JNU was established in 1966 by the act of Parliament [Jawaharlal Nehru University Act 1966, (53 of 1966)]. On the occasion of celebration of the birthday of Jawaharlal Nehru, the university was formally inaugurated on November 14, 1969, with the objectives embodied in the Article 4 of the Act 1966: 'to disseminate and advance knowledge, wisdom and understanding through teaching and research and by the example and influence of its corporate life and in particular the objects set out in the First Schedule'. This university is an academic monument established in recognition of the contribution made by Jawaharlal Nehru in the freedom struggle in the British period and building the nation as the first Prime Minister of independent India. It is evident from the First Schedule of the Act of 1966, which states that: 'the university shall endeavour to promote the study of the principles for which Jawaharlal Nehru worked during his lifetime, namely, national integration, social justice, secularism, a democratic way of life, international understanding and scientific approach to the problems of society'.

This First Schedule of the Act 1966 also entrusted the university with various tasks including, (i) fostering the 'composite culture of India', (ii) undertaking 'special measures to facilitate students and teachers from all over India to join the University' and (iii)' promoting 'in students and teachers an awareness and understanding of the social needs of the country and prepare them for fulfilling such needs'. Thus, the objectives of JNU have an inbuilt mandate to make its campus diverse and respect the same.

For the translation of mandate into reality, JNU always strives to make policies and implement the same effectively and meaningfully as well as to introduce academic programmes which could enrich and make a qualitative and distinct addition to the human resources of the country, and in turn contribute to the nation building. The university carefully avoids mere quantitative expansion of academic activities and facilities. Importantly, JNU provides quality education with equity and equal opportunity. JNU focuses on academic programmes that are of relevance in the life of students as well as for social and economic progress of the nation.

JNU was planned essentially for postgraduate teaching and

research. Presently, it is broadly structured into ten schools. Out of these, three schools have Centres, totalling thirty-seven in number. In addition to these, there are three functionally independent Special Centres. Apart from these, JNU has recognized various prestigious Defence Institutions as well as Research and Development Institutions across the country which also reflects the true national character of the University.

JNU offers PhD, MPhil, MTech and MPH (Master of Public Health) programmes in more than sixty disciplines, MSc/MCA programmes in five science disciplines, MA programmes in twenty-three disciplines. It also offers undergraduate programmes in nine foreign languages and Advanced (PG) diploma in Bioinformatics. In addition, Certificate, Diploma, and Advanced Diploma Courses are available in languages.

JNU has maintained high standards of teaching and research, updated and revised the curriculum on a regular basis, introduced new courses and academic programmes to suit the needs of time. Unlike, many other institutes, the teaching and research go together in JNU and gives opportunities to students to participate as well as learn the process of creation of knowledge and its dissemination. There is no gap between students and teachers, and as an effect their close interactions are immensely beneficial to the latter. Enough space is available for debate, discussion, dissent and creativity.

Apart from this, the talented pool of faculty members, from all parts of the country, is the main asset of the university. Their scholarly approach to teaching makes students to think, and shape their minds for scientific scrutiny, logical questioning and critical analysis, which gives enough strength to their wings to fly high and succeed. The teachers themselves are very active in research and most of them have made original contributions to their respective academic fields. It is evident from their combined effort that during the academic year 2005-06, around a hundred books, 253 books' chapters, 518 research papers and articles in reputed journals, 906 participations in conferences, seminars, symposiums and workshops, and 518 lectures delivered outside JNU and 239 research projects concluded. The teachers organize national and international seminars, conferences, symposiums and workshops.

The campus is full of such activities throughout the year. The teachers play a major role in governance of the university.

The scholarly output and other academic activities of faculty members of JNU, is continued. During 2014-15, the faculty published 133 books, 303 chapters in books, 943 research papers in journals, 1,786 participation in conferences and seminars, 974 lectures deliverd outside JNU and 450 research projects. Compared to 2005-06, the faculty output and their academic activities have increased. During 2013-14, JNU awarded 404 PhD and 603 MPhil degrees. It means, JNU produces one PhD and two MPhil students every day. It has contributed significantly to the generation of knowledge and its dissipation. It has also created a talented pool of educated people, and in turn an asset for the nation. JNU alumni, spread all over the the country and world, serve India in their own ways.

Admission Policy

Keeping in mind the goals set for the University, the founding faculty members have prepared the admission policy, which could ensure to identify the talent and potential to execel and achieve the highest academic goals. On admission, such studends could be groomed into a national asset, which would contribute to nation building in various ways and capacities. JNU is proactive in implementing the reservation policy and attracts a large number of students from unprivileged sections of society. In addition to reservation policy, the university has developed its own affirmative action and created an opportunity in admissions for students form backward regions of the country.

Through a Unique Admission Policy, JNU attracts students from all over the country (presently from thirty-five states/union territories) representating every section of society. It is quite evident from the admission profile of the students for the last five years from 2002-07 (Table 1) that shows social, economic, religious, spatial and linguistiy diversity, and in turn makes JNU a mini India and enriches its unique composite culture.

Table 1. Diverse Background and Regional Profile of JNU Students in Last Five Years (2002-07) Admissions

Students' Group	*Average of the Last Five Years (%)*
Scheduled Castes	14.89
Scheduled Tribes	08.84
Other Backward Classes	>21.0
Minorities	>10.0
Differently-abled	02.79
Men	65.86
Women	34.14
Rural Background	35.87
Urban Background	64.12
Public School Background	27.21
Other School Background	72.77
Income below Rs. 3,000 p.m.	21.37
Income Rs. 3,000 to 6,000 p.m.	21.84
Income above Rs. 6,000 p.m.	56.77

Compiled by the Author from the JNU Annual Reports

Entrance Test at Doorstep

JNU conducts an all India entrance test every year at more than seventy centres all over the country, for admission to its various academic programmes, including in two SARC nations. JNU is perhaps the only university which goes to the doorsteps of the candidates so as to enable them to appear for the entrance test. Due to this, JNU becomes easily accessible to students from every part of the counry, particularly for those who are from rural and remote places as well as from poor and underprivileged backgrounds.

Since, the JNU is keen to get good students from different parts of the country, all the outstation students who cleared the Entrance Test for various MPhil/PhD programmes and called for *viva-voce* are paid travel allowance. The purpose of the *viva-voce* examination is to ascertain the potential of candidates to undertake research and to generate new knowledge or contribute further to its advancement. For the MA, MSc and MCA programmes of study, there is no *viva-voce* examination. The admissions are granted for these programmes on the results of a written test. This JNU entrance test is a long exercise, almost every teacher participates in some or other way.

It may be mentioned here that the number of admission seekers both at the national and international level to JNU has been steadily growing. In the year 2005-06, around one lakh students had applied for admission, out of which around 1,400 could secure admission.

Affirmative Action for Social Justice

The social order (or disorder?) did not allow education to be democratized in the country. An uneven spread of education empowered and enabled an elite section of society and members of upper castes, although small in numbers, to occupy almost all available space, posts and positions, and in turn control the national resources and institutions as if they were their own property. On the other hand, for the remaining majority of people non-accessibility to education pushed them back, adversely affecting their development, progress, and prosperity. Since differential diffusion of education was governed by the caste system, most of the *Shudra* and *Ati-Shudra* (also referred to as *Panchamas*) castes, remained socially and economically backward. Even after achieving independence, in our country, no special measures were taken for the education of Shudra castes now called OBCs, particularly in matters of admissions to various institutions, colleges, and universities which were either directly or indirectly under the control of the central government. However, JNU has taken the initiative on its own as part of securing social justice, and devised an affirmative admission policy to encourage the students belonging to the OBC (Other Backward Classes) communities to seek admission*. According to this policy:

> OBC candidates [excluding creamy layer as mentioned in column 3 of the Schedule to the Government of India, Department of Personnel & Training, O.M. No. 36012/22-93 Estt.(SCT) dated September 8, 1993], as per the lists drawn by the Government of India, and excluding Income Tax Payers, are awarded ten deprivation points to women candidates and five deprivation points to men candidates.

Like social disparity, inequality in education is clearly visible

* 27% reservation in admission is provided to OBC in the year 2006.

between the urban and rural India. To a great extent, there is lack of access, equity, equality and quality in education imparted to the students from the rural part of the country. Such regional imbalance may have serious consequences and efforts are therefore needed to be made to bridge the regional divide. JNU is probably at the forefront to address this particular concern and took necessary measures to bridge the educational gap. For this purpose, JNU undertook an extensive exercise to characterize and categorize all the districts of the country and grouped them state-wise (placed in different Quartiles) according to their backwardness. On this basis, five and three deprivation points for Quartile-1 district and Quartile-2 respectively are awarded to all candidates (including the OBCs).

There is little scope here to either elaborate the method/ procedure used in determining the regional backwardness of the districts or for placing them in different Quartiles. Information is available in this regard in the prospectus of the university published every year and other sources in public domain. For the benefit and information of readers, some part is reproduced below. In brief, the lists of districts were prepared from every state and grouped as Quartiles-1 and 2 on the basis of mainly following three criteria:

(i) 'Literates as percentage of total population (excluding child population in the age group 0-6 years) as per the provisional figures of the Census of India 2001'.
(ii) 'Non-agricultural workers (main and marginal) as percentage of total (main+marginal) workers (as per the provisional figures of the Census of India 2001)', and
(iii) 'Agricultural productivity per hectare (averaged over 1997-98 and 1998-99)'.

It is understood that characterization and categorization of all the districts of India was done by Professor G.S. Bhalla in his pioneering research work which JNU adapted to give weightage to students coming from backward districts.

Many students are being benefited from the Affirmative Policy of JNU. For example, around twenty-one per cent students belonging to the OBC category are admitted to various programmes of study every year (Table 1). If the OBC students from the creamy layer are included, their overall percentage could be higher. The rural-urban composition of the students' population in JNU could also be seen in Table 1. Almost thirty-six per cent students with a rural background join the university per year. Although slow, the number of students taking admission with a rural background is increasing. It is evident that 34.33 and 38.14 per cent of students who took admission in the year 2002-03 and 2006-07 respectively were from rural areas. The data of the last five years (2002-2007) is indicated that the rate of increase in enrolment of students from rural parts of India, was more than one per cent.

As mentioned earlier, presently, students from twenty-eight States and seven Union Territories are on the campus. It is important to note that the candidates who passed their qualifying examination in various programmes of studies last year are from more than 130 Indian universities/institutions/boards. Another interesting feature of the students on JNU campus is that only twenty-seven per cent students had their Public School academic background and seventy-three per cent students came from Municipal and non-public schools (Table 1).

Although, no mechanism is available to keep count of all the social groups like minorities, however, a rough estimate is suggestive of the presence of more than ten per cent Muslim students on the campus. If the students belonging to other minority groups like the Christians, Sikhs, etc. are included, the number of minority students on the campus is likely to increase (Table 1).

Although higher education is expanding, at the same time, it is being converted into a profit-making business by private players. On the other hand, with a few exceptions, the quality of education is deteriorating in institutions, colleges, and universities which are in the public domain. In such situations the poorer sections of society are doubly disadvantaged. They have no money to get a good education and therefore are forced to send their wards to the low grade institutions and colleges which makes economically poor students educationally disabled. The students equipped with low quality education are nothing but national wastage. To get maximum social returns, it is necessary to provide access to quality education to such poor students. The share of economically poor students in population is significantly high. With this backdrop, it is important to note that a large number of students from the families with relatively low incomes have been joining JNU (Table 1). It can be seen that 21.37 and 21.84 per cent students come from the families whose incomes are less than Rs 3,000 and between Rs 3,000 and 6,000 per month respectively.

The significance of educational needs of women has now been well recognized, as the spread of education especially higher education among them is crucial in the development of the nation. Perhaps in pursuance of the same, women students have been encouraged to join JNU by awarding them 5 deprivation points more than the male students. Presently these deprivation points are given to girls belonging to the OBC category. This benefit is likely to be extended to all women candidates from the following academic year onwards. As a result of the award of deprivation points, the enrolment of women students has been gradually increasing every year. It is evident from the enhancement from 31.15 to 38.34 per cent in admission of women students in the academic year 2001-02 and 2006-07 respectively. The net increase of women candidates within five years is seven per cent. An average break-up of women and men students admitted the JNU for the last five years (from 2002-03 to 2006-07) is 34.14 and 65.86 per cent respectively (Table 1).

Owing to unfortunate circumstances the people in large numbers had to migrate from the Kashmir region. They had been living with the feeling of being refugees in their own country. In this hour of suffering, these uprooted people need to be cared for. Accordingly, efforts are being made to extend all possible help at different levels. JNU has also joined the nation in its own way and made some provisions for them on its campus. As far as admissions are concerned, all Kashmiri migrants are awarded five deprivation points.

JNU has close links with the Defence Ministry through the recognition or accreditation that it granted to its various prestigious institutions and also in the process contributing indirectly to national security. It has always shown respect for the sacrifices made by the defence personnel during the times of external aggression and internal disorders including natural calamities. It is reflected in some of the measures taken by the University. For example, wards or widows of defence personnel are given five deprivation points as mentioned below:

a. 'Widows/Wards of defence personnel killed in action.
b. 'Wards of serving personnel and ex-servicemen disabled in action.
c. 'Widows/Wards of defence personnel who died in peace time with death attributable to military service; and
d. 'Wards of defence personnel disabled in peace time with disability attributable to military service'.

Reservation in Admissions for SC and ST Students

JNU has been making concerted efforts for effective implementation of the reservation policy of the Government of India in admissions. Twenty and a half per cent reservation is provided to SC and ST students (15 and 7.5 per cent for SC and ST respectively) in each programme of study. Further, all the SC and ST students 'who have passed the qualifying examination are eligible to apply for admission irrespective of their percentage of marks'.

Strict observance of the reservation policy of the Government of India enabled JNU to attract SC and ST students in large numbers every year. It is evident from Table 1, which shows the social profile of JNU students in respect of the last five academic years (2002-2007) with regard to admissions. On an average, 14.89 per cent SC students and 8.84 per cent ST students are admitted to the University. It may be mentioned that in the academic year 1991-92, 8.96 per cent of SC students and 5.50 per cent of ST candidates were given admissions to different academic programmes. This intake was lower than their prescribed quota. However, thereafter, the intake of the SC and ST students increased gradually and came close to the prescribed share for them in the year 1999-2000. Then from the academic year 2000-01 onwards, the intake of the SC and ST students slightly exceeded even the quota limit. It is quite clear that JNU is perhaps the only Central University which protects the interests of the SC and ST students in admission at all levels of study. JNU is also the only Central University where the highest number of SC (more than 360) and ST (around 180) students are presently pursuing PhD degree programmes. In terms of total enrolment of students, JNU is one of the smallest universities. Thus, through effective implementation of the reservation policy, JNU achieved success in providing access to quality education to SC and ST students.

Reservation for Physically Challenged Candidates

The persons with Disabilities Act, 1995 provides reservation to disabled persons. JNU has been making efforts to do the same through effective implementation of the reservation policy framed for them. In pursuance of the said Act, three per cent of reservation is provided to the Physically Challenged (now called differently abled persons) students in all the programmes of study. According to JNU rules, the differently-abled candidates, 'who have passed the qualifying examination, are eligible to apply for admission irrespective of their percentage of marks.'

The success achieved by JNU is distinctly visible from the intake of differently- abled candidates. As shown in Table 1, JNU has been admitting around 2.8 per cent students belonging to this category every year for more than five years. It must be noted that just one per cent differently-abled students were admitted to JNU in the academic year 1991-92 and then gradually increased every year. Their presence is almost three per cent in the academic year 2006-07. It is also important that JNU became active quite early to make its campus barrier free, and probably the first university to take up such measures. Thus, JNU was also able to fulfil the statutory obligations through strict implementation of the reservation policy.

Facilities for Field Work

The University facilitates field work abroad by students engaged in research programmes in International Studies, if it is necessary to access the source material for his or her research. Other Schools also encourage their students to go abroad, to participate in international conferences and present their research work, as well as try to send their students to undertake some part of study/research abroad through the exchange programmes. If not all, many students are exposed to international level academic debates and discussions. Such measures are likely to motivate many to perform and excel in academics. Such facilities give international exposure to SC and ST students. Many SC and ST students have undertaken field work and participated in international conferences.

Hostel Facilities on the Campus

On the JNU campus, there is no gap between students and teachers. Being a residential university, 'the academics and accommodation are in close vicinity'. The inmates of hostels come from different parts of the country as well as from abroad. These students with different backgrounds live together like members of a single large family. This togetherness creates the bond of fraternity and good will, enables them to understand the culture of each other and promotes cooperation. Importantly, the hostel life in JNU integrates the nation. At night, after dinner, JNU campus becomes lively. The students organize various functions in the hostels. Apart from cultural programmes and other events, students invite eminent personalities and academicians to give talks on contemporary issues and other burning topics. Students can be seen in open common places discussing among themselves every issue and subject under the sky. Such discussions, interactions and sharing experiences expand their academic and intellectual horizons. It is therefore, sometimes mentioned that students in JNU learn more outside class than inside the class. Another important feature is that celebrations and protest marches are taken out by students mostly at night. Indeed, the hostel life in JNU, to a great extent shapes the personalitry of students. JNU provides accommodation to more than four thousand students in its sixteen hostels. There are more than sixty wardens, four provosts and one associate Dean who assist the Dean of Students to run these hostels smoothly. Student Committees comprised of elected representatives also 'assist the hostel authorities in smooth running of the hostels'.

Information which can be seen in Table 2 has significance from the diversity point of view. Minorities, particularly, Muslims, the SCs and STs are considered to be underprivileged groups of society. There are 12.69 per cent SC, 7.77 per cent ST and 10.43 per cent Muslims students in JNU hostels. It is important that the share of students in hostel occupancy is very close to their respective share in Indian population.

Table 2: Social Composition of Students in JNU Hostels (2006-2007)

Category	*Male*	*Female*	*Total*
SC	416 (09.52%)	136 (03.11%)	552 (12.69%)
ST	209 (04.78%)	131 (02.99%)	340 (07.77%)
Muslims	409 (09.36%)	47 (01.07%)	456 (10.43%)
Others	1822 (41.70%)	1199 (27.44%)	3021 (69.11%)
All	2856 (65.37%)	1513 (34.63%)	4369 (100%)

Compiled by the Author from the information available with the Inter-Hall Administration (IHA), JNU.

Out of 4369 hostellers, girls are thirty-five per cent (1513) and boys sixty-five per cent (2856). However, the representation of girls belonging to SC, ST, and Muslim communities is just 3.11, 2.99, and 1.07 per cent respectively, in student population residing in all hostels (Table 2). The Gender Ratio (Male: Female) in different social groups is shown in Table 3. It is the highest for the Muslims (8:70) and lowest for the ST (1:59), and for the SC (3:06). Out of the total 456 Muslim students girls are just forty-seven. The SC girls (136) are also less when compared to the SC boys (416). Since, the intake of girl students is increasing every year the gender gap might

Table 3. Gender-wise Social Groups of the Inmates in JNU Hostels (2006-07)

Social Group	*Male*	*Female*	*Total*	*Male to Female Ratio*
All categories	2856 (65.37%)	1513 (34.63%)	4369 (100%)	1.88
SC	416 (75.36%)	136 (24.63%)	552 (100%)	3.06
ST	209 (61.47%)	131 (38.53%)	340 (100%)	1.59
Muslims	409 (89.69%)	47 (10.31%)	456 (100%)	8.70
Others	1822 (60.31%)	1199 (39.69%)	3021 (100%)	1.52

Compiled by the Author from the information available with the Inter-Hall Administration (IHA), JNU.

be minimized soon. Gender-wise social composition is shown in Tables 4 and 5. The share of ST girls among the total girls' population in the hostels is 8.66 per cent which is more than the prescribed 7.5 per cent quota for their community. On the other hand, the Muslim girls are only 3.11 per cent, almost three times lower than even the SC (8.99 per cent) girls. The social composition of male students is very close to their respective share in the Indian population. As mentioned above eighty-five per cent students of JNU stay in hostels, and within that the strength of the OBC students is more than twenty-one in the hostel accommodation.

Table 4. Female Students in JNU Hostels (2006-07)

Category	*Female Students*	*Percentage*
SC	136	08.99%
ST	131	08.66%
Muslims	47	03.11%
Others	1199	79.24%
All	1513	100%

Compiled by the Author from the information available with the Inter-Hall Administration (IHA), JNU.

Table 5. Male Students in JNU Hostels (2006-07)

Category	*Male Students*	*Percentage*
SC	416	14.56%
ST	209	07.32%
Muslims	409	14.32%
Others	1822	63.80%
All	2856	100%

Compiled by the Author from the information available with the Inter-Hall Administration (IHA), JNU.

The need for hostel accommodation is imperative for SC and ST students especially on account of the unfortunate traditional and conservative social attitude. It is difficult for students from these communities to get private accommodation. Even if available, most of them are not in a position to hire the same because of their poor economic background (Kale, 2007). Probably keeping this aspect in mind, JNU has made provision to allot hostel accommodation on priority to all the students belonging to SC and ST communities. Moreover, as per UGC guidelines, 'the SC and ST students are exempted from payment of hostel fees (room rent)'. The results of such proactive measures taken by JNU are clearly visible. Almost all SC and ST students are provided hostel accommodation. All differently- abled students, except residents of Delhi, are provided hostel accommodation on priority basis and are also exempted from payment of hostel fees.

Hostel accommodation is one of the major attractions for students to join JNU. A large number of students from every part of the country apply for admission. This number is increasing every year. Importantly, the JNU hostels are not just a place to stay but are also centres for debates and discussions. After dinner, discourses and debates on important issues in hostels make the campus very vibrant and active. In the JNU campus students learn a lot outside their classrooms and seminar halls through the interaction among themselves and with the teachers, whose residences are in the close vicinity of the hostels. As, in the last few years, the infrastructure development is lagging behind the academic expansion, and also the demand for hostel accommodation has gradually increased over the years. The shortage of hostel accommodation has compelled the university to prioritize the allotment as given below. For the benefit and clarity of readers particularly for interested students the same is reproduced from the hostel manual and prospectus of the university:

'*First Priority*: (a) Students admitted to full-time programme of study and who have passed their qualifying examination from places outside Delhi, and are not residents of Delhi except those who are admitted to a programme at a level at which the student already has a degree or has pursued studies in JNU (at the same level) with hostel accommodation; (b) Students who have passed their qualifying examinations from Delhi but have stayed in recognized University/College Hostel and are not residents of Delhi; and (c) Students who have passed their qualifying examination from Delhi-based Institutions by making their own private arrangements for accommodation but at the same time do not have their family residence in Delhi.'

'Second Priority: Outstation students who are admitted to a programme at a level at which the student already has a degree or has pursued studies in JNU (at the same level) with hostel accommodation'.

'Third Priority: V and XI Semester (SLL and CS) MA, V Semester MPhil, IX Semester PhD and local students in that order.'

Thus, students can come to JNU from different places, stay in hostels and pursue their higher studies without much worry, as they are provided hostel accommodation with priority.

Proactiveness of JNU is also reflected in the social composition of Day Scholars (Table 6). Out of 5,134 JNU students, only 765 stay outside the campus which could be due to non-availability of hostel accommodation, residence in Delhi, or as their own choice. It could be seen that just one student each from SC and differently- abled group stays outside the JNU campus and significantly none from the ST category (Table 6). This indicates that because of the proactive nature of JNU policies, all the students those who belonged to disadvantaged sections of society (SC/ST, differently-abled

Table 6. Day Scholars in JNU (2005-07)

Group	*Male*	*Female*	*Total*
General	280 (36.60%)	427 (55.81%)	707 (92.42%)
SC	1 (0.13%)	NIL	1 (0.135)
ST	NIL	NIL	NIL
DA	1 (0.15%)	NIL	1 (0.15%)
Muslims	24 (3.14%)	12 (1.56%)	36 (4.76%)
FN	9 (1.17%)	11 (1.43%)	20 (2.61%)
Total	315 (41.17%)	450 (58.82%)	765 (100%)

Compiled by the Author from the information available with the Inter-Hall Administration (IHA), JNU.

SC: Scheduled Caste; ST: Scheduled Tribe; DA: Differently-abled; FN: Foreign National persons, etc.), get hostel accommodation on priority. Another important observation is that only a few students belonging to the Muslim community stay outside the campus. Out of 456 Muslim students on the role of JNU, thirty-six were Day Scholars. Thus, most of the Muslim students (more than ninety per cent) also get hostel accommodation. Among the Day Scholars (765) the majority belong to general category (707). Since, in this category girls (427) are more than boys (280), it appears that more girls than boys from Delhi state join JNU.

Scholarships, Fellowships and Other Welfare Schemes

Apart from the UGC-CSIR Junior Research Fellowships, JNU awards other scholarships and fellowships in large numbers are available for the needy, deserving, and meritorious students. It also provides free studentships to such groups of students.

JNU has established the 'Student Aid Fund' out of the contributions it received from the students and teaching and non-teaching staff members as well as other sources. From this fund, financial assistance is given to poor and needy students. This assistance might not be a solution to the financial crisis but definitely lessens its burden and likely to be a turning point in the life of some students.

JNU has created the 'G Parthasarathi Endowment Fund for Economically Weaker Sections'. Out of this fund financial assistance is provided to students belonging to socially and economically weaker sections of society.

From the current academic year, the university has enhanced the number and amount of Merit-cum-Means (MCM) scholarship which would cover a large number of students. Indeed, practically there would not be any student on the JNU campus without some or other fellowships and scholarships. As a result, on joining JNU, students would pursue education without becoming a burden on their parents.

Fee Structure

Considering the diversified nature of students who take admission in the university, especially economically poor and socially backward sections, the fee structure of JNU is made affordable.

Indeed, the fee is almost negligible compared to other institutions of higher learning. SC, ST and differently-abled students who appear for the Entrance Test, conducted by the University for admission to various programmes of studies, have to pay fifty per cent of the entrance examination and processing fee as compared to the general category students.

A student has to pay, at the time of admission, on an average Rs. 240 as annual tuition fee and about Rs. 155 on account of other miscellaneous charges (sports, medical, security deposit, I-card, etc.), and even out of this security deposit Rs. forty is refundable. This comes to Rs. twenty per month on account of tuition fees and about Rs. ten on account of other miscellaneous fees. In case some students who are not able to pay the fees, they are provided financial assistance out of the Students' aid fund, as indicated earlier.

JNU has introduced an innovative scheme called 'Earn as You Learn' for the benefit of those who are in need of financial assistance and not getting any fellowship or scholarship from any source. Students are supposed to contribute their free-time in any Office, School or Library, and are paid at the rate of Rs fifty per hour with a maximum limit of Rs 1,500 per month.

Thus, JNU tries to attract students belonging to economically weak and socially backward and unprivileged students on the campus by undertaking several welfare measures.

Equal Opportunity Office

One of the important features of JNU is Pursuit of Excellence with social responsibility. Being sensitive towards 'the needs and constraints of the disadvantaged social groups', it established an Equal Opportunity Office (EOO), 'to oversee the effective implementation of Policies and Programmes for disadvantaged groups and to provide them guidance and counselling with respect to academic, financial, social, and other matters and enhance diversity on the campus.' At present, JNU is perhaps the first and only university which has such an office. The UGC adapted the concept and issued guidelines to establish the EOO in colleges and universities. Among its many functions, EOO makes every effort 'to sensitize the University community regarding the problems associated with social exclusion as well as the aspirations of the marginalized communities'. It helps 'individuals or a group of students belonging to the disadvantaged sections of society to contain the problems related to discrimination.'

Academic Excellence and Diversity

From the aforementioned facts, it is well-established that the degree of diversity achieved by JNU is very high. More importantly, it continued to sustain the same. The representation of students belonging to underprivileged sections of society is very close or equal to their share in the population of the country. It is also clear that achievement of diversity and its sustenance on the JNU campus could be attributed to the strict implementation of the reservation policy of the Government of India for SC, ST, and differently-abled persons, adaptation of the affirmative policy, as well as various measures taken by the University to attract good students from different parts of the country.

Many in our country consider that the reservations and affirmative policies adversely affect the standard of education. Had this been true, then JNU should have been the worst university of the country. On the contrary, it is perhaps the best. In this context, it must be mentioned that JNU is one of the first few universities to receive the recognition of University with Potential of Excellence (UPOE) from the University Grants Commission. Not only that, 'JNU is the only university in India that has found a place in the global ranking of universities or institutions of higher learning.' It must also be noted that, JNU has been climbing the ladder of global ranking. The success story of JNU disproves, without any ambiguity, that reservations and affirmative policy affect the quality of education. Possibly, an enhancement in academic performance and achievements of JNU as well as increase in the degree of diversity in the student population on its campus, for the last several years may not be just coincidence and could be closely interlinked.

It is pertinent to mention that JNU has also achieved diversity to a great extent in appointments of faculty and non-teaching posts. The degree of diversity on its campus, possibly, is the highest compared to other universities. It could be due to strict implementation of reservation policy in recruitments. JNU was able to attract and appoint some candidates who belonged to reserved categories, even against un-reserved posts, because of their merit. The recent recruitment drive has shown that reseved category candidates were equally meritorious, and some cases better than others. Apart from academic excellence, the perception of equality and equal opportunity and academic freedom on its campus, JNU attracts people from different walks of life, and contributes to its diversity.

Conclusion

India is a country of diversity. However, its diversity has intrinsically been exclusive in nature, which did not allow education to spread evenly among the masses. Traditionally, the education has served the interest of few and these same few controlled it making non-accessible to the remaining others. After independence, several measures were taken to expand education and make it accessible to the masses. It is important that the Sachar Committee had recommended education as inclusive in nature in colleges and universities by attracting students from different sections of society. In this context it was quite significant that the founding faculty members of JNU introduced and subsequently evolved the admission policies and academic programmes which ensured an access to education at JNU to all the sections of society. JNU admission policy not only honoured constitutional provisions for underprivileged but also went beyond and incorporated the Affirmative Action for others. JNU has always been sensitive to social realities and remained proactive from its inception, compared to other campuses.

Apart from academic excellence, effective implementation of reservation policies of the Government of India, its own affirmative policy for other social groups, entrance examinations at the doorsteps of students, affordable fee structure and hostel facilities; provisions like establishment of Equal Opportunity Office and other facilities enabled JNU to get students from every part of the nation from different socio-economic backgrounds. As a result, JNU could achieve diversity in its student population on campus.

One of the features of JNU is its pursuit of excellence with social responsibility. Importantly, the JNU experience proves that academic excellence and diversity on campus are not mutually exclusive. Further, the diversity could be achieved by taking up various measures, e.g. affirmative action and strict implementation of the guidelines and directives of the government on reservations for the underprivileged social groups like the SC, ST, OBC and differently-abled persons. Since, the diversity is expected to ensure the uniform spread of education and its democratization, its social returns would be very high which in turn might accelerate the inclusive growth and development of the nation. Keeping this in mind, every institution of higher learning, college, and university should undertake various of initiatives to promote diversity on their campuses. JNU has shown the way. Other universities should follow its example.

REFERENCES

Annual Reports of Jawaharlal Nehru University (2002-2006).

Kale, R.K. (2008). Enrolling or Rolling Out: SC and ST Students in Central Universities, *University News*, A Weekly Journal of Higher Education, Association of Indian Universities, New Delhi, Part I, Vol. 46, No. 21, pp. 9-13 and Part II, Vol. 46, No. 22, pp. 6-10.

Prime Minister's High Level Committee Report on Social, Economic and Educational Status of *the Muslim Community of India* (2006), Cabinet Secretariat, Government of India.

8

Higher Education and Development of the Nation

Introduction

In *India 2020: A Vision for New Millennium*, Dr. A.P.J. Abdul Kalam with Dr. Y.S. Rajan (1998) have discussed the potential of India to be a developed nation and suggested the ways to accomplish the same. According to them, concentrated efforts need to be made in around five identified areas, and as a result those would lead to a major transformation of the nation. Most importantly, they have mentioned our billion people as a resource for the transformation of India into a developed nation. It is pertinent to mention that human capital is known to play an important role in economic growth and development (Gautam and Tripathi, 2004). *The Human Development Report* published in 1990, opened with the statement; 'the real wealth of a nation is its people'. The experience of various countries in the last more than four decades suggested that the mere physical and capital resources alone are not sufficient to make a country developed (Sudha Rao, 2002). The acquisition of material gains and affluence might lead to economic development, but not necessary to social development. On the other hand, it could cause inequalities and distortions in the distribution of wealth (Alam and Jhon, 2004), and widen the gap between the poor and rich.

Importance of human resource and the role of education in development have been well recognized. Therefore, the progress witnessed by the world could be attributed to education and knowledge creation. The transformation from an agriculture society into industrial and subsequently into a knowledge society occurred due to educational advancement. The invention of machines caused the industrial revolution in the past, and technology development with geometric proportion, digitisation and innovation through technological combinations have been contributing to economic development and shaping the world. These events, past and present, have been the result of planned investment in education. The countries with a strong educational base, generated talented and skilled human resource and with support of scientific research developed new technologies and used the same for their own benefit to emerge as a developed nation. Halsey et al. (1961) some years ago have rightly stated that 'the economies of advanced industrial countries/societies were found to depend to an unprecedented extent, on the result of scientific research, on the supply of skilled and responsible manpower and consequently on the efficiency of the education system'. The Task Force on Higher Education and Society appointed by the World Bank and UNESCO in 2000 suggested that without more and better education, developing countries would find it difficult to benefit from the global-knowledge-based economy.

Education, particularly higher education, is known to empower and convert the population into a national asset. If the pool of educated people is large enough, it works as a driving force for growth, progress and development of the country. In this context, progress made by Japan is an exemplary. Japan is one of the small countries with almost no land for cultivation, limited or no natural resources and devastated by the two atomic bombs just two years before our independence. However, Japan overcame several constraints and emerged as a developed nation and became the second highest economy in the world in a relatively short time. We also started building our nation almost at the same time. Even after more than 65 years of independence, India still remained in the developing phase. With relatively abundant natural resources and availability of agricultural land, India should have become developed earlier than Japan. Education is one of the main reasons behind the success of Japan and lack of it for the failure of India. Japan provided education to the masses and in turn generated huge educated and skilled human resource. It is evident from its increased GER for higher education from nine per cent in 1968 to forty-two per cent in the mid-1990s. It invested in higher education particularly in science and technology. On the other hand, India failed to spread education among the masses and also to develop technologies. When Japan achieved forty-two per cent GER in the mid-1990s, our GER for higher education was just seven per cent. We continued with the British style education in its form and function which was confined to a small section of society. As a result, the large population of the country remained uneducated and unskilled. Unlike Japan, India failed to generate enough human resource required to make India developed. Had India expanded the higher education to a greater extent it would have contributed to generation of wealth, prosperity of people, economic growth and development of the country. South Korea succeeded. China planned major changes in higher education in 1997-98 and took over India.

The year 2020 is approaching fast. It is just a few years away. Indeed, we are at its doorsteps. In such a short period, is it possible to succeed? Does the present higher education system have a potential to convert our huge population into national assets? Will we be able to accelerate the growth and development? These and other related concerns are kept in mind, while discussing the higher education and its close link with the development of the nation.

Higher Education in India

At present there are around 247 Universities and 98 Deemed to be Universities, more than 60,000 colleges, 97 lakh students and 4.5 lakh teachers in India in 2004-05*. When India became independent, there were just 19 universities, 500 colleges, 2.28 lakh students and about 25,000 teachers. These figures in Table 1 show that the massive expansion of higher education has taken place after 1947. However, it is not true, as basal numbers are small.

Although, the enrolment of 97 lakh students appears to be quite high, but it accounts only for less than one per cent of the total population of India. In other words, more than 99 per cent population of our country is out of the higher education system. In terms of GER it is around just seven per cent. The large population

* In the year 2011-12, 18.80, 34.80, 47.52 and 42.76 fold increase could be seen in universities, teachers, colleges and students compared to 1950-51.

Table 1. Some Basic Information on Higher Education in India

S. No.		*1947*	*2003-2004*
1.	Universities	18	345
2.	Colleges	500	16000
3.	Students	228804	9463821
4.	Teachers	<0.24 lakh	4.36 lakh
5.	Budget	55 crores	>78000 crores

in the relevant age group either has no access or cannot afford to go in for higher education. Therefore, efforts need to be made to provide access to higher education to as many people as possible. Access to education is essential for the empowerment of people.

Table 2. Number of Universities in Some Leading Countries

S. No.	*Country*	*Population (crores)*	*Universities*
1.	Japan	12.7	684
2.	USA	27.6	2364
3.	UK	5.98	104 (231*)
4.	Germany	8.2	330
5.	India	100	247+98**

*autonomous institutes, ** deemed to be Universities

Table 2 shows the number of universities in some of the leading and important countries along with their population. Japan for its 12.7 crore people has 684 Universities. USA with 27.6 crore population has 2,364 Universities. In UK and Germany, there are 104 Universities (in addition to 231 autonomous institutes) and 330 Universities whose populations are 5.58 and 8.2 crore respectively. However, as mentioned above, for more than 100 crore Indians, we have 345 Universities. It is indicative of the acute shortage of universities in India and the need to establish more to provide access to higher education particularly to people from rural areas. To come close to Japan and USA, roughly six to nine thousand universities need to be established in India. It took nearly 60 years to establish 300 universities. Can we add at least another 300 universities in the next 14 years and enhance the enrolment significantly? It seems to be almost impossible!

The young Indians between the age group of 17 and 26 years

are also large in number. This age group of students is expected to be enrolled in higher education. However, most of them (approximately ninety-three per cent) are out of the higher education system, perhaps due to lack of access to higher education to many. A mere six to seven per cent of the said age group is enrolled for higher education. In countries like Canada, USA and Australia, the students' enrolment of the same corresponding age group is between 80 and 88 per cent. We are even behind Thailand, Brazil and Indonesia where enrolment in higher education is 19, 12 and 11 per cent respectively (Table 3). The main objective of the Tenth Plan of UGC is to raise enrolment in higher education from the present seven to ten per cent by the end of the Plan Period. It will be a great achievement, if we succeed in enhancing the enrolment by three to four per cent by the year 2008.

Table 3. Student Enrolment in Higher Education in Some Selected Countries

S. No.	*Country*	*% Enrollment*
1.	Canada	88
2.	Australia	79.8
3.	USA	80.9
4.	UK	52
5.	Thailand	19
6.	Brazil	12
7.	Indonesia	11
8.	India	6

Education needs to be evolved, diversified and extended in its reach and coverage, as higher education is known to enhance the advancement of technology as well as skill of human resources. The World Bank Document (1994) has also shown a direct correlation between the development of higher education and economic development. Since the spread of higher education in India is quite slow and inadequate, it remained confined to very limited people. In such a situation, the present higher education system cannot be effective to enhance the skill of human resources as well as to develop technology. With an inadequate education system and in turn with limited human resources; it would be difficult to make India developed in such a short period of time.

Dr. D.S. Kothari (1964-66) in his Report had given an importance to education in the development of nation and made several recommendations. We have ignored some of them while implementing. According to him, higher education is essential for any country to achieve sustainable development. As the enrolment in higher education at least twenty per cent is imperative for economic progress of any country (Pundir and Singh, 2004), it is essential for India to expand its higher education system and cover as many eligible young Indians, as possible. The continued efforts need to be made to achieve the same. We should remember that it took almost 60 years to provide higher education to only six to seven per cent of young Indians. Otherwise, our dream to be a developed nation would never be realized and remain a dream.

Funding Higher Education

Although, education is known to be an investment both at the individual and society level, there has been apathy towards higher education in our country. It appeared that higher education has never been the priority of the Government of India. The interdependence of various levels of education was ignored and over emphasis was given to literacy and primary education. The equal importance also should have been given to higher education which is known to contribute immensely to economic growth and development. Probably, 'the development of primary education, at the best elementary education was considered to be enough for the development of India' (Tilak, 2004). This resulted in decline in the flow of funds for higher education. Table 4 shows the financial

Table 4. Financial Support for Indian Higher Education in Terms of GDP

S. No.	*Year*	*Percentage*
1.	1971	1%
2.	1981	0.8%
3.	1991	0.6%
4.	2001	0.4%

Source: Rajeshekar Pillai: Statement in *The Hindu*, Delhi Edition of March 21, 2006

support for Indian higher education in terms of GDP. It continuously decreased from one per cent in 1971 onwards to reach 0.4 per cent in 2001 (Pillai, 2006). As a consequence, Indian higher education has been starved of funds and its magnitude increased with time. Allocation to higher education in the Eighth and Ninth Plans reached all-time bottom levels. We failed to achieve a target of spending six per cent of GNP on education as recommended by the Kothari Commission way back in 1964-66.

Table 5. Funding the Higher Education in Terms of GDP in Some Selected Countries

S. No.	*Country*	*% of GDP*
1.	USA	6.5
2.	France	5.8
3.	Germany	4.6
4.	Thailand	5.0
5.	Kenya	5.2

Countries like USA, France and Germany spent 6.5, 5.8 and 4.6 per cent of GDP respectively on higher education. We are even far behind countries like Thailand and Kenya, who spent five per cent and 6.2 per cent GDP respectively on their higher education (Table 5). It is experienced that whenever, there is a cut in public expenditure on education, it is the quality and more importantly the equity get adversely affected. According to Tilak (2004), we are rapidly marching towards laissez-faireism (minimum state intervention and allowing activities to take their natural course) in higher education in India.

As in the globalized world, the internationalization of higher education is taking place faster than expected, India needs to orient and reform its higher education suitably so as to harvest the gains and exploit the opportunities of globalization. However, the present fund-starved Indian higher education system is neither strong nor widespread. It is unlikely, to help to gain from the globalization and contribute towards making India developed. It may be mentioned that the report of UK's National Committee of Inquiry into Higher Education under Sir Ron Dearing has suggested that the investment into higher education is an investment in the future.

It is therefore necessary that the government should liberally fund, expand and democratize education. Otherwise, making India developed will remain just a dream. It is a matter of some consolation that the government for the first time announced that it would increase the funding on education to six per cent of GDP. Let us hope this encouragement may not be short-lived.

Scientific Research

It is assumed that India with its vast infrastructure in science and technical education has created a niche advantage in the globalized economic environment. It is also assumed that India is poised to develop as the knowledge superpower. However, ground realities seem to be quite different. The details can be seen in the thought-provoking article written by Prof P.N. Srivastava (2005) in which he has diagnosed the sickness of science education and research.

In most of the developed countries, universities are nerve centres of research activities. New discoveries, technologies and innovations have emerged from such centres. However, Indian universities were not made main places of research activities. Instead, the universities were confined mainly to teaching and ignored scientific research. Because of this their contribution to scientific research remained meagre. The teaching of science was detached from research activities. As a result, Indian universities failed to produce the required human resource for scientific research and the technologies which adversely affected the progress of the nation. Our neglect of universities forced the country to buy technologies from other nations.

It is pertinent to mention that while discussing the science education and scientific research in Indian universities, Srivastava (1989, 2005) has always reminded us that 'the value of silicon chip does not lie in the sand from which it comes, but it lies in the microscopic architecture engraved upon it by an ingenious human mind. Although, the most promising super conductors are made from ceramics and new materials, the value does not come from the materials, but from the human imagination that will build the new millennium out of sand and clay'. Therefore, the sound knowledge in basic science as well as its applications is necessary. Such knowledge can be transformed into technology for the development of the nation. With this background, it will be interesting to see the present status of science and scientific research in India.

Table 6. Level-wise Students Enrolment in India for the Year 2001-2002

S. No.	*Level*	*Enrolment*	*% of Grand Total*
1.	Graduate	76,62,588	89
2.	Postgraduate	8,16,335	9
3.	Research	60,516	0.7
4.	Diploma/certificate	81,656	0.9
	Grand Total	88,21,095	

Source: University News: 42 (52), 2004 December-2005 January

The enrolment of students at different levels in India during the year 2001-2002 is given in Table 6. Around 89 per cent students are at the graduate level. Out of these, nearly 80 per cent students drop out and only 9 per cent and 0.7 per cent go to postgraduate studies and research respectively. Unlike other countries, very limited numbers of students go for research as a career. In a country of billion populations, the total enrolment for research is just about 65,000. Further, each year approximately 11,000 research scholars are awarded doctoral degrees in all subjects. The US produces more than 60,000 PhDs per year. Therefore, a pool of active researchers in India is very small, making the country almost handicapped in the generation of new scientific knowledge and its advancement. This reflects from our poor contribution to research publications. In 10 years from 1995 to 2005 a total of 3,08,81,012 research papers

Table 7: Patents Relative Position of India

Country	*No. of Applications*
India	24,505
China	1,73,327
Japan	4,27,000
South Korea	15,70,000
Taiwan	47,841

Ref: DST Report 2007-08

were published in the world. Out of these, India published just 6,89,938. In the 1970s and 80s, when compared, India's contribution to scientific research was more than 8.2 per cent, and that of China 2.3 per cent. However, this situation is now just reversed, and India is lagging behind China. According to the UNCTAD technology and innovation report, in 2007 China published 56,806 research papers and India 18,194. Table 7 shows that in filing the applications for patents, India is also miles behind Asian countries. Countries like China, Japan and South Korea filed application for patents in lakhs. Even Taiwan has filed more (47,841) applications than India (24,505), in 2005-06. Recently, the World Intellectual Property Organization's, Statistics on Patents showed that in 2011 the total number of China's patent applications were 5,26,412, whereas India's were 42,291 only. It could be due to a small pool of scientific researchers in India (Table 8). According to the DST Report of the year 2007-08, on average more than five thousand scientific researchers per million populations are in Europe, USA and Japan. Unbelievably, India has just one hundred and forty. In the same DST Report it has been shown that 3.91 lakh personnels are in the R & D establishment of India. Out of that thirty-three per cent provide administrative support. The fifty-five per cent of the total personnel have postgraduate or above degrees as educational qualifications. Therefore, actual active and creative researchers at both senior and junior level are limited. On the basis of a small pool of human resource and limited R & D, it would not be possible to make the nation developed.

Table 8. Scientific Researcher Per Million Population

Country	*No. of Researchers*
India	140
Finland	7681
Sweden	6139
Singapore	5713
Japan	5546
Denmark	5277
USA	4651

Ref: DST Report 2007-08

Table 9. Faculty-wise Student Enrolment for the Year 2000-2001

S. No.	*Subject*	*%*
1.	Sciences	19.7
2.	Arts	42.7
3.	Commerce (including management)	20.7

Source: UGC Report 2000-2001

The supply line of our scientific research is also choked, which is evident from tne subject-wise enrolment shown in Table 9. Only nineteen per cent students enrolled for the science stream (UGC Report 2000-01). The poor interest among students for science is a matter of concern. In 1980, around 35 per cent students had chosen science. Even in 1950, the enrolment in science was 32 per cent. Within 20-25 years of the period, it decreased almost by 50 per cent. The basic science of today is always considered to be engineering and technology of tomorrow. This declined interest in science would prove to be detrimental to basic education, scientific research and technology development. Many students opt for medical and engineering, but emphasis in both streams is on teaching. On completion of their studies, as mentioned earlier, very few opt for research as a career.

The performance of Indian science during the last 60 years is sliding down. In depth research made by *Nature* (Vol. 308, 1984 and Vol. 366, 1993), a scientific journal of very high repute, has shown the continuing declined trend in academic science. Even in a recent 2004 survey, there is not a single Indian University (not even the Indian Institute of Science, Bangalore) among the top 100 universities of the world. In the list of 500 best Universities and Institutes of higher learning, there are 168 universities from USA, 40 each from Germany and UK and 30 universities from Japan. There are only three from India who are almost at the bottom of the list. The same trend is still continuing. In terms of publications of scientific research in the world, India ranked eighth during the 1980s, slipped to thirteenth during the 1990s and has nose-dived to the 21 position in the new millennium (Srivastava, 2005). According to Virk (2004), the rank of India after introducing a measure of 'quality' had dropped to 119 (Science Citation Index) (Table 10). The number of research papers, cited among the top

Table 10. International Standing of India in Scientific Research

S. No.	Year	Rank
1.	1980	8
2.	1990	13
3.	2000	21
4.	On the basis of citation index	119

one per cent in the world, is 205 from India, 375 from China and 23,723 from USA (Chopra and Suri, 2005). As mentioned earlier, it is known that India in the 1970s and 80s used to contribute 8.2 per cent to the world scientific research, whereas it was 2.3 per cent for China. This trend has changed. India is now contributing around two per cent and China more than eight per cent. China's contribution is increasing every year.

Although, it has been claimed that India is very rich in scientific manpower, we have not produced any significant research which can be considered as an original breakthrough at the international level after 1946 (Krishna, 2001). Our inability to provide 'Health for All till 2000', even after 60 years of independence is an excellent example of our scientific failure. The promises made in the Bhore Committee (1948) and Alma Declaration (1978) are yet to be fulfilled. We are still not able to control most common diseases like TB, malaria and leprosy. These and other diseases keep resurfacing, affecting and killing lakhs of people every year in India (Kale, 2003). Considering these aspects, probably, it would not be wrong to state that in India, science is not progressing, only a few scientists are progressing and fluorishing.

The liberal funding is essential for scientific research. The volume of Indian higher education increased due to a progressive increase in the number of universities and enrolment of students. With the same proportion funding for scientific research was not made available. We kept our universities starving. The universities are considered as fountains of knowledge. We almost capped these fountains, knowingly or unknowingly. In advanced countries, thirty per cent of R&D budget goes to the university system. In the case of India it is six to ten per cent. Sufficient funds are required to establish sound infrastructure and physical facilities. Presently, Indian universities are in a crisis. Inadequate funding has paralyzed the research activities in almost every university, and in turn cutting edge scientific research and technology development.

Technical Education

In the recent past, technical education expanded rapidly. New colleges and institutes teaching engineering and technological courses are being added every year. The vast technical education system gives the impression that India has a large pool of technical professionals. However, the number of technical professionals per thousand in India is 0.3 compared to 7.1 in Japan, 4.0 in USA, 5.9 in Israel and 0.6 in China. The total enrolment in the higher S&T education of the relevant age group is also quite low and it accounts for less than two per cent. On the research front, technical education is also quite weak. In 2002, India produced just 739 PhDs in technology and engineering, mostly from the IITs. These 739 doctorates include 200 PhDs from departments of pure sciences and humanities. The number of S&T PhDs per million populations in India is around four compared with 89 in USA, 75 in Japan and 52 in South Korea. It may be mentioned that the Indian higher education system took almost a 100 years to produce the first PhD in the Technical/Engineering subject, after the establishment of the first three universities (at Bombay, Calcutta and Madras) in 1857.

At present, only a few institutes of technical education are engaged in research. This may be a reason for the small number of patent applications from such institutes. In 2003, CSIR and MNCs in India filed 354 patent applications (which include 169 from CSIR, 50 from IITs and the rest from MNCs) compared to 5,300 from Taiwan and 3,952 from Korea. Refer to Chopra and Suri, (2005) for more details. The total application from India and some other countries for the year 2006 is already mentioned above.

According to the Census 2001, released in June 2005, among the technical graduates, almost 32 per cent were found to be unemployed. The McKinsey Global Institute study about emerging global market is perhaps an eye opener for us. Despite the one-third of million plus engineering graduates we produce every year, MNCs found only 25 per cent employable. Out of these 25 per cent, only six per cent are unsuitable in their own specific disciplines.

The same trend continues todays. With incease in the size of Indian technical education, its quality decreased. The rapid expansion of the system and lack of qualified teachers accelerated the deterioration of technical education (Agrawal, 2005). Because of the poor health of technical education, it failed to contribute scientifically to the development of new technologies.

Table 11. Technologies used in Indian Industry

S. No.	*Foreign/Indigenous*	*Status*	*% in Use*
1.	Foreign	Used without alteration	50
2.	Foreign	Modified and adapted to suit our need	45
3.	Indigenous	-	5

Kulandaiswamy (2005) refers to a conference of scientists designated as 'Science Summit 2000' organized at the initiative of C. Subramaniam, in which Dr. P. Rama Rao, former Secretary, DST, gave the information related to the technologies used in our industry, the share of indigenous and foreign technology. As shown in Table 11, we have developed indigenous technology, which account for just five per cent and the remaining 95 per cent is foreign technology used with or without alterations/modifications. As a result, the contribution of Indian Industries per se has been just 0.7 per cent of world exports. Our industries, un-surprisingly, have not produced a single global brand (Vivek Kumar, 2005, 2006). Unlike in advanced countries, Indian industries did not support scientific and industrial research. Instead of investing in research activities, industries preferred to buy and import technologies. Technical and engineering education is responsible, to some extent, for this poor performance of Indian Industries. Had we supported the research, Indian industries, in return, would have benefited.

Our IITs also failed to develop technologies appropriate to our condition (Mohan, 2004) and could not make the country self-sufficient. The very purpose for which IITs were established has failed to a great extent. Consequently, we did not get the desired social returns from the IITs and other technical institutes. Such a weak and non-performing engineering and technical education cannot support the growth and development.

The UNESCO World Conference on Higher Education in the Twenty-First Century was held from October 5-9, 1998 in Paris. India was one of the participants and presented the country paper entitled, 'Higher Education in India: Vision and Action'. In that paper, the Government of India highlighted the views of Dr. B.R. Ambedkar on education at two places. One of the views is, 'No plan for the future development of the country can be deemed to be complete, which does not provide for technical and scientific training. This is an age of machines and it is only those countries who have risen to the highest pitch, that will survive in the struggle that will commence when the war is over, for maintaining decent standards of living for their people.' Dr. Ambedkar's statement made during the Second World War is still relevant and makes us think about what we should have done after our independence to develop indigenous technology to become self-sufficient. We should have perhaps built a corpus of scientists and technocrats as the Soviet Union, which was of more than two million first class scientists and matched the technological progress of the US despite having a twentieth of its per capita income (Jha, 2006).

It is pertinent to mention again that on April 1, 2005, according to the DST Report (2007-08), 3.91 lakh personnel were in the R&D establishment of our country. As 33 per cent provided administrative support and 55 per cent had postgraduate or above qualifications, the actual number of active and productive scientists must be small.

How can our dream to become developed by 2020 be realized, when we do not have an adequate number of scientific and technical human resourses, quality engineering and technical education and ability to develop technologies?

Green Revolution

Every Indian feels proud of the green revolution as it freed the country from the humiliating imports. Our food grain production increased from 51 million tons in 1951 to 212 million tons in 2003-04. There was a substantial increase in the production of major commercial crops (Table 12). For instance, between 1950-51 and 2003-04 production of sugarcane increased from 57 to 236 million tons, oil seeds from 5.16 to 25.14 million tons and cotton 3.04 to

Table 12. Success of Green Revolution

S. No.	*Production*	*Quantity (Million tons)*	
		1950-51	*2003-04*
1.	Food grain	51	212
3.	Sugar	57	236
4.	Oilseeds	5.16	25.14
5.	Cotton	3.04	13.79

13.7 million lint (Mungekar, 2005). However, the green revolution failed to wipe out the tears of poor and hungry. While about 50 to 60 million tons of food grain stock are in godowns but not accessible to many, about 50 to 60 per cent population lives below the poverty line. The benefits of the green revolution were not shared by the poor section of the society and continued to remain hungry as before. Even the farmers continued to commit suicides, sadly their number is increasing. An unequal distribution of the benefits of the green revolution was mainly due to highly unequal ownership of land and other productive assets in the rural areas.

With poor, hungry and uneducacted population in huge numbers no country in the world has progressed and developed. India first needs to eradicate poverty and hunger, and spread education among the masses, with focus on the most socially backword and unprivileged. Our present approach to development is making rich people richer and poor people poorer. As a consequence, India continued to maintain its status as a rich country of poor people.

Disadvantaged Section of Society

The demography factors indicated that the large population of the country is disadvantaged and marginalized. The disadvantaged section of society consists of SC (16.2 per cent), ST (8.2 per cent), women (48 per cent), minorities (19 per cent) and differently-abled (three per cent), which comes to 94 per cent compared to the total population (Table 13). On including the other backward classes, the effective number of disadvantaged people would be quite high.

Table 13. Population of Disadvantaged Sections

S. No.		*% in total*
1.	Women	48
2.	SC	16.2
3.	ST	8.2
4.	Minorities	19
5.	Differently-abled	3

Source: *Census of India 2011*

It would be difficult to achieve sustainable growth and development in this fast changing technology-driven world without empowering the disadvantaged and marginalized sections. It is necessary to educate and make them a national asset. The country needs a critical mass of educated and skilled people to achieve developmental goals. It would be impossible for the present microscopic population belonging to elite, urban rich and upper castes to take the country on the path of progress and development. Further, the 21st century is a century of knowledge, where there will be an explosion of information. It will be a challenging task to store, retrieve and apply such accumulated information. Further, this century would also witness the development of new technologies with geometrical proportion, unprecedented use of combination of technologies to make new gadgets and machines, and fast disappearance of atoms and molecules due to digitization. Other countries like the US, have already taken the lead and developed new technologies in these areas. India is several decades behind. Minimizing this technological gap itself would be an almost impossible task. However, India cannot afford to remain behind and backward. Therefore, India has no other option but to educate its huge disadvantaged population at the earliest to get the necessary trained human resources as well as technologies. Perhaps, we may learn from the experience of China which increased its GER in a relatively short time. To achieve this, special targeted schemes for disadvantaged sections have to be planned and implemented through which India would get the largest pool of educated and skilled human resources.

Indian society is a rigid cluster of castes. The hierarchical structure and function of the caste system made the untouchables, presently called SCs, social slaves with only duties and no rights. They were pushed to a sub-human status. The caste system did not allow them to have property, occupation (business and trade) and education. They faced intense discrimination and inequalities; and were subjected to all kinds of exploitation for centuries. The condition and sufferings of Scheduled Tribes also were not very different. They were isolated and completely neglected.

Education was historically confined to a small section of society with complete exclusion of SCs and STs (Thorat, 2004). Although the British were not very keen due to customs and traditions of Indian society, they took some initiative to provide them education. Early efforts were made by Mahatma Phule and others for the upliftment of the unprivileged with emphasis on their education. Dr. Ambedkar took the work of Phule forward and remained at the forefront for protecting the interest of the unprivileged. After independence, while framing the constitution, a conscious decision was taken to undo the historical wrongs by providing the reservations in education, services and legislation to SCs and STs. It was important that, formally, education became accessible to SCs and STs in 1950 through constitutional provisions. On the other hand, education became available almost exclusively for the elite and upper castes way back in 1835 when Macaulay wrote the minutes. Thus, there is a gap of more than a hundred years between SCs/STs and others for the accessibility to education.

The reservation policy has helped SCs and STs to a great extent. One estimate indicates that out of seven lakh SCs in the higher educational institutes, most of them are because of reservation. However, the spread of education among the SCs and STs has been very slow compared to other sections of society. Table 14 shows the percentage of SC and ST students in higher education in the 1970s and 1980s. It is quite clear that the rate of increase of their enrolment is just around one per cent. Very few go for post-graduation and research. The data for the 1990s and 2000s was not available (even with the UGC and HRD ministry), the picture for these years may not be very different. Recent enrolment of SCs and STs as well as variation in their enrolment in different sources is already discussed in another section. Although, the enrolment has shown some increase, its wide gap between SCs/STs and others

Table 14. SC/ST Students in Higher Education

S. No.		*1970s*	*1980s*
1.	SC	7.0%	7.8%
2.	ST	1.6%	2.7%

Source: Srinivas Rao, 2002

still persist. Since the social returns from the education of SCs/STs are very high, the slow spread of education among them is expected to be detrimental to their interest and also of the nation.

To spread higher education among SC and ST, their dropout rate, particularly at school level, has to be reduced. There is interdependency in all the levels of education. According to the statistics of the year 2002-03, the dropout rate for the general population for the fifth, eighth and tenth standards is 34.89, 52.79 and 62.59 per cent respectively. In the case of SCs, it is 41.4, 0.93 and 71.92 per cent; and for ST it is 51.37, 68.67 and 80.29 per cent respectively (Mungekar, 2006). The symbiotic relation in terms of interdependency in all the levels of education needs to be maintained for maximizing the social returns.

Table 15. Poverty and its Distribution in India

S. No.	*Population*	*Crores*
1.	Total population	>100
2.	Below poverty line population	26.03
3.	Below poverty line population rural	19.32
4.	Below poverty line population urban	6.72

As shown in Table 15, out of 2,602.50 lakh Indian people who live below the poverty line, SCs constitutes 1932.29 lakh (Janaki, 2005). Since, education can uplift people socially and economically, measures could be taken to provide them access and at the same time implement the schemes to retain them in the education system (Kale, 2005). At present, the post-matric scholarship is the only major scheme for SC and ST students. Even this scheme is inadequate. The amount paid in the form of scholarships is meagre and varies from state to state. The scholarship amount should be determined on the basis of living costs and revised from time to time keeping inflation in mind. More targeted schemes may be introduced. In the changed time the nation cannot ignore SCs and STs which constitutes one-fourth of the Indian population. It is, as mentioned earlier, almost double the population of Japan and close to USA. It is also three times and four times higher than that of Germany and UK respectively. Can we offered to ignore such huge population? Can India become a knowledge society without SCs and STs as well as without involving them in knowledge generation? Can India become a developed nation without educating them?

There is the large population, apart from SCs and STs, which was stigmatized by the British branding as criminal tribes (Criminal Tribe Act 1871) and ignored by its own government after declaring them as Denotified Tribes (DNT) through repealing this draconian act in 1952. These communities, also carrying the past burden of social stigma, humiliation and exploitation, are continued to be isolated from society, even in the post-independent period. Social isolation as a separate category and its detrimental effect on their lives, could be mitigated mainly by providing them easy access to education. This population which has been suffering from the British times, needed some constitutional guarantee for their socio-economic progress. Otherwise this quite large human resource would remain un-utilized for the betterment of the nation.

Because of the socio-cultural mindset, girls/women are not given education, particularly higher education. Under the pretext of traditions and customs, women were denied education for centuries. They were considered to be unequal and subordinate. In independent India steps were taken to create new avenues and opportunities including education. Despite several measures, the enrolment in higher education increased slowly which is evident from their twelve to fifteen per cent GER. The steady increase in the enrolment of women in higher education is sometimes wrongly termed as phenomenal (Table 16). Only six per cent of women reach the level of college education and beyond, due to a heavy drop out from schools. According to a rough estimate the rate of increase of their enrolment in higher education is just 0.6 per cent per year. The educational gap between males and females is still persisting. The gender disparity is known to lead to serious economic and

Table 16. Enrolment of Women in Higher Education

S. No.	*Year*	*Women Enrolled*	*%*
1.	1950	43,126	10.9
2.	1960	1,70,455	16.2
3.	1970	6,55,822	21.9
4.	1996	21,14,511	34.1
5.	1997	25,14,511	36.7
6.	2002-03	36,96,000	40.05

social imbalance, making the nation weak. Renewed efforts need to be made to spread education with greater speed. Education is a premier instrument for promoting equality of status, opportunity and, empowerment which would enable women to participate in the development of the nation.

In India, differently-abled (physically challenged) are around three per cent of the total population. They have their place and significance in the demographic setup of the nation. To ensure the same, the Indian parliament has passed the Act called the Persons with Disabilities (Equal Opportunities, Protection of Right and Full Participation) Act 1995. UGC has issued instructions from time to time to all universities to ensure implementation of the 33 and 39 Section of this Act to empower persons with disabilities. To use the differently-abled as a national asset, we must provide them educational opportunities. Many of them are already serving the society and nation.

The minorities including Muslims (13.4 per cent), Sikhs (1.9 per cent), Christians (2.3 per cent), Buddhists (0.8 per cent), Jains (0.4 per cent) and others (0.6 per cent) collectively constitute around nineteen per cent of the Indian population. The importance of the empowerment of these communities and their possible role in nation building to make it developed has been recognized. This aspect could be discussed separately, as every minority community is not educationally backward. Among these communities, Muslims are economically and educationally more backward. A detailed account of their status and recommendations are available in the Sachar Committee Report. Once they are educated, this large population would become a national asset.

Few to Teach and Many to Learn

Indian universities are afflicted by several problems like inadequate number of teachers and too many students. This observation was made way back in 1984 by *Nature,* one of the most prestigious scientific journals. The situation has further gone from bad to worse (P.N. Srivastava, 2005). National Eligibility Test (NET) has added fuel to the fire (Kale, 2006). Those who want to be teachers in higher education have to pass the NET. The impact of NET is discussed in some detail in the next section.

More than five lakh increase is seen in the enrolment of students every year in the university system of education. Therefore, at least 40 to 50 thousand additional teachers are required every year to teach them. Further, a large number of teachers retire every year. When taken together, India needs more than 65 to 70,000 additional teachers annually. The UGC-NET can identify between two to four thousand eligible candidates with potential to teach in 75 subjects of social sciences for more than 300 universities and 16,000 colleges in the country. In other words, the NET makes just one teacher available every year for three colleges assuming that every eligible candidate is selected for the post of lecturer. The situation is the same also in natural sciences. Although in recent past the pass percentage has been increased, but even that was not enough to meet the need. Instead of providing solutions, the NET has been creating the acute and chronic shortage of manpower required for teaching; and forcing the colleges and universities to engage ad hoc, part-time, contributory or temporary lecturers to run the academic programmes and in turn converting the temples of learning into tuition shops (Kale, 2006). Apart from non-availability of the qualified and competent teachers, lack of financial resources and rapid growth of private colleges and universities facilitate the entry of non-suitable candidates as teachers into the education system (Jafri, 2006).

In many universities, there has been no regular recruitment of teachers for more than 15 to 17 years. No recruitment for a long time and non-replacement for retired teachers resulted in continuous decrease in the strength of teachers and that too when the enrolment of students is being increased every year. If this situation continues, the higher education system will be collapse sooner or later. It may not be out of context to mention that out of the 13,150 colleges in 2000-02, only 5,238 satisfied the minimum requirement specified by UGC under Section 2(f) of the UGC Act.

The situation in technical education could not be very different. Rapid growth of engineering and technical institutes, has increased the demand of teachers. The shortage of well quality and competent teachers has created a serious problem (Agarwal, 2005). The Report of the Board on Faculty Development of the AICTE (March 2004) projected the need of 95,924 as on March 31, 2003. The level-wise requirement comes to: Professors 13,703, Associate Professors 27,407 and Lecturers 54,814. As per the qualifications, the requirement of teachers with PhD was 41,110 and with MTech it was 54,814. Instead, 7,536 with PhD and 11,983 with MTech were in service. This created the gap of 33,574 and 42,831 with PhD and MTech respectively. Annual increase of enrolment created more complications. Consequently, AICTE had reduced the admissions by 25,335 in 1,346 engineering institutes.

The relevance of education in IITs is discussed earlier and required no further elaboration. However, it may be mentioned that the famous Shanghai Jiao Tong University's Academic Ranking of World Universities 2003 study, IIT of Delhi and Kharagpur have been ranked in the 451–500 slot. IIT Madras, Kanpur, Bombay and Roorkee did not figure at all. This shows where we stand exactly in technical education. Such ranking is now regularly published. Occasionally one or two of our academic institutes figure at the button. The government spends more than Rs. 1,400 crore every year on IIT-IIM education (Mungekar 2006), but these elite institutes failed in their social responsibilities. Their social auditing may reveal more. As far as teaching is concerned, all IITs are also experiencing the shortage of teachers. These days this issue is being debated and written widely in the electronic and print media.

Technical or non-technical education, the shortage of competent regular teachers is going to be detrimental to the education system. It will produce unemployable graduates and make them a liability instead of a national asset.

Conclusion

The year 2020 is too close to plan and execute the same to achieve the status to be a developed nation, as suggested by Dr. Abdul Kalam. At least a critical mass of educated and skilled human resource is required to make any country developed. As education converts people into a national asset, its one billion population makes India potentially rich in human resource. However, we failed to transform this potential into kinetic and subsequently to harvest and reap its benefits as education remained confined to a small but dominant section of the society, mainly to descendants of beneficiaries of British education. Naik (1974), mentioned thirty-five to forty years back that 'basically, Indian education is discriminatory in nature. The entire education system has been oriented mainly to meet the requirement of one-third of the population ignoring the interest of the rest'. By design, for their own benefits, the upper castes, elites and urban rich did not allow the spread of education among the marginalized section of the society, whose share is more than three-fourth in the total population. When targeted schemes like reservations in education, scholorships and fellowships for educating the underprivileged were introduced, this small group resisted. Being in administration and policy making, the members of this same group implemented these welfare schemes detrimentally. Such discriminatory actions resulted in acute shortage of human resource. By doing so, they have not only harmed the underprivileged, particularly SCs and STs, but also the nation. It is necessary to make upper castes, the elite and urban rich understand the significance of reservations in education and other welfare schemes, whose success could generate human resource required to accelerate our progress and take India to the status of an advanced country.

In the interest of our country, education particularly higher education has to be carefully planned and made accessible to the disadvantaged and marginalized sections of society, to enlarge our pool of human resource. It is never too late to start something beneficial and useful. We may have to learn from the experiences of some countries like Japan, South Korea and Taiwan and apply them after modification to suit our diversity to overcome the educational crisis. To begin with, higher education has to be expanded particularly in the public sector to reach the large population by increasing the number of colleges, institutes and universities from the present level, and run in mission mode with emphasis on quality both for teaching and research. Increase in number of colleges, universities and academic institutes does not affect the quality of education (*The Hindu*, Delhi, May 18, 2006), but the way we run.

Today, production of new technologies with geometric proportion, innovations, combination of technologies and digitization, are mainly contributing to generation of wealth. Advanced countries like the US have taken the lead and gone ahead in these fields. India is left far behind. In between our contribution to scientific research progressively went down. Although late, new initiative must be taken with set goals and achieve the same at the earliest. For this, the universities have to be made the main place of research activities and supported with liberal funding, as done in advanced countries. By enriching science education in the universities, it will generate scientific and technical human resource, which could be deployed in the national laboratories and institutes to accomplish targeted R&D projects. Along with science, care must also be taken to nurture and enrich the humanities and social sciences which help to make people socially sensitive and feel pain and suffering. Other problems like poverty and hunger are pulling us back. Since, most of these poor people belonged to the disadvantaged and marginalized section, the solution lies in education.

It is quite clear that education, particularly higher education, is intimately linked with development. Being confined to the small section of society, Indian higher education needs to be spread among the disadvantaged and marginalized population, to produce human resource required for development. Therefore, without educating marginalized people, it would not be possible for India to be a developed nation before or after 2020.

REFERENCES

Abdul Kalam, A.P.J. with Rajan, Y.S. (1998). *India 2020: A Vision for New Millennium*, Penguin Books, New Delhi.

Agarwal, Pawan (2005). Engineering Education in India: Changing Global Realities and Responses, *University News*, Vol. 43, No. 39, pp. 35-41 & 67.

Alam, Anwar and John, A.G. (2004). Education: An index of Human Development, *University News*, Vol. 42, No. 46, pp. 25-29.

Chopra, K.L. and Suri, R.K. (2005). Knowledge Based Technical Education, *University News*, Vol. 43, No. 39, pp. 42-47.

Gautam, N.C. and Tripathy, S.K. (2004). Engagement of Universities with the Society: A Model for Promoting Non-Formal Education Through Universities, *University News*, Vol. 42, No. 46, pp. 30-32.

Halsey, A.H., Floud J. and Anderson, C.A. (1961). *Education, Economy and Society*, The Free Press, New York, p. 177.

Jafri, H.A.S. (2006). Scrap or Review it, *University News*, Vol. 44, No. 19, p. 30.

Janaki, D. (2006). Universities as Boundary Breaker for Empowerment of the Socio-Economically Weak in India, *University News*, Vol. 43, No. 37, pp. 119-123.

Jha, Prem Shankar (2006). Teach Us a New Lesson. *Hindustan Times*, New Delhi, May 19, p. 8.

Kale, R.K. (2003). *Understanding the Indian Science: A Dalit Perspective*, International Dalit Conference, held on 15-16 May 2003, Vancouver, Canada.

Kale, R.K. (2005). Special Schemes of UGC for Empowerment of SC/ST, *University News*, Vol. 43, No. 47, pp. 45-54.

Kale, R.K. (2006). National Eligibility Test (NET): Is It a Solution or a Problem, *University News*, Vol. 44, No. 10, pp. 1-6.

Krishna, V.V. (2001). Reflection on the Changing Status of Academic Science in India, *International Social Science Journal*, 168, UNECSO, Paris, pp. 231-246.

Kulandaiswamy, V.C. (2005). Reconstruction of Higher Education in India, *University News*, Vol. 43, No. 27, pp. 6-11 & 15.

Mohan, Surendra (2005). Society's Expectations from Indian Universities. In: *Challenges Facing Indian Universities*, Arun Kumar (ed.), Collection of papers based on a seminar organised by JNUTA on October 2, 2004 in Jawaharlal Nehru University, New Delhi, pp. 62-67.

Mungekar, Bhalchandra (2005). Economic Planning for Growth and Social Justice, *University News*, Vol. 43, No. 48, pp. 18-20.

Mungekar, Bhalchandra (2006). Asamanjaspanachi Spardha (Marathi), *Maharashtra Times*, Mumbai, May 18, p. 6.

Mungekar, Bhalchandra (2006). *Maharashtra Times*, Mumbai, May 21.

Naik, J.P. (1974). Crisis in Indian Education: A Search for Alternatives. Monograph.

Pillai, Rajashekaran (2005). *The Hindu*, Delhi, March 21.

Pundir, J.K. and Singh, R.P. (2004). Engagement of Universities with Society: New System Fulfilling Needs or Forcing Exploitation,

University News, Vol. 42, No. 46, pp. 41-43.

Srinivasa, Rao S. (2002). Equality in Higher Education. The Impact of Affirmative Action Policies in India. In: *The Role of Higher Education in Diverse Democracies*, Beckhman, Edgar (ed.). Association of American Universities and Colleges, Washington D.C., pp. 41-61.

Srivastava, P.N. (1989). Resource Constraints and Educational Development, *Higher Education Policy*, 1989.

Srivastava, P.N. (2005). Science Education in Indian Universities: Shouldn't Someone Be Concerned About It? *University News*, Vol. 34, No. 39, pp. 7-12.

Sudha Rao, K. (2002). *Educational Policies of India: Analysis and Review of Promise and Performance*, National Institute of Educational Planning and Administration, New Delhi.

Thorat, Sukhadeo (2004). Marginalized Groups and Democratization of Higher Education. In: *Challenges Facing Indian Universities*, Arun Kumar (ed.), Collection of papers based on a seminar organised by JNUTA on October 2, 2004 in Jawaharlal Nehru University, New Delhi, pp. 44-47.

Tilak, J.B.G. (2004). Laissez-faireism Higher Education in India, In: *Challenges Facing Indian Universities,* Arun Kumar (ed.), Collection of papers based on a seminar organised by JNUTA on October 2, 2004 in Jawaharlal Nehru University, New Delhi, pp. 62-67.

Virk, H.S. (2004). *Indian Association of Physics Teachers Bulletin*, Vol. 21, pp. 51-53.

Vivek, Kumar (2005). Understanding the Politics of Reservation: A Perspective from Below. *Economical & Political Weekly*, Vol. XL, No. 9, pp. 803-806.

Vivek, Kumar (2006). Devoid of Merit, *Times of India,* Delhi, April 17.

9

National Eligibility Test (NET): Is it a Solution or a Problem?

The Government of India set up interim UGC by a resolution and began to function from the last week of December 1953 with the renowned scientist, Dr. Shanti Swarup Bhatnagar, as its chairman together with eight members. Before the first meeting of the members of the commission, Dr. Bhatnagar wanted to do something 'dramatic' that would catch the attention of the universities. For this, he proposed to raise the salaries of the university teachers by twenty-five per cent immediately. However, the then finance Minister, Dr. C.D. Deshmukh, strongly opposed the said proposal on the ground that it would lead to limitless increase in expenditure. These conflicting views laid the foundation for the periodic revision of salary scales of university and college teachers (Sharma, 2003).

The issue of adequate remuneration and academic qualifications for university and college teachers had been going on since 1955. UGC had considered/examined these issues from time to time. In 1983, UGC appointed a committee under the chairmanship of Prof. R.C. Mehrotra to review and revise the pay scales of teachers in universities and colleges. The committee submitted its report in May 1986. Among many significant things, qualifying in National Eligibility Test (NET) was recommended as an essential condition for recruitment of the post of lecturer (now Assistant Professor) in universities, colleges and other academic institutes. For the first time, such a test for teachers was recommended by any committee. On accepting NET, it replaced the earlier provision introduced by the Sen Committee (1973) that MPhil or PhD can be an essential qualification for recruitment to the post of a lecturer. The Sen Committee had linked salaries to the qualification of teachers. It was stated in the report that a mere Master's Degree was not enough for the post of a lecturer. Further, it was stated that there should be teaching research or advanced study qualifications beyond the post graduate degree as found in developed countries. The committee appointed under the Chairmanship of Dr. R.P. Rastogi (1994-1995) also recommended a good academic record, i.e. at least fifty-five per cent at the Master's level together with qualifying in NET or an equivalent accredited examination as an essential minimum qualification for recruitment of lecturers. The national test was also consistence with the Programme of Action of the National Policy of Education (1986).

To implement the recommendation of the Mehrotra Committee, UGC introduced the national level test. Thus, UGC conducts a national level test for eligibility for lectureship and Junior Research Fellowship (JRF) in seventy-eight subjects at seventy-four selected university centres around the country, in the Humanities (including languages), Social Sciences, Computer Applications, Electronic Sciences and Environmental Sciences. The National Level Test for determining the eligibility of candidates for award of Junior Research Fellowship/Lecturership in science subjects (Chemical Sciences, Physical Sciences) is conducted jointly with the Council of Scientific and Industrial Research (CSIR), New Delhi. However, the present study is confined to UGC-NET. The test is conducted twice in a year in the month of June and December. In addition to NET, UGC has already given an accreditation to conduct State Level Eligibility Test (SLET) to many states on the recommendation of the NET Review Committee (1998).

NET, first recommended by the Mehrotra Committee, was aimed to remove the disparities in the standard of evaluation and teaching that prevailed among a large number of universities, colleges and academic institutions. UGC assumed that NET would ensure quality and uniformity of standards at the recruitment level and in turn in higher education. With this backdrop, an attempt has been made to examine the implications of NET and also to see whether UGC was able to achieve aims and objectives set out for NET.

Findings and Discussion

More than 50,000 students appear in JRF test held twice a year, i.e. in June and December. Out of these, around 350 students qualify for the test. Amazingly, the success ratio is very low for this test. Figures in Table 1 show that just less than one per cent students are able to clear the test.

It may be mentioned that importance of research in the university system has been well recognized. In the National Policy on Education 1986, the significance of the symbiotic relationship between higher education and research has been highlighted. The report on the Education Commission (1964-66) also stated that research is essential for quality in education. In all the advanced countries, universities constitute the strong centres of research. India has, as of May 31, 2003, 247 universities and ninety-eight deemed to be universities.* Candidates who qualify for award of JRF are eligible to pursue research in the subject of their postgraduation or in a related subject in any of the above mentioned universities and deemed to be universities. The awardees are also eligible for lectureship. The universities can select the JRF awardees for full-time research work in accordance with the procedure prescribed by them. Apart from universities, academic institutes and other national organizations can also select the JRF awardees for full-time research work.

Since, approximately 700 students** qualify the test (held twice a year in June and December), every university is likely to get only two JRF on an average. In such a situation, it is difficult to understand how these, i.e. one or two, JRF awardees, would contribute in supporting higher education and help in maintaining the symbiotic relation between research and education in the university. It is like cooking a grain or two of rice for a hungry family of many members. Instead of making good quality researchers available for the Universities, JRF-NET is making them

---

* In February 2012 there were forty-three central universities, 297 state universities, 129 deemed to be universities, hundred private universities and sixty-five institutes of national importance and other university level institutions.

** June 2010 onwards, more than 3000 students per year cleared the NET.

Table 1: Result of the National Level Test Conducted by UGC for Junior Research Fellowship

Exam	*Registered*	*Appeared*	*Qualified (%)*
June, 2000	42542	34147	354 (1.036)
December, 2000	54929	44637	352 (0.788)
June, 2001	54268	42726	301 (0.704)
December, 2001	62394	50690	343 (0.676)
June, 2002	54098	4529	354 (0.832)
December, 2002	46812	35490	357 (1.005)
June, 2003	57892	45768	365 (0.797)
December, 2003	65128	51834	399 (0.769)
June, 2004	63255	50328	397 (0.788)

Figures in parenthesis show the percentage of successful candidates compared to the total number of candidates who appeared for the test.
Source: University Grants Commission, New Delhi

non-available leading to research starvation; and in turn converting the Universities into coaching centres and teachers into tutors or wage earners. It is a matter of great concern. This situation is likely to be detrimental to the advancement of knowledge and creation of new knowledge in the university system through enquiry and investigation. Indeed, this effect is distinctly visible in some universities. Among these a few universities were known for their academic excellence in the past.

The poor quality of research, particularly in the university system, always dominated the debates and discussions and attracted the attention of policy makers and its implementers. There has never been a doubt about the urgent need to improve the quality of research, to achieve this goal, as one of the measures, the JRF test was introduced by UGC. However, because of a relatively small number of fellowships, i.e. 700 JRF for more than 300 universities with around seventy subjects, NET could not make any significant impact. In fact, it failed to enhance the quality of research.

The decline in the quality of research could be seen from the published works from the universities. With few exceptions, the research carried out in the last fifteen years in the university system is not internationally competitive. Recently, Professor Nian Chai Liu and his colleagues at Shanghai Jiao Tong University in China spent two years collecting and analysing the output of two thousand universities/institutes worldwide. On the basis of academic performance and excellence they had ranked five hundred universities. None of the Indian Universities figured in the Top 500 (Vivek Kumar, 2005).

The eligibility test for sciences (CSIR-UGC JRF) could be discussed separately. However, it may be mentioned that even CSIR-UGC JRF seems not to have played any significant role to improve the quality of research in general and the university system in particular. In terms of publications of scientific research in the world, as mentioned earlier, India ranked eighth during the 1980s, slipped to thirteenth during the 1990s and has nose-dived to twenty-first position in the new millennium (Srivastava, 2005). The rank of India after introducing a measure of 'quality' has dropped to one hundred and nineteenth position (Science Citation Index) (Virk, 2004). India's contribution to the world of science is merely five per cent where China's is twelve to fifteen per cent (Neha Mehta, 2005).

From the above, it appears that only the individual awardees were benefited from JRF-NET and not the higher education system. It is also quite clear from the available information that beneficiaries of NET are mostly from urban area of India, especially from metro cities. The students from the rural areas also qualify for the test but they are few and rich. These few and rich migrate to cities like Delhi to get access to good quality education. Although, the elite and rich are small in per cent, they are large in absolute numbers. They grab limited available opportunities including the JRF-NET scheme. In fact, the elite and rich have benefited from the education system and different related schemes right from British India. Looking critically at the implementation of different schemes and policies on education, it gives the impression that these are designed to benefit the elites and/or rich from the metro cities. The disadvantaged group of society, particularly SCs and STs, is the most affected by the UGC-NET. Since implementation of the reservation policy is, in general, found to be detrimental, it does not make much difference to SC and ST students whether they have qualified NET or not. This aspect is discussed in detail in a recent study on implementation of the reservation policy (Kale, 2006).

Table 2 shows the result of last nine lectureships eligibility tests held from June 2000 to June 2004. Although, the number of candidates who appeared in the eligibility test during the period mentioned above remained almost the same, the pass percentage of students continuously decreased from 9.54 to 2.22 during the period June 2000 to June 2004. Take the example of the eligibility test for lectureship held in December 2000 and June 2003, 6,792 and 1,644 candidates cleared the test out of 75,732 and 73,738 candidates respectively*. It was a decline of 5,148 in the number of successful candidates. Results of the December 2002 test showed an increase in pass percentage. However, the reality is different. For this December test, 73,322 students registered, out of these only 53,854 actually appeared which caused an enhancement in percentage.

Table 2: Result of the National Level Test Conducted by UGC for Lecturership Eligibility

Exam	*Registered*	*Appeared*	*Qualified (%)*
June, 2000	72260	56186	5365 (9.54)
December, 2000	96855	75732	6792 (8.96)
June, 2001	99165	75776	2400 (3.16)
December, 2001	114047	89946	2037 (2.26)
June, 2002	98186	74324	1861 (2.50)
December, 2002	73322	53854	1976 (3.66)
June, 2003	96727	73738	1644 (2.22)
December, 2003	105886	81714	4632 (5.66)
June, 2004	105685	81503	3291 (4.03)

Figures in parenthesis show the percentage of successful candidates compared to the total number of candidates who appeared for the test.
Source: University Grants Commission, New Delhi

In any system, it is necessary to maintain the balance between demand and supply. However, the decline of successful candidates (both in percentage and absolute number) in the NET examination, has disturbed the balance. On an average, there is a 4.5 lakh increase in the enrolment of students every year in the university system of

* Between June 2005 and December 2011, 5267 to 13859 candidates per year cleared the NET and the pass percentage varied from 1.66 to 7.73.

education (Table 3). Considering forty students in a class, there is a need of at least 10,000 new classes every year. Further, according to the Annual Report of UGC, in 200-2001, total teaching staff in universities and affiliated colleges was 3.95 lakhs as against 3.51 lakh teachers in the previous year. It is an increase of 0.44 lakh teachers. In 2002-2003, the total teaching staff increased to 4.36 lakhs. This increase is likely to be continued for the coming years. Therefore, it is difficult to understand the reason(s) or logic to reduce the number of eligible candidates to be teachers when they are more in demand. Is it that the decline has resulted from the lack of potential to be a teacher among the candidates? Or is it that the Lectureship Eligibility Test itself lacks the potential to identify the eligible candidates to be teachers? Although, there is an enhancement in qualified candidates in the lectureship eligibility test held in December 2003 and June 2004, it cannot answer the above questions.

As mentioned earlier, there are around 300 universities and 15,000 colleges in India. Every year around 5,000 candidates become eligible for the position of college or university teacher. Thus, the eligibility test provides just one teacher every year for three colleges assuming that every eligible candidate is selected for the post of lecturer. In other words, NET makes more candidates ineligible and keeps them away from the job of teacher resulting into acute as well as chronic shortage in manpower. Education is supposed to help in human resource development. It may also be mentioned that all those who become eligible do not join teaching jobs. Quite a large number of candidates take to other avenues and opportunities as a teacher does not have status and respect similar to personnel in other services. The teachers are honoured and respected only in books, academic functions and sometimes in the social programmes.

Therefore, lectureship is the last option for many. This leads to further decline in availability of eligible candidates. Thus, the eligibility test creates the shortage of manpower required for teaching in higher education. Like grocery shops in the market, the colleges and universities cannot be closed down. Therefore, they are forced to engage part-time contributory or temporary teachers to run the show. It is quite clear that the Lectureship

Table 3: All India Growth of Student Enrolment: 1982-83 to 2002-2003

Year Enrolment	*Total*	*Increase Over the Preceding Year*	*Percentage*
1982-83	3133093	181027	6.1
1983-84	3307649	171556	5.6
1984-85	3404096	96447	2.9
1985-86	3605029	20933	5.9
1986-87	3757158	152129	4.2
1987-88	4020159	263001	7.0
1988-89	4285489	265330	6.6
1989-90	4602680	317191	7.4
1990-91	4924868	322188	7.0
1991-92	526886	341018	6.9
1992-93	5534996	269080	5.1
1993-94	5817249	282283	5.1
1994-95	6113929	296680	5.1
1995-96	6574005	460076	7.5
1996-97	6842598	268593	4.1
1997-98	7260418	417820	6.1
1998-99	7705520	445102	6.1
1999-2000	8050607	345087	4.5
2000-2001	8399443	348836	4.3
2001-2002	8821095	421652	5.0
2002-2003	9200000 (app)	400000 (app)	4.35 (app)

Source: University Grants Commission, New Delhi

Eligibility Test failed to provide adequate manpower required for teaching in colleges and universities. The total enrolment in all courses and levels is close to ninety lakhs. Out of these, nine per cent and seven per cent students pursue postgraduate and research programmes respectively. It means India has 8.5 lakh postgraduate students and 0.65 lakh research scholars as a pool of young talent with potential to teach. This huge reservoir of educated people needs to be tapped to meet the increasing demand of teaching. If necessary, eligibility may be lowered. Lowering the eligibility does not mean lowering the quality. Therefore, UGC must review the policy related to NET and make suitable changes to meet the demand without compromising the quality. By creating a shortage of teachers, NET has directly affected the teaching in the university system.

As mentioned earlier, way back in 1984, *Nature*, one of the prestigious science journals, devoted twenty pages on science in India and observed that Indian universities are afflicted by a host of problems like inadequate teachers and too many students (*Nature*, Vol. 308, 1984, 591-611). According to P.N. Srivastava (2005), this situation has gone from bad to worse. It is not known whether NET contributed in arresting or accelerating this collapse of our university system. Only ten of India's young people complete their higher education compared to substantially higher percentages in the developed countries. The present situation in the university system is one of the reasons for high dropouts in India. The main objective of the tenth plan is to raise enrolment students (of eighteen to twenty-three years age group) in higher education from the present six per cent to ten by the end of the plan period. Increase in enrolment would put immense pressure on NET which has no strength to bear the same. While the advanced countries are moving towards mass higher education (Table 4), India has only six per cent of the age group entering the portals of universities. Considering the increase in population and requirement of higher percentage of the age group there would be a need for massive increase in opportunities for higher education (Kulandaiswamy, 2005). NET cannot meet this need. We have to plan something different.

Table 4: Age Group Entering Higher Education in Some Advanced Countries (2000)

Country	*Enrolment (%)*
Canada	88
Australia	80
USA	80
Finland	74
UK	52
India	06

Source: Modified from Kulandaiswamy (2005) and UGC Report

Keeping the requirement of teaching in higher education in mind, many state governments have introduced the SLET. However, the candidates who had cleared the SLET, accredited by

UGC for eligibility for Lecturership held prior to June 1, 2002 are exempted from appearing in NET. For SLET held from June 1, 2002 onwards, the qualified candidates are eligible to apply for the posts of lecturer only in the universities/colleges belonging to the state from where they have cleared their SLET. The action of UGC to give accreditation to SLET conducted by different states defeated the purpose for which NET was introduced, because it is not possible to maintain the uniformity and quality in teaching throughout the country, when the separate eligibility tests are conducted by each state. UGC may claim that it maintains the standard of SLET through the process of reviews. However, the way systems function and policies are implemented in our country; it is difficult to accept that the state can successfully maintain the standards of SLET as equivalent to NET. The de-accreditation of SLET of some states by UGC supports this doubt. It is also important that the SLET has a geographical barrier. The SLET is valid only for the universities and colleges which belong to the state from where the candidates have cleared the test. The geographical barrier also supports that the standards and conduct of examinations for SLET are not equivalent. It differs from state to state. Further, if the states are allowed to conduct their own test, then what is the use of having NET? At the most UGC can conduct the NET for central universities. An expenditure of Rs 2.5 crore is incurred every time on conducting NET. UGC by confining the NET to central universities may save a substantial amount which could be used for welfare schemes.

It is important that the candidates who have passed their MPhil degree by December 1993 or have submitted their PhD thesis to a university on or before December 31, 2002 are exempted from appearing in NET. The total enrolment for research is about sixty-five thousand. Each year approximately 11,000 research scholars are awarded the Doctoral Degree. For example, during 1998-99 and 1999-2000, 11,107 and 11,067 scholars were awarded the degree. The situation cannot be dramatically different for the years other than above. It is quite significant that 11,000 candidates with Doctorate Degree exempted from NET were/are available each year along with 2,000 to 4,000 students who had cleared UGC-NET for lectureship. The number of candidates with UGC-NET is very small compared to the candidates with Doctorate Degrees. Thus, the pool of eligible candidates available for the recruitment for the post of lecturers was dominated mainly by the candidates with Doctorate Degrees. By exempting the candidates from appearing with Doctorate Degrees till the end of December 2002, UGC itself has contributed in non-maintenance of minimum standards for entrants in the teaching profession. It is an open secret that the decision to exempt the candidates with doctorate degrees were taken under pressure and not for academic reasons. However, it is a matter of fact that NET failed to ensure the uniformity and quality for the recruitment at the level of lecturer.

NET was one of the important measures taken by UGC to improve and reconstruct the system of higher education. Indeed, the introduction of lectureship eligibility test could be considered as a historic decision. However, NET was not effective in removing the country-wide disparities in teaching and research prevailed in the higher education system, to the extent that it should have been. UGC-NET failed to maintain uniformity and equality in the recruitment of teachers. It created the shortage of manpower required for teaching in higher education and in turn adversely affected the normal and smooth running of the colleges and universities. Because of UGC-NET, the teaching profession became accessible to the few that are rich and elite. The action of UGC to give accreditation to SLET conducted by the states defeated the very aims and objectives of NET. Further by exempting the candidates from appearing in NET with Doctorate Degrees from time to time, UGC itself contributes in the non-maintenance of standards for entrants in the teaching profession. Being small in number, the Junior Research Fellowships were/are not able to maintain the symbiotic relations between research and higher education. JRF-NET also could not enhance the quality of research in the university system. The present scenario of higher education suggests that UGC-NET created more problems than have been solved.

Education empowers indivuals. It playes an important role in social change, economic growth and development, as it produces the required human resource.The experience of various countries in the last four decades has indicated that mere physical and capital resources alone are not sufficient inputs for developing a nation. Education improves the socio-economic condition of people. Improvement in the quality of people is a necessary condition for achieving sustainable and accelerated development (Sudha Rao, 2002). A useful classification of the benefits of education has been provided elsewhere (Jean Dreze and Amartya Sen, 1995). The UGC-NET should have played a catalytic role and contributed in making higher education an instrument of social change through human resource development. In view of the above, it is necessary that every policy related to education needs to be carefully examined and implemented. Unfortunately education has never been a priority on the agenda of the nation right from independence. Even when the first draft of the First Five Year Plan was prepared, education was almost completely ignored (Cabinet Secretariat Resolution, No.1-1© 150; Silver Jubilee Souvenir, CABE, 1960 and Kaur Kuldip, 2003). It seems there was no discussion on the role that was expected of education in planning. It was a different matter that the final draft had all praise for education.

A number of committees, commissions, conferences, panels, workshops, meetings of educationists and administrators have discussed educational problems and suggested the measures to improve and reconstruct the system of education. However, most of the measures were/are curative in nature rather than preventive. The curative measures are always accompanied by a certain degree of risks in the form of side effects. The UGC-NET was introduced to prevent the deterioration in higher education. However, it got transformed into a problem. In view of the above, it is necessary to review UGC-NET or scrap it altogether to avoid its adverse effects on the education system.

The UGC has been making efforts to improve the process of NET examination. For example, it has taken a major decision, on December 22, 2011, to conduct UGC-NET completely in an objective mode from June 2012 onwards so as to make the examination and evaluation process more interactive and less prone to subjectivity. The answer keys of all the question papers are made available in public domain as they are uploaded on the web site as a measure to promote transparency. The candidates having any grievances with regard to answer-key(s) can approach UGC within one month from the date of the declaration of results. It is advisable and also a requirement to improve the examination system. However, as fewer candidates pass the NET than the requirement of the education system, the shortage of qualified teachers thus created has not been addressed and found the solution by the UGC. There is a serious imbalance between supply and demand. Thus, NET continues to create a shortage of teachers in higher education. Figures in Table 5 convincingly support this fact. Recently, Rukmini (2014) has reported in *The Hindu*, that a large number of faculty positions are vacant in the central universities and centrally funded academic institutions. Around forty per cent teaching courses in central universities are presently vacant. Surprisingly, 52.89 per cent posts out of 1,706, are lying unfilled in the University of Delhi. Being one of the oldest and premier universities of high repute and in the capital of the country, it failed to attract potential teachers and fill the vacant posts. The situation is worse in some of the new central universities established in 2009. For example, in the central university of Tamil Nadu, eighty per cent teaching posts are reported to be vacant. Like central universities, thirty-nine per cent posts are also vacant in IITs. In the case of IIMs, on average more than twenty per cent posts are vacant. It is important that the teaching vacancies have been persistently remained unfilled for long.

Table 5: Faculty Positions in Central Universities and Centrally Funded Academic Institutions

Sr. No.	*Universities/ Institutions*	*Sanctioned Posts*	*Posts Filled*	*Vacant Posts*
1	CUs	16,114 (100%)	10,091 (62.62%)	6,023 (37.38%)
2	IITs	6,653 (100%)	4,087 (61.00%)	2,566 (39.00%)
3	IIMs	766 (100%)	598 (78.00%)	168 (22.00%)

Modified from: Ministry of Human Research Development (2014) and Rukmini (2014).

CU: Central University, IIT: Indian Institute of Technology, IIM: Indian Institute of Management.

The NET could be beneficial to SC and ST students as it augments their prospects to get an appointment as Assistant

Professor even against an unreserved post. It becomes difficult for the selection committee to ignore or reject them, if suitable. The NET gives confidence to SC and ST students.

As mentioned earlier in another section, the caste discriminations are practised on campuses. Even the NET passed suitable SC and ST candidates are likely to be rejected, on appearing before the hostile selection committee. Otherwise, many SC and ST candidates with NET would not be found wandering on the roads in search of jobs. The NET or no-NET that does not matter much but the mindset of persons, who are running colleges and universities, and those who are on the selection committees, certainly matters.

NOTES

1. Rukmini S. (2014): Forty Per Cent Faculty Posts Vacant in Central Universities. *The Hindu*, Wednesday, December 3, 2014, p. 13.

REFERENCE

Annual Report 2000-2001, UGC Higher Education, University Grants Commission, New Delhi, p. 24.

Cabinet Secretariat Resolution (Planning), No. 1-1(C)/50, New Delhi.

Dreze, Jean and Sen, Amartya (1995). *India: Economic Development and Social Opportunity*, Oxford University Press, Delhi.

Kale, R.K. (2006). Implementing of Reservation Policy for SC ST in the Colleges Affiliated to University of Delhi, *University News*, A Weekly Journal of Higher Education, Association of Indian Universities, Vol. 44, No. 4, pp. 1-6.

Kaur, Kuldip (2003). *Higher Education in India (1781-2003)*, University Grants Commission, New Delhi and Centre for Research in Rural and Industrial Development (CRRID), Chandigarh.

Kulnadaiswamy, V.C. (2005). Reconstruction of Higher Education in India, *University News*, A Weekly Journal of Higher Education, Association of Indian Universities, Vol. 43, No. 27, pp. 6-15.

Kumar, Vivek (2005). Understanding the Politics of Reservation: A Perspective from Below, *Economic and Political Weekly*, Vol. XL, No. 9, pp. 803-806.

Mehta, Neha (2005). Wanted: Critical Mass for Science, *Sunday Hindustan Times*, New Delhi, October 9, p. 12.

Rukmini, S. (2014). Forty Percent Faculty Posts Vacant in Central Universities, *The Hindu*, Wednesday, December 3, p. 13.

Sharma, Kavita A. (2003). *50 Years of University Grants Commission*, A Publication of the University Grants Commission, New Delhi, pp. 21-23.

Silver jubilee Souvenir, Central Advisory Board of Education, Ministry of Education, Government of India, 1960, pp. 347-348.

Srivastava, P.N. (2005). Science Education in Indian Universities: Shouldn't Somebody Be Concerned About It? *University News*, A Weekly Journal of Higher Education, Association of Indian Universities, Vol. 34, No. 39, pp. 7-8.

Sudha Rao, K. (2002). *Educational Policies of India: Analysis and Review of Promise and Performance*, National Institute of Educational Planning and Administration, New Delhi, pp. 1-114.

Virk, H.S. (2004). *Indian Association of Physics Teachers Bulletin*, Vol. 21, pp. 51-52.

10

Past and Present: A Summary

The British introduced the present education system in India. They came as traders in 1612. On reaching the Indian coast, the East India Company established its factory at Surat and started trading. Subsequently in a short period the trade was expanded to Bombay, Madras and Calcutta. After trading for 145 years, the Company got the first opportunity to gain the political supremacy in the form of the Battle of Plassey in 1757. The company defeated Sirajud Daula in this famous battle and became rulers. Thereafter, the British went on expanding their wings and ruled for 190 years. Coorg and Punjab were the last two geographical territories which came under their control. As traders and rulers, the British stayed on the Indian social scene for 335 years.

The East India Company had no mandate to spread education among the Indian population. However, its officers took an interest in educating Indians, with focus on the top layer of the hierarchical society, consisting of members of royal and aristocratic families as well as elite, rich and upper castes, with the aim to win good will and subsequently attract and involve them in administration and in turn get support directly or indirectly of this section, who had complete control over the entire population to rule the country smoothly. The establishment of the Madrasa at Calcutta (1787) by Warren Hastings and Banaras Sanskrit College (1792) by J. Duncan indicated this possibility. In 1813, while renewing the Charter of the East India Company, a new clause was introduced in the East India Company Act of 1813, which gave responsibility to spread education in India. It was the first legislation on the right of education in India and Rs. one lakh was allotted for its implementation. While planning, the controversies erupted soon between the Anglicists and Orientalists on the nature of education to be imparted. The Orientalists who dominated the Central Committee of Public Instructions introduced the orientalist education. It was evident from the establishment of Sanskrit College in Calcutta and Oriental College at Agra and Delhi as well as patronage of *Pathshalas* and *Madrassas*. However, oriental education did not last for long. T.B. Macaulay introduced the anglicist education policy in 1835, which laid the foundation of the present education. Macaulay wanted to form an elite class that was 'Indian in blood and colour, but English in taste, in opinion, in morals and in intellect'.

When English was made a language of administration (1837) and employment avenues available for Indians (1844), people in large numbers particularly from upper castes rushed for Western education. After 100 years as rulers, in response to the Dispatch of 1854, British established three universities in 1857, one each in Calcutta, Madras and Bombay. That year, only 5,309 students were studying in 27 colleges. In 1947, when India became independent, there were 19 universities, 496 colleges and 2,41,369 students. Of these universities, two were in princely states, one in Mysore and another in Hyderabad. During this long period of 90 years of rule (1857-1947), the British added fourteen universities, 469 colleges, with increase in enrolment by 2,36,060. When the British left this country, only 0.06 per cent of population availed themselves of higher education.

Although, the Dispatch of 1854 made provision for English education to the Indian masses, it remained confined to the 'elite class', defined by Macaulay. While implementing, the British kept the education system small in size and restricted its spread among the masses; probably to avoid emergence of the intelligentsia which would pose a threat to their empire. It could be possible that they had the American experience in mind. The loss of America as a colony was attributed, as one of the reasons, to education given to their own people, who settled there. In course of time, the same people revolted and liberated themselves from British clutches and declared America as an independent country. Possibly, to avoid such a repeat, the British planned the Indian education mainly to rule and generate revenue with the help of 'elite' natives, to make

Britain more prosperous. Expectedly, the 'elite class' supported and helped the British in governance and administration. These native beneficiaries of British education, mainly from the upper castes, opposed the same for the downtrodden under the pretext of customs, traditions and religious sanctions. This created the educational gap between them and people belonging to depressed classes which continued even after independence. The British were also not very keen to educate the unprivileged section of the Indian society, as they could not afford to antagonize the Brahmins and upper castes.

We have a long history of education and proudly refer to the Gurukul system, Taxshila, Nalanda and other such centres of learning. However, since ancient times to the recent past, education was not accessible to the people belonging to untouchable castes, which at the bottom of the pyramid of the social order were supposed to serve those above them, without any returns. The untouchable castes had no rights including education, but only duties. Any deviation from their assigned social duties could invite severe punishment. Their desire to acquire education became visible during the British time. The British, who were more interested in protecting their own interests, had focused on the education of upper castes and Brahmins to form the 'elite class'. Subsequently they succeeded. On the other hand, as mentioned earlier, the British had no interest in imparting education to untouchables as no gain, in any form, was foreseen in strengthning and sustaining of British rule, and shifted their own responsibility to the 'elite class' belonging to the upper castes which had been against the education of untouchables. For education of untouchables, the British adopted the 'trickle-down' approach, wherein, first, the top layer of society was educated and which in turn would educate the lower one. However, the British conveniently ignored that Indian society consisted of hierarchical non-permeable layers of castes which made it impossible to' trickle-down' education from top to bottom.

It was significant that in course of time, social reformers and leaders emerged from their own untouchable communities who awakened, mobilized and united them to fight together for their rights including education. Because of their own initiatives and support and help from others like the great Chhatrapati Shahuji Maharaj and Narayan Guru as well as Christain missionaries, the untouchables could gain access to education. It must be mentioned that the British were not rigid like the upper castes of Hindu society, therefore, the educational avenues, to some extent, became available for untouchables during the British period.

In independent India, education and the education system fell into the lap of the elite, rich and upper castes who continued to have a hold on governance and administration. Instead of nurturing education, and making efforts for its equal spread and democratization, keeping the interest of the entire society and overall development of the nation in mind, the elite and upper castes carefully kept the education system smaller in size as well as its form and function given by the British. Under them, higher education expanded mainly in urban India, particularly in metro cities where elite and upper caste people were concentrated. On the other hand, the need and interest of the rural part of the country was ignored. No high schools were opened even in small towns for a long time in the early phase of independence. India was and is in villages and small towns. The elite and Brahimin increased their hold on education and restricted its accessibility to the rural poor, particularly the downtrodden. This approach widened the educational gap between the urban rich, upper castes and, rural population, particularly the underprivileged.

Apart from the above, in independent India, several commissions, committees and task forces were constituted and, conferences were held to reform higher education. There is a long list starting right from the University Education Commission (1948-49), to the Knowledge Commission (2006), which produced numerous reports. However, their recommendations were not taken to a logical end. As a result, from the larger social context, the country lost precious time as it could not develop a long-term education policy and reap the benefits. This failure adversely affected national development and social progress particularly of the unprivileged section of the society. Japan, South Korea and recently China succeeded in enhancing the GER and generating educated and skilled human resources which contributed to the economic and social development of their respective country.

Education was a state subject upto 1976. All the state universities of the country were/are under the state governments. The funds were provided to these universities mainly by the state governments and had a role in appointments to the statutory posts and statutory bodies. Importantly, the organizational and academic structure, inherited from the British, was kept intact, which enabled the state governments to regulate these universities. Indeed, the education system being in the control of the elite, urban rich and upper castes, the state universities were actually governed and administered by them for their own benefit. Further, the universities and colleges were located in the cities and big towns, it was not possible for the poor from villages particularly SC and ST students, in small numbers who could complete school education, to go to such places, stay there and pursue higher education. The schools and high schools should have been established, as mentioned earlier, in villages and small towns in a planned manner immediately after independence for young children who after completing schooling would have joined higher education.

The founding fathers of independent India were aware that the country could not be built and developed without social and economic equality. To achieve the same, they made provisions of reservations in the Constitution for SC and ST communities in the educational institutions. Since these institutions were governed and administered by the elite, urban rich and upper castes, the reservation policy was implemented detrimentally. It was vident, for example, from the order No. F.No.6-30/2005 U5 dated December 6, 2005 of MHRD, blaming the UGC for its failure in implementing the reservation policy effectively in the colleges and universities. In response, the UGC prepared guidelines on reservation for SC and ST for its strict implementation in 2006. However, resistance to reservation persisted on campuses. Even today, the University of Delhi has not fully implemented the reservation policy.

In JNU, a section of teachers in 2010 openly opposed the reservation for SC and ST at the level of Associate Professor and Professor. Surprisingly, many retired Professors and Former Vice-Chancellors of JNU also joined these teachers. JNU is considered to be the hub of intellectuals and progressive people. Most of the

Vice-Chancellors appointed to this university were of great eminence and very high academic credentials. At the national level, the scenario is the same. The UGC had to conduct inquiries related to reservation issues against some colleges, central universities and deemed to be universities.

The government started several schemes, including post-matric (PMS) for SC and ST to enable them to gain access to education. However, to avail of this scheme, one had to first complete school and high school education. Non-availability or lack of school facility in villages kept SC and ST children away from the PMS scheme and higher education. The acute poverty did not allow them to go to towns and cities for education. Had there been schools in villages and also Pre Matric Scholarships for SC and ST students, that would have worked as a wonder to reach higher education. The government opened the hostels for SC and ST students in towns and cities. However, due to the small intake capacity, insufficient and untimely release of grants; the hostel scheme had very limited success. Despite several difficulties, some SC and ST students could enrol in colleges and universities, and complete their higher education because of the PMS scheme. In the absence of other financial sources, SC and ST students had to depend almost solely on the PMS scheme for higher education.

This PMS scheme enabled the SC and ST students to come to towns and cities after schooling. However, procedural delay in sanctions of scholarships, longer time taken for its release and finally reaching the relevant people, forced many students to dropout in between. Although in the early phase of its introduction, an amount of PMS was probably adequate but did not enhance periodically as time passed; and whenever enhanced, it was not sufficient to meet the minimum daily requirement. Such a detrimental approach also forced the SC and ST students to dropout or not to go for higher education.

Surprisingly, Post-Matric scholarship is not available to every SC and ST students because of family income ceiling for eligibility. It is more surprising that sufficient funds are available under the Scheduled Caste Sub-Plan (SCSP) and Tribal Sub-Plan (TSP), and remained under-utilized year after year. However, such income ceiling is not applied to the scholarships and fellowships given to others by the organizations like CSIR and UGC. Why was there selective restriction of income in case of exclusive schemes for SCs and STs? It should be remembered that at least, first and second generations of SCs and STs are always in a transitional state and did not become economically independent because of poverty. Importantly the welfare policies for SC and ST are formulated not just to eliminate their poverty, but uplift them socially. The welfare policies, therefore, should be implemented with that spirit. The government provides many benefits in terms of subsidies and tax exemptions to corporate and other sectors which run into several thousand lakhs. For example, for the period from 2005-06 to 2011-12 it comes to around Rs. 26 lakh crore (Table 1). The favour could have also been shown to the SC and ST communities. However, the government seemed to be not liberal in spending on SCs and STs, which was evident from the just thirty scholarships given to SC and ST students under the Overseas Scholarship scheme for Master/PhD Programmes. Out of 1.2 billion Indian population, SCs and STs are almost 25 crore (16.2 per cent SC and 8.2 per cent ST) and Overseas scholarships are 30 which is less than the total number of states and union territories of the country. Not even one scholarship per state/union territory.

Table 1: Total Revenue Forgone from 2005-06 to 2011-12 (in crores)

Corporate Income Tax	Rs. 3,95,878
Excise duty	Rs. 9,55,726
Custom duty	Rs. 12,22,438
Total	Rs. 25,74,042

The reservations are provided in admissions but are not supported by the schemes like scholarships and fellowships, with adequate numbers and amounts to reap the benefits of reservations. Presently, these are just two schemes worth mentioning. One is PMS and another Rajiv Gandhi Fellowships (RGF). The PMS are available in large numbers, but its scholarship amount is inadequate with the ceiling of family income for eligibility. The fellowship amount of RGF is quite adequate but its number is inadequate considering around 25 crore population of SCs and STs. Moreover, the PMS and RGF schemes are of the Ministry of Social Justice implemented by the UGC, and not of the MHRD. There was ample scope and opportunities for UGC and MHRD to formulate thir own targeted schemes for SCs and STs with adequate numbers like Research Fellowships, Research Associateships and Teacher Fellowships to carry out the research in India and abroad as well as liberal funding for hostel construction on university campuses. The budgetary provision under the SCSP and TPS should have been used for such scemes. The scholarship, fellowship and hostel facilities are essential for the education of SC and ST students. Although, a statutary body, the UGC traditionally resisted the reservation policy for SCs and STs, right from its inception. As mentioned above, the UGC was severly criticized by the MHRD in the communication of December 6, 2005, for its failure to implement the reservation policy effectively.

Mention has been made about the SCSP and TSP. The government had prepared a separate development plan called TSP for STs in 1976 followed by the special component plan for SCs in 1978, recently named as the Scheduled Caste Sub-Plan (SCSP). Under these plans, every department/ministry is expected to make provision in its budget to the extent of proportion to the population of SCs and STs for their overall development. The funds allocated under SCSP and STP cannot be diverted to other projects or schemes, and have to be used exclusively for the welfare of SCs and STs by developing targeted schemes. It is seen that most of the departments and ministries have not earmarked the funds at the required level (15 per cent SC and 7.5 per cent ST) or diverted to other projects and schemes. According to the recent study by the Centre for Budget and Governance Accountability (CBGA), a Delhi based think tank, reported by Subodh Varma in the *Times of India*, Ahmedabad, Thursday, March 15, 2012; that in 2011-12, SCs were deprived of about Rs. 23,890 crore and STs of Rs. 12,187 crore by deficient allocation by the central ministries. Thus, in reality, SCSP and STP remained on paper. From 2004-05 till 2010-11, the CBGA has shown that the allocation for SCs has ranged between four and eight per cent instead of fifteen per cent, and allocation for STs between three and five per cent instead of 7.5 per cent. The situation is also the same in the case of state governments.

It is understood that MHRD is heavily funded for educational development of SCs and STs. It should have developed various schemes like scholarships, fellowships and hostels in large numbers for SC and ST students. After a long time, the SCSP and STP were discussed and debated seriously only in the academic year 2012-13. The MHRD is now insisting on the Central Universities to allocate 22.5 per cent (15 per cent SC and 7.5 per cent STs) budget under SCSP and STP. However, there are no targeted schemes at the university level.

Meanwhile, the government started withdrawing slowly from higher education, which was evident from the gradual decrease in funding from one per cent in the 1970s to 0.4 per cent of GDP in the early 2000s. This decrease of 0.2 per cent of GDP per decade crippled the higher education system. Further, the government did not take an interest in expansion of higher education and made it difficult for SCs and STs to access the same. Therefore, the educational interests of SCs and STs were most adversely affected. Subsequently, the government also encouraged privatization of higher education, and more aggressively after the 1990s, on the pretext of its inability to meet the increased demand of education. Its withdrawal from higher education and encouragement to privatization was probably reflected in the response of the government towards increased aspirations of the underprivileged for higher education and their demand for strict implementation of reservation policies. Awakening among SC, ST, OBC and their readiness to fight for rights was probably seen by the higher castes as a threat to their status and progress.

The private institutions started mainly professional courses with high fees. The students particularly belonging to the middle class from the elite group and upper castes could access professional education which had more employability. SCs, STs and other unprivileged had no option, but to go for traditional social sciences, humanities and natural sciences with declined quality in government and government-aided academic institutions, colleges and universities. This trend is clearly visible in Table 2. Surprisingly, in some private academic institutes, the presence of SC and ST students is non-existent or negligible. According to a self-study report of one private college named SCMS School of Technology and Management, Aluva, Cochin (2014), submitted to NAAC for accreditation, there was only one SC student enrolled in the last four years, although it follows the rules of the state government and affiliating university.

Table 2. Representative Enrolment of SC/ST Students in Different Types of Colleges

S. No.	*Category*	*Government College**	*Aided College***	*Private College****
1	SC	28.41%	4.54%	0.58%
2	ST	2.55%	0.88%	0.00%

Source: Prepared from information embodied in SSR of Government College, Kadapa, AP (2012)*; Lal Bahadur Arts & Science and S.B. Solabanna Shetty Commerce College, Sagara, Karnataka (2014)** and SCMS School of Technology and Management, Aluva, Kerala (2014)***; submitted to NAAC, Bangalore.

During this period, the increased flow of students of rich and higher caste students towards private institutions and SC and ST students towards public institutions was clearly visible. Their increased flows towards professional courses indicated that the rich and upper castes wanted to be competitively ahead of SC, ST and other backward classes, to maintain their control and dominance.

The change in the medium of instruction turned out to be most detrimental to SC, ST and other backward communities. Apart from withdrawing from higher education, the government changed the medium of instruction from English to the vernacular language which contributed greatly to the deterioration of the quality of education. It created a language barrier, arrested mobility and personality development and in turn made students educationally disabled. Importantly, the policy change in the medium of instruction was not complete, but partial as the government also allowed the English medium to continue. Thus, there were two types of educational institutions, one with vernacular medium and another with English medium.

Such a dual approach made a perfect divide, sometimes referred to as Bharat and India. Vernacular education mainly for SC, ST, OBC and poor from rural India and English medium education for the elite, urban rich and upper castes concentrated in towns and cities. It has increased the language as well as the regional gap, which is still continued. Presently, the GER of urban India is three times higher than the rural. The information on educational status is available for 584 districts, out of which 373 districts could be considered as educationally backward as their GER is significantly lower than the national average. Some districts even have GER less than three to six per cent. The educational gap among social groups is also not significantly narrowed. The social groups such as SC, ST and OBC are lagging three, three and two times behind respectively compared to others. If the drop-out rate is considered, the actual spatial and social gap would be quite high.

It is a matter of great concern that out of 1.02 billion population of the country, around one crore students were enrolled in higher education, amounting to around just one per cent of the total population, keeping almost 99 per cent Indians out of higher education. As far as the young people with the relevant age group between 18 and 24 are concerned, out of them, only eight to nine per cent were in higher education, when globalization was at their doorstep. Implementation of the higher education policy, differentially beneficial to small, but the dominant section of society, created acute shortage of educated and skilled human resource required for the development of the nation particularly in this era of globalization.

Everyone is shouting from the roof tops that India has a demographic advantage compared to many other countries. The population of India is projected to increase from 1.02 billion in 2001 to 1.7 billion in 2060. Importantly, working age population (between 18 and 59 years old) is also suggested to increase from 58 per cent to 64 per cent till 2016. Although, this working age population would stabilize after 2016 in relative terms, it would increase in absolute terms due to increase in population. Therefore, India has a rare opportunity to reap the demographic dividend; and if failed, the possible demographic dividend would turn into a demographic disaster. The year 2016 is about to end and the present GER is around 15 to 16 per cent for higher education. In such a situation, it appears difficult to harvest the demographic benefits fully. Had higher education been democratized with an accelerated rate at the early phase of independent India, it would have been ready to reap the demographic dividend. It is well known that 240 million people skill gap across twenty-two sectors was reported for the period 2008 to 2012. In the sector like auto and auto-components, building and construction industry, textile and clothing the skill gap is reported to be 35, 33 and 17 million people respectively. Even in the unorganized sector, 37 million skill gap could be seen. In higher education itself, around 40 to 50 teaching positions are vacant. The rough estimate suggested that, every year higher education needs more than sixty to seventy thousand additional teachers due to expansion and superannuation.

It is pertinent to note that observations made by Ashok Upadhyay (2013) on a survey by Gallup, found that a large number of people (100 million) from populous countries, including India (10 million) are likely to migrate to the US permanently. The Migration Policy Institute (MPI) at Washington D C conducted a study in 2011, which revealed India's contribution to the American economy. The study also revealed how much middle-class urban Indians feel proud to migrate to the US.

In 2008, the US had around 1.6 million Indian-born migrants. According to MPI, in relation to other groups, the Indian-born population in the US grew rapidly to 1.2 million during the 1990s to 2000s with about an increase of 65,000 per year, (which surpassed the Chinese and Hong Kong) to become the third largest group. Of those, who came to the US during this period of 1990-2008, three quarters were with at least a bachelor's degree. Out of these, very few came back to India. It is known that the US economy welcomes immigrants because they are cheaper than native workers. The migrants work more for far less than the natives. As mentioned earlier, 10 million Indians are likely to migrate to the US, which will make it a demographic nightmare (as a result of an aging population), a dream; and turn into a competitive labour market. At the end Ashok Upadhyay (2013) concluded that India's demographic shift could become America's dividend. Keeping such situations in mind, India has to plan and take appropriate measures not to allow our demographic dividend to turn into a demographic disaster (Ashok Upadhyay, *The Hindu Business Line,* Wednesday,

March 27, 2013, p. 6), which could be avoided by educating SCs and STs as well as other socially backward communities.

On the economic front, assuming an average annual growth rate 7.25 per cent between 2010 and 2040, increase in GDP of India is estimated to be eight fold to reach US$ 32 trillion, higher than the GDP of USA (US$ 29 trillion) during the same period (Merchant, 2010). Presently, in the USA, the GDP is $14.70 trillion and that of India is US$ 4 trillion (by purchase power parity). In 30 years, the Indian economy is likely to be larger than USA. Further, Merchant (2010) refers to the work of Virmani (2010) 'in an attempt that departs from the traditional procedure of ranking countries in terms of per capita income, and examines the two components of per capita income, i.e. gross domestic products (GDP) and population separately as well as evaluate the GDP of various countries not in terms of actual exchange rate, but in terms of purchasing power parity'. The world is visualized as tripolar by 2040 that includes US, China and India. Recently, the *Economist* has predicted that India would take over China soon. From the studies stated above, it is posited that India is to become one of the largest economies of the world. However, to convert this potential into reality, at least, a critical mass of educated and skilled people are needed, which, India presently does not have. The economic growth is known to rely on sustained improvement in human capital, institutions and governance (Dani Rodrik, *The Financial Express*, Ahmedabad, August 14, 2012). For a sustained improvement of human capital and its generation, the country needs a healthy education system, which India does not have. Indeed, India could be termed as educationally backward, as around one per cent of its population is in the realm of higher education, with GER of about twelve to fifteen per cent.

In view of the above, it was necessary to spread quality education to the width and breath of the country to reap demographic dividends and achieve inclusive sustainable economic growth. Probably, because of national academic need and rapid changes taking place in the world, the government had set a target of twenty-one per cent GER by the Twelfth Five Year Plan, against the interim target of fifteen per cent GER by 2012, by the end of the Eleventh Five Year Plan.

To achieve the target of fifteen per cent GER by 2012, according to the estimate of UGC, the enrolment was to be increased to 8.4 million at the annual rate of about nine per cent between the years 2006 and 2012. In terms of capacity and to meet the GER target, additional 400 to 800 universities and more than 2,000 colleges were required.

Against these projections, the government had planned to establish 30 new universities, 8 IITs, 20 NITs, 3 IISERs, 7 IIM and 2 SAP as well as 373 new colleges in educationally backward districts with GER below the national average. The provision was also made for 1,000 new polytechnics particularly in unserved districts including new community polytechnics and 210 new community colleges. Fifteen universities and 373 colleges are yet to be established. Their fate is not known. Out of the proposed thirty universities, sixteen were established in 2009.

This expansion is considered to be the second wave of education and the Eleventh Five Year Plan is termed as the educational plan. For the first time in India, education was expanded to such a great extent with the emphasis on equity. More than 60 years after independence, the importance of education and its intimate link with inclusive growth and development was recognized, and measures were taken for its equal and uniform spread among the Indian society particularly making it more accessible to SC, ST and OBC communities by implementation of the reservations policy and other affirmative actions.

However, the steep resistance to reservations from the people belonging to higher castes is still continued, particularly in the publically funded institutions which are imparting professional education. Because of the past legacy, these people became highly educated, captured academic institutions and used as their own. On the other hand, the welfare schemes like reservations for SCs and ST, were implemented detrimentally by them. The data shown in Table 1 indicates the same.

It is understood that the information (as on March 31, 2013) contained in Table 1 was given to the Parliament last year. The percentage shown in parenthesis was calculated for clarity. It is seen that just 7.33 per cent SC and 4.26 per cent ST faculty members are in the above institutions of higher education established by the

Table 2: Faculty Positions Across Institutions

Institution	*Total in Positions*	*SC*	*ST*
Central Universities	10,070	703 (6.8%)	507 (5.03%)
NITs	1064	252 (23.68%)	73 (6.86%)
IIITs	118	2 (1.69%)	0 (0%)
IISc	498	29 (5.82%)	11 (2.20%)
IIMs	508	02 (0.39%)	01 (0.19%)
IITs	1387	33 (2.37%)	03 (0.21%)
IISERs	295	01 (0.33%)	0 (0%)
Total	13940	1022 (7.33%)	595 (4.26%)

Note: Scientific and Technical Institutions provide reservations in faculty positions at the entry level.

Government of India. If the data, i.e. 23.68 per cent (252) SC and 6.86 per cent (73) ST of NITs (out of the total 1064) is ignored, the presence of SCs and STs in these institutions come down further. It is notable that NITs were able to attract and appoint SC and ST candidates as faculties in large numbers. However, in other centrally funded academic institutions like IITs, IISC, IIMs, NITs and IISERs, the representation of SCs and STs in faculty positions is quite poor. Some of the IIMs and IITs were established in the late 1950s, and early 1960s. However, there are still two (0.39 per cent) SCs and one (0.19 per cent) ST out of the total faculty position of 508 in IIMs. Similarly, among 1,387 faculty members in IITs, there are 33 (2.37 per cent) SC and three (0.21 per cent) ST. During this long period, many SC and ST students might have joined IIMs and IITs and completed their studies successfully. Some of them must have been suitable to rejoin their alma mater as faculty members. The small number of SC and ST in the faculty indicated that these IITs and IIMs either failed to attract them or rejected them on appearing in the interview.

IISERs and some IITs are relatively new and had a chance to get SC and ST candidates as scientists at the lowest rung. It appears these institutions did not make efforts as is evident from the poor representation of SC and ST in faculty positions. There are just two (1.69 per cent) out of 118 and one (0.33 per cent) SC out of 295 in IITs and IISERs respectively. Surprisingly, there is no ST teacher in both these institutions. It is understood that the Search Committee travelled abroad including US to find and recommend candidates for appointment as scientists or faculty members in these newly established professional institutions. The Committee met and addressed students and researchers in an open house at various places. It is reported that at least in one such meeting in the US, Dalit students raised points directly or indirectly related to preference being given to candidates with a certain background. From the proceedings of such a meeting, the Dalit students perceived that the Search Committee travelled a long distance with very short vision. Being new, care must be taken not to make these institutions rehabilitation centres for scholars and researchers of a certain section of society or for students of some scientists and teachers.

The situation of social inclusiveness in IISc compared to other institutes is slightly better with 29 (5.82 per cent) SC and 11 (2.2 per cent) ST teachers but, still, far below the prescribed 15 per cent and 7.5 per cent for SC and ST respectively. India has a few centres of excellence and IISc is one of them. However, such islands of excellence are isolated and not connected to the society. They are liberally funded and had greater autonomy, and live in their own world.

The central universities have not opposed reservations openly. However, JNU came openly against reservation. Almost all central universities have been passive and carefully careless, which is evident from the above Table 2. It can be seen that out of the total 10,070 teachers (in 39 central universities), the share of SC was 703 (6.98 per cent) and ST 507 (5.03 per cent). It may be noted that the UGC source showed a total of 2,273 teachers in Central Universities on March 31, 2013. Out of these, SC were 703 (4.3 per cent) and ST 507 (3.11 per cent). Interestingly, there was a significant difference in SC and ST teachers in terms of percentage between these two sources, but not in their absolute number. In Table 2, the reserved posts are compared with the existing strength, whereas UGC compared it with sanctioned posts. It is known that the statistics always comes to the help of its user. Even if both the sources of information are seen together or separately, the representation of SC and ST in faculty positions is still far below the prescribed 15 per cent and 7.5 per cent respectively. In 39 central universities, just 26 (1.14 per cent), 79 (1.75 per cent) and 557 (6.53 per cent) teachers of SC were at the level of Professor, Associate Professor and Assistant Professor respectively. In the case of ST, there were twenty (0.88 per cent) Professors, 56 (1.24 per cent) Associate Professors and 338 (4.79 per cent) Assistant Professors in all these 39 universities. It can be noted that the UGC regularly monitors the implementation of reservation policy through its Standing Committee and Monitoring Committee on SC/ST. It had also issued the guidelines for strict implemention of the reservation policy. In spite of this, the representation of SC and ST in faculty position is quite low. It is clear that the past practice of non-implementations of reservation policy, by design or default, is still continued in the present day. It was possible that no candidates belonging to SC and ST communities were available in the 1970s, 1980s and even to some extent in the 1990s. The suitable candidates are now available. The time has changed. Similarly, there is need to change the mindset of people involved in governance and administration as well as faculty members on the reservation issue. It is necessary to sensitize and make them understand the historic background and reason for providing the reservations and importance of upliftment of the unprivileged in the interest of the nation. They also need to be informed that the progress made, the status achieved and privileges enjoyed by the members of the higher castes have flown down through the successive generations as a legacy from their forefathers who had oppressed and suppressed the downtrodden.

It is equally applicable in case of an implementation of reservation policy in admissions. An explosion of protest resulted as a reaction against 27 per cent reservation extended to OBC in the centrally funded institutions of higher education in 2006, after the 93rd amendment in the Constitution by inserting the Article 15(5). The protest spread all over India like wild fire. The steep opposition came mainly from the institutions of professional education. The students and faculty members of institutions like IITs, were at the forefront with the demand that the admissions should be made solely on merit and not on caste-based reservations, as it, according to them, adversely affects the quality of education. It implies that the reserve category students are not meritorious; and merit is a copyright of only the upper caste students.

Surprisingly, this class of meritorious students and faculty members never uttered a word, went on strike, came on to streets and roads and paralyzed the country or knocked on the doors of the High Courts and Supreme Court with PIL in hand against the admissions on the basis of donations and capitation fee with lowered marks and merit, in medical and engineering courses in private colleges and institutions. It is difficult to understand how an admission on the basis of money and lower marks of upper caste students does not adversely affect the merit and equality of education.

It would be pertinent to refer to an article entitled, 'Unreserved on the Roll', written by Anuradha Raman (*Outlook,* the weekly news magazine, July 8, 2014, pp. 18 and 19) on the performance of OBC candidates in the test for an admission in seventeen IITs for the academic year 2013-14, in which the merit argument is debunked, as more than 1,000 students from OBC had made it to IITs in the general category. She reportd that the students this year, were supposed to appear first in the JEE Main Examination, conducted by the Board of Secondary Examination and need to clear to become eligible for the JEE Advanced Examination. More than 3 lakh students took the examination, out of which 1.5 lakh became eligible to appear in the JEE Advance Examination. Finally, 9,867 candidates who had qualified for admission in these seventeen IITs, 4,841 are from the general category, 2591 OBC, 1,431 SC and 720 ST students. 4,188 students belonging to the OBC category were called for counselling (or interview) of which 2,591 were declared eligible for BTech courses. Another important aspect she mentioned was that the difference in qualifying marks between the general category students and OBC students was negligible. Further, out of 4,841 successful general category students, more than 1,000 belonged to the OBC category. Thus, OBC students in large numbers made it to the hallowed portal of the IITs without reservation. In view of the above facts, the urban elite and upper castes who have been opposing the reservation on the ground of merit and quality, need to change their attitude and mindset. It would not be surprising, on seeking such success of OBC candidates, the elite and upper castes in IITs may think of changing the admission policy on some or other pretex.

Voltaire once said, 'The human brain has the power to make

man find reason to continue believing in what he wants to believe'. It is a well-known that the students belonging to the elite group and upper castes spend a lot of time and money to get coaching in the private coaching centres and learn how to score high marks in the competitive examinations such as JEE conducted for admissions in IITs, rather than understanding the subject. Mastering the trick by rote learning to score high marks is claimed to be academic merit, which is acquired by making heavy payment. The poor, particularly, SC and ST students do not have money to acquire such merit. However, it is seen that on getting equal educational opportunities, SC and ST students also perform well in the examinations, and sometimes do better than unreserved category students. Such a possibility is supported by the report of Sreeniwas Janyala, in *The Indian Express* (Mumbai, Saturday), dated May 18, 2013, according to which the students belonging to extremely poor SC, ST and other backward communities, who study in schools run by the Andhra Pradesh Government's Social Welfare Department, performed extremely well (94.22 pass per cent) in the SSC or Class X examination of the year 2013 beating pass percentage (88 per cent) and outperformed students tutored in expensive private schools. The parents of these unprivileged students are either manual labourers or daily wagers. Of 279 such schools in the state, one hundred and one schools secured a hundred per cent pass results. Out of this, 13,213 students got the highest grade. If these students get proper guidance and opportunities, they would excel in competitive examinations like JEE for IIT admissions.

It is known that the IIT students who leave the country immediately on graduating mainly belong to the elite section and upper castes. Their migration defeats the very purpose of establishing the IITs. On the other hand, the students belonging to OBC, SC and ST communities are expected to stay back in large numbers and remain connected with their motherland. In such an event, social returns would be quite high. Therefore, from the social inclusion in IITs, the country will benefit more than before.

Our obsession with commissions and committees still continues. The constitution of UGC/AICTE Review Committee to review the function of UGC/AICTE, in the wake of changes in higher, professional and technical education in India and the demand of a new knowledge economy under the Chairmanship of Prof. Yash Pal, was notified on February 28, 2008, which is popularly known as the Yash Pal Committee. It was renamed as the Committee to Advise on Renovation and Rejuvenation of Higher Education (CARRHE) by the notification on October 14, 2008, without change in its composition and terms of reference. However, its scope was widened (Prof. Yash Pal's letter to the Ministry of HRD, dated November 1, 2008). The committee submitted its interim report in March 2009 and Final Report in May/June 2009. It identified various issues like the need for a division between research bodies and universities, lack of learning across disciplines, neglect of undergraduate education, fine balance between quality and affordability, resource management, financing, poor governance and the erosion of democratic space. Considering such important aspects of higher education, the committee gave several recommendations, including subsuming of all regulatory bodies with the National Commission for Higher Education and Research (NCHER), improvement in the method of selection of Vice-Chancellors and internal working of universities, introduction of public-private partnership, to invite from abroad, a substantial number of potentially great academics and scientists instead of importing mediocre foreign universities to set up shop here.

The National Knowledge Commission (NKC) was constituted with Dr. Sam Pitroda as its Chairman, on June 13, 2005, almost three years before the Yash Pal Committee, and worked for three years from 2006-09. The committee was required to give its views on the twenty-seven per cent reservations for OBC in centrally funded institutions of higher education. Its support to reservation for OBC was highly qualified, with the view that reservations required only affirmative action. Two members apparently resigned because they did not agree with the formulation of NKC. The Vice-Chairman of the committee who was pro-reservation also resigned because of differences with the Chairman. Therefore, the NKC was reconstituted. The terms of reference related to higher education were: Build excellence in educational systems to meet the knowledge challenges of the 21st century and increase India's competitive advantage in the world of knowledge. It concentrated on five key areas such as: to access, concepts, creation, application and services to build the knowledge society. The commission considered three fundamental challenges related to demography, disparity and development. In its recommendations related to higher education, it focused on expansion, excellence and inclusion in education. It suggested, among other things, to increase GER to fifteen per cent and above by 2015; to increase the financial support to higher education, to create 1,500 universities by 2015, to set up an independent Regulatory Authority for higher education (IRAHE); and reformation in structure and function of their universities including academics.

The NKC Report on higher education was considered by the CABE and most of its recommendations were rejected. Its recommendations had overtaken by the recommendations of the Yash Pal Committee which suggested the establishment of the National Council of Higher Education and Research (NCHER). The proposals made by NKC were seen to be ambitious and ambiguous by the academicians (Kolhatkar, 2012). The Yash Pal Committee Report was also criticized as it focused too much on an idealist concept of universities and ignored the fact that knowledge has other important dimensions like commercialization and marketing. The report is also oblivious to the role played by professional councils in the maintenance of standards (Bhusan Sudhanshu, 2009).

Perhaps for the first time in the history of Indian education, one high power committee and another high power commission were constituted almost at the same time and worked in parallel with a great degree of overlap on the issues related to higher education. It created the confusion in the mind of the educationists and those in education.

In broad spectrum, it looked alike and both were doing the same thing. One had focused on the process of production and impartment of the knowledge and another on the product itself. It may be noted that the NKC recommended an umbrella body called IRAHE, and to have a standing committee on the sub field of higher education. UGC was reduced to a mere agency of disbursement of grants to and maintenance of public institutions. The Yash Pal Committee proposed to establish the NCHER which would subsume UGC. Thus, the UGC was dissolved by this committee as a solute into the solvent called NCHER. It is seen that in the last few years the UGC has been the subject of criticism. It is perceived as a bureaucratic organization which has lost both its autonomy and soul, and occupied a diminished space (Kolhatkar, 2012). Some have considered UGC as a failed organization. However, the interest of SCs and STs was crushed between NCHR and IRHE.

UGC is one of the organizations among the several other organizations, institutions, agencies, departments, councils and commissions of the country. Is the UGC the only organization which failed? Is the very purpose defeated for which it was established? Is its structure and functions irreversibly damaged beyond repair? If so, then who is responsible? How is one sure that the new structure and function called NCHER would not go the same way as that of UGC and collapse one day? Indeed, the failure and success of any organization should be measured in terms of its social returns. In India, there is provision for financial audit, but not for social audit. If the social audit is carried out most of the departments, councils and commissions would score poorly. Compared to others, the performance of UGC would definitely be better. With limited financial resource and autonomy, the UGC has contributed to a great extent in the generation of educated and skilled human resource. Its policies and their implementation are more inclusive than other departments, institutions, councils and commissions. Some of these organizations have shown steep resistance to reservation policies of government for SCs and STs. Although, the UGC was unwilling and slow on implementations of reservations in the 1960s to 1980s, became proactive only in the middle of the 2000s. Now the UGC has been giving emphasis to enhancing the access to higher education with equity and equality of opportunities through various schemes and programmes such as the establishment of Equal Opportunity Cells for SC and ST (in 1066 colleges, 101 state universities and 27 central universities), establishment of Residential Coaching Academy for SCs, STs and minorities in universities (in 5 central universities), Remedial Coaching Scheme for SC, ST, minority and OBC students (in 22 central universities, 154 state universities and 10 deemed to be universities). Rajiv Gandhi National Fellowships for SC and ST students (10,707 and 4,163 fellowships awarded to SC and ST students respectively from 2005-07 to 2011-12), Post-doctoral fellowships for SC and ST students (491 fellowship awarded from 2006-07), postgraduate scholarship for SC and ST students in professional courses (3,936 scholarship awarded from 2007-08 to 2011-12), establishment of SC/ST cell (128 cells are functioning in various universities till March 31, 2012), Women's Hostels in colleges located in ST predominant states (27 states) and the establishment of centres in universities for study of Social Exclusion and Inclusive Policy (35 centres till 2011-12). In general, the Indian society is benefited relatively more from UGC than other organizations. Instead, individuals like scientists and educationists were benefited more from other councils and commissions. It can be noted that DBT has been funding postgraduate programmes in Bio-technology located in more than thirty universities. The DBT is the only department among others, which has contributed through such programmes in generating human resources in a vital academic and scientific field. At some or other stage, a few people with short or no vision, probably involved directly or indirectly in governance and administration of the UGC, might have taken certain decisions or actions which adversely affected its structure and functions. Along with taking corrective measures, the UGC should have been expanded and changed its structure and function with change in time, by the policy makers and implementers. However, the NCHER Bill was introduced in the Parliament on May 3, 2010. The Yash Pal Committee made provision of NCHER, which would subsume UGC and other councils. The Bill finally confined probably to just UGC and AICTE as the other councils were removed from its purview. There was a steep opposition to this Bill in the Parliament House and outside. Now the survival of the NCHER Bill appears to be difficult and it has to wait for its natural death. Although, the NKC and Yash Pal Committee reports generated considerable interest and hope but, not much, emerged in terms of policies from both the reports. It appears that a lot of time and efforts have gone waste. Both reports have now become a primary source of information on Indian education, and gather dust in the archives awaiting scholars and research for their use.

Mention has been made in the Kothari Commission Report, 'that history has shown numerous instances, where a small group and elite have used education as the prerogative of their rule and as a tool for maintaining their hegemony and perpetuating the values upon which it has rested'. The report also saw the Indian society as hierarchical, stratified and deficient in vertical mobility. These observations made by the Kothari Commission Report most probably referred to the Indian tradition of the supremacy of Brahmins and other upper castes. Although, the Kothari Commission Report has not elaborated on social issues, its social sensitivity was visible from this suggestion. While writing the Report, it must have been felt necessary to make special mention on the education of children from backward classes which includes SC, ST, Denotified communities and a few nomadic and semi-nomadic groups. Further, the Report also suggested that education has to be used as an instrument of social change, apart from economic and political change. In this context, it could be mentioned that social democracy and economic democracy are known to be muscle fibres of the political democracy.

To provide strength to these three democracies and intimately interlink them, the democratization of education is essential. With this backdrop, the suggestion to make special efforts for the education of the unprivileged section of society has a great significance. Indeed, knowingly or unknowingly, the Kothari Commission had taken forward the educational agenda of social reformers like Mahatma Phule and Dr. B.R. Ambedkar, who throughout their lives worked for the upliftment of the unprivileged section of society. The social concerns and depth of their understanding was not visible in both NCK and Yash Pal Reports. Some of their recommendations were considered to be detrimental to the educational interests of SC, ST, OBC and other unprivileged sections of society.

Recently, several steps have been taken by the government to reform the education system in India. These reforms were mainly guided by the recommendations of NKC and the Yash Pal Committee. Around twelve Bills were drafted between 2009 and 2013 and introduced in the Parliament. When they were passed and became laws, education expected to be overhauled in terms of governance, administrative structure, and function leading to make qualitative changes in teaching and research. Perhaps for the first time more than sixty years, such major changes are proposed through the legislations. Most of these Bills, however, have become controversial to some extent and have been opposed both inside and outside the Parliament, and as a result have remained pending. Of these Bills, a few are mentioned below:

1) *National Commission for Higher Education and Research (2010)*: It is one of the most controversial Bills and widely debated in the country. However, as mentioned above, due to reported opposition, it is not likely to see the light of day.
2) *The Foreign Education Institutions (Regulation of Entry and Operations) Bill, 2010*. According to this Bill, foreign education institutions could set up independently or in collaboration with an Indian education provider, institutions that provide education resulting in a degree, diploma or certificate in India. There was steep opposition from different corners and was seen as protecting the interest of corporate and elite social groups as well as of America and other foreign universities. It is also seen as a business venture and with no space for poor and socially backward castes.
3) *National Accreditation Regulatory Authority for Higher Education Bill, 2010*: The provision has been made in this Bill to make accreditation (by independent accreditation agencies) mandatory for higher educational institutions, educational programmes, and educational infrastructure. The Bill has also made a provision for establishing an independent statutory authority. It is likely to enhance and maintain the quality of education, provided its provisions are implemented without fear and favour. If it comes into existence, the authority should also insist on inclusive education.
4) *Educational Tribunal Bill, 2010*: It is mainly to provide the system of adjudication of disputes relating to education that involve teachers, employees, students, universities, institutions and statutory authorities. Therefore, the National Education Tribunal was established to resolve intra and inter-institutional disputes. This Bill as the most non-controversial should have been passed without much

difficulty. However, when taken in the Parliament, it was severely criticized by none other than the members of Treasury benches.

The landscape of Indian higher education is changing very fast. The education system is being shifted towards the US model in case of academic programmes, with not much change in the British style of model of governance and administration, which has been followed for long. As mentioned earlier, the higher education is expanding in an unprecedented manner in the private sector almost in the business mode. Instead of nurturing, the education in the public sector is allowed, by default or design, to collapse and, at the same time over regulated by the government.The professional and technical courses in academic institutions and traditional courses in public institutions have divided the society vertically, which was already divided owing to the medium of instruction. This dual system has created two classes of educated population.

The first generation of national leadership includes those who studied abroad and made efforts to find Indian solutions to Indian problems. The education was seen, by them, as an instrument of social change. The new generation of leadership particularly those who studied abroad in countries like USA, provide Western solutions to Indian educational problems. Individual perceptions and understanding of a select few guided and influenced the educational policies and their implementations. As time passed, the quality of education deteriorated. However, the academic institutions run by elites, and for elites maintained the quality at the cost of public sector institutions. At the individual level, many rich parents send their children abroad for higher education and pay fees between $20,000 and $70,000 per year to keep their supremacy at the social and economic level. According to the Open Doors Report, released on November 14, 2016, there were a record enrolment of 1,65,918 students from India, during 2015-16 academic year in USA colleges and universities. As mentioned elsewhere, the Open Doors Report is published annually, by the Institute of International Education alongwith the US Department of State's Bureau of Education and Cultural Affairs. The increase of 25 per cent from the previous year (2014-15), made India leading country which exports students to US. Now, one out of every six international students in the US, is Indian. If all the countries taken together, the number of Indian students studying abroad will be very high. Any way, our education system continues to produce well educated and qualified youth from a small, but dominant section of the society. At the same time, it also produces non-employable and skill deficit youth in large numbers from the remaining section of the society, particularly from the poor and underprivileged.

The resolution dated June 21, 2012, published by the Department of Higher Education, Ministry of Human Resource Development (F.No.9-6/2012-SC/ST) suggested a realization on the part of the Government of India about the uneven spread of higher education and the need of protection of educational interests of SC, ST and other social groups. As a result, it constituted a National Monitoring Committee (NMC) for Education of SC, ST and PWD, under the Chairmanship of the Union Minister of India, Ministry of Human Resource Development; with two Ministers of State for Human Resource Development, 18 Ex-officio nominees which includes the Education Ministers of different states, two Lok Sabha nominees, two Rajya Sabha nominees, 26 academics, activists and administrators connected with SC, ST and PWD; three organizations and eight officials as its members.

The Committee was supposed to advise the government on all matters pertaining to education and its pursuit for SCs, STs and PWD. In addition, the committee was asked to review the functioning of various schemes launched by the ministry for the purpose of promoting SCs, STs and PWD in education. Its first meeting was held on June 27, 2012. After detailed discussions on various issues, challenges and strategies related to education, in this very first meeting of NMC, apart from the fifteen members Standing Committee with Prof. S.K. Thorat as its Chairman, six Task Force teams were set up on various subjects. Accordingly, all the Task Forces worked and submitted their reports and recommendations. The standing committee also finalized draft guidelines for implementation of Scheduled Caste Sub-Plan (SCSP) and Tribal Sub-Plan (TSP) and submitted to MHRD (on April 1, 2013). These draft guidelines were placed before the NMC in its second Meeting, held on June 12, 2013. The guidelines for implementation of SCSP and TSP framed by the Standing Committee and duly approved the NMC, were finalized with approval of the Minister of Human Resource Development and circulated to concerned departments, centrally funded educational Institutions and other agencies, on October 1, 2013, for its implementation (F.No. 9-21/2012-SC/ST, the Ministry of Human Resources and Development, Department of Higher Education). Importantly, the status of implementation of SCSP and TSP in MHRD for the year 2014-15 was reviewed in the third meeting of NMC, held on December 21, 2014.

While implementing the policy decisions, the past of thousand years of social slavery, exploitation and oppression of SC/ST has to be kept in mind. The welfare schemes for SC and ST should not be considered as just measures to free them from the clutches of poverty or redistribution of the wealth. The purpose of such schemes is to undo the historic wrongs and bring equality in Indian society. Therefore, one has to think and act beyond fifteen and 7.5 per cent reservations as well as SCSP and TSP. Specially, new targeted welfare schemes have to be developed. Most importantly, welfare schemes have to be implemented effectively so as to get desired outcomes. The social backwardness is a disease and that needs to be treated for its complete cure. Education is a broad spectrum and an effective medicine.

Education is known to be a social and economic equalizer. In this context, as stated earlier, it is important to note that social democracy and economic democracy are muscle fibres of political democracy. Therefore, educating Dalits and Tribes means making Indian democracy strong, and in turn India as a progressive and prosperous country.

REFERENCES

Bhusan, Sudhanshu (2009). *Restructuring Higher Education in India,* Rawat Publications, Jaipur and Delhi.

Dani, Rodrik (2012). *The Finacial Express,* Ahmedabad, Tuesday, August 14.

Janyala, Sreeniwas (2013). *The Indian Express,* Mumbai, Saturday, May 18.

Kolhatkar, M.R. (2012). *Survey of Indian Education (1947-2007),* Concept Publishing Company, New Delhi.

Merchant, Minhaz (2010). New Triangle in an Emerging Tripolar World, Stewardship of India's Foreign Policy Needs Firmer Hands, *The Times of India*, Ahmedabad, May 1.

Raman, Anuradha (2014). *Outlook*, The Weekly News Magazine, July 8, pp. 18-19.

Upadhyay, Ashok (2013). *The Hindu Business Line*, Wednesday, March 27, p. 6.

Varma, Subodh (2012). *The Times of India*, Ahmedabad, Thursday, March 15.

Virmani, Arvind (2010). *From Unipolar to Tripolar World*, Academic Foundation, New Delhi.

Index